A Moon for the Misbegotten
on the American Stage

A Moon for the Misbegotten on the American Stage

A History of the Major Productions

LAURA SHEA

McFarland & Company, Inc., Publishers
Jefferson, North Carolina, and London

LIBRARY OF CONGRESS CATALOGUING-IN-PUBLICATION DATA

Shea, Laura.
   A moon for the misbegotten on the American stage : a history of
the major productions / Laura Shea.
      p.   cm.
   Includes bibliographical references and index.

   ISBN 978-0-7864-3563-0
   softcover : 50# alkaline paper ∞

   1. O'Neill, Eugene, 1888–1953. Moon for the misbegotten.
2. O'Neill, Eugene, 1888–1953 — Dramatic production.   3. O'Neill,
Eugene, 1888–1953 — Stage history.   I. Title.
PS3529.N5Z79698   2008
812'.52 — dc22   2008001639

British Library cataloguing data are available

On the cover: Eve Best as Josie Hogan and Kevin Spacey as James
Tyrone, Jr. in the Old Vic Theatre Company production of *A Moon for
the Misbegotten* in 2006, directed by Howard Davies (photograph by
Simon Annand); background lighting ©2007 Shutterstock

Manufactured in the United States of America

*McFarland & Company, Inc., Publishers
   Box 611, Jefferson, North Carolina 28640
   www.mcfarlandpub.com*

For my father,
Robert B. Shea

Acknowledgments

Although writing is a solitary endeavor, no one works alone when producing a manuscript, and there are a number of people to whom I owe a debt of gratitude.

At Iona College, I am grateful to Dean Alexander Eodice for his support of my scholarship. I received a sabbatical leave for the 2003–2004 academic year, and this is when the project took shape. I would not have been able to complete the manuscript without a course remission, for which I thank Dean Eodice as well as Iona's English Department, chaired by Dr. Hugh Short. Funding from the Committee on Faculty Travel and Development has enabled me to attend a number of conferences that have expanded my interest in all things O'Neill, particularly the O'Neill Society's International Conference in Bermuda in January 1999, followed by the conference in Tours, France, in 2003.

I extend my sincere thanks to Zander Brietzke, editor of *The Eugene O'Neill Review*, for his interest in the project, which led to the publication of the first chapter, in a slightly different form, in 2005. The publication of the article, entitled "Eugene O'Neill, the Theatre Guild, and *A Moon for the Misbegotten*," led to the development of this material into a book-length manuscript. *The Eugene O'Neill Review* has granted permission to use material from the article in this book.

I offer thanks to Deborah Williams, colleague and friend, for her willingness to read and comment on the manuscript, when her own free time is at a premium. I also wish to thank Cyrus Patell for his invaluable assistance, particularly in times of technological crisis.

7

Acknowledgments

A number of research librarians and archivists guided me to the resources of their collections, beginning with Laurie M. Deredita in the Department of Special Collections of the Charles E. Shain Library at Connecticut College, home to the Louis Sheaffer-Eugene O'Neill Collection. This is where the search began. With seemingly endless patience, Jeremy McGraw at the New York Public Library for the Performing Arts helped me to acquire several of the photographs used in the book, and Tom Lisanti at the New York Public Library assisted me in obtaining the permissions to use them. I would also like to thank the staff at the Beinecke Rare Book and Manuscript Library at Yale University, the Theatre Collection at Harvard University, and the Rare Book and Manuscript librarians at Princeton's Firestone Library for their attentive and expert assistance.

At the American Repertory Theatre, Katalin Mitchell and Jan Geidt were extremely generous in sharing their time and their knowledge as well as their photographs. I also wish to thank Dan Bauer at the McCarter Theatre Company and photographer Eric Y. Exit for their generosity in providing images used in the book. From London, Simon Annand sent not one but a series of photographs from which to choose. For filling in those essential details on the history of these productions, I wish to thank Steven Scarpa at the Long Wharf Theatre, Mark Turek at Trinity Rep, Erin Moore at the Goodman Theatre, and Teresa Mensz at the Yale Drama School Library. I have also found Harley J. Hammerman's electronic O'Neill archive (eOneill.com) to be indispensable to my teaching and scholarship.

Several events have added to my experience of O'Neill's works. In 1995, I participated in an NEH Summer Seminar at Columbia University, directed by Howard Stein, which renewed my interest in the plays of Eugene O'Neill. Listening to Jose Quintero speak at the Playwrights Theatre Forum in 1998, particularly his unforgettable discussion of *A Moon for the Misbegotten*, enhanced my experience of this play and others through his insistence that we "make ourselves vulnerable to the material." In 2001, as a Critic Fellow at the O'Neill Playwrights Conference in Waterford, Connecticut, I paid several visits to nearby Monte Cristo Cottage and began to see the place not as a stage setting but as a home that once housed actual inhabitants, a place where you "go to the source and touch the ghosts," to borrow the words of Brian Dennehy, spoken at the 2004 celebration of O'Neill's birthday at the O'Neill Theater Center.

Acknowledgments

I wish to thank my friends for their willingness to share in the experience of O'Neill, often through seeing the plays in production. As a testament to the longevity of our friendship, Karen Galatz and I saw *A Moon for the Misbegotten* from the second-to-last row of the Morosco Theater in 1974 and from the orchestra of the Brooks Atkinson in 2007. The Broadway revival in 2000 and the production at the McCarter Theatre in 2006 increased my understanding of the play. A final set of thanks go to my sister Sally Sweeney, Laureen Griffin, Betsy Fox, and Tom Doherty for their unfailing encouragement of my work.

Contents

Acknowledgements   7

Preface   13

Introduction   15

The Plot   21

1. The Original Production, 1947   27

2. New York Premiere and Broadway Debut, 1957,
   and Off Broadway Debut, 1968   53

3. Broadway Revivals, 1973 and 1984   75

4. Broadway Revival, 2000, and Regional Productions   107

5. Broadway Revival, 2007   137

Conclusion: "What's past is prologue."   161

Production Chronology   173

Works Cited   177

Index   187

Preface

A Moon for the Misbegotten is one of Eugene O'Neill's most frequently revived works, and the major American revivals of the play have been instrumental in securing its place in theater history. The landmark production in 1973 is seen as the moment when the play finally achieved greatness, but the complicated history of the play, spanning over 60 years, has led to a number of misconceptions regarding the success or failure of the productions that preceded or followed it. Beginning with the original performance in 1947, this study of the major American productions of *A Moon for the Misbegotten* will separate the myth from the reality regarding the production history of one of O'Neill's greatest works. For the most part, these productions have occurred on Broadway, which serves as the focal point for American drama. Whether for good or ill, a production on Broadway receives more attention than it would in any other theatrical venue. The recent spate of transfers from the London stage, including the 2007 production of *A Moon for the Misbegotten*, seems to confirm this assessment. If a play is to make a lasting impression, so the theory goes, it must be seen on Broadway, not only to demonstrate the weight and seriousness of the enterprise but also to garner the attention of a worldwide audience.

Originally, I had planned to pursue my interest in O'Neill's stage directions, those specific instructions regarding the physical and emotional dimensions of the plays, which leave nothing — and everything — to the imagination. Having written on the subject of the stage directions in *Hughie*, in an essay that appeared in *The Eugene O'Neill Review* in 1999, I intended to study the progression of the stage directions as they moved from manuscript to typescript throughout the playwright's career, thus giving serious consideration to this vital aspect of O'Neill's drama.

While a Critic Fellow at the O'Neill Playwrights Conference in Waterford, Connecticut, in 2001, I paid my first visit to the Louis Sheaffer–Eugene O'Neill Collection at the Charles E. Shain Library at Connecticut College in nearby New London. There, I examined materials relating to the original production of O'Neill's *A Moon for the Misbegotten*, a production that was sent out of town in 1947, never to return for its intended run as part of the Theatre Guild's 1946–1947 season. The enterprise suffered from an array of difficulties, not the least of which was the author's extensive list of demands, and when the production closed, it was summarily dismissed. In fact, a closer look at the production materials, seen through the eyes of the actors, directors, designers, and even the critics, reveals that the production was not the catastrophe that has been described. I was intrigued and chose instead to study the disjunction between the accepted fact and a documented reality, resulting in an essay, entitled "Eugene O'Neill, the Theatre Guild, and *A Moon for the Misbegotten*," that appeared in *The Eugene O'Neill Review* in 2005. In time, my research extended to the Beinecke Rare Book and Manuscript Library at Yale University, the Theatre Collection at Harvard University, and the Rare Book and Special Collections of the Firestone Library at Princeton University, and the essay became the first chapter of the first book-length study of the play's production history. In discussing the major revivals that followed the original production, on Broadway in 1957, 1973, 1984, 2000, and 2007, Off Broadway in 1968, and in a number of regional theaters from 1979–2006, my intention remained the same: to separate the flawed perception from the reality of the play in production, and in the process, to demonstrate how each revival has added to the growing reputation of an increasingly celebrated play.

Introduction

Most plays are written to be produced, so their production is a topic worthy of study. While it is impossible to recapture the evanescent moment, this volume will give readers an understanding of what has gone into the making of *A Moon for the Misbegotten*, and how the productions have been essential in transforming the play from its uncertain start into an occasion for greatness. The play was completed in 1943, at a time when O'Neill was depressed both by his own ill health and by the events of World War II: as he wrote to his son Eugene, "Pearl Harbor exploded when I was writing the most difficult part" (*Selected Letters* 526). The play was championed by Lawrence Langner at the Theatre Guild, an organization eager to renew its reputation as the producer of serious drama on Broadway. Despite Langner's effusive praise for the play, calling it "one of the truly great tragedies of our time" (402), the key selling points were, in fact, O'Neill's name and reputation, and the opportunity to attach both to a Guild production.

Though no production makes the transition from the page to the stage without incident, *A Moon for the Misbegotten* was plagued by a variety of problems, from casting difficulties to a controversy over censorship. Having mandated an all–Irish cast and creative team, O'Neill was still dissatisfied with the play in rehearsal and insisted on an out–of–town tryout, providing his own list of cities in the Midwest in which the production could tour. At several of the venues, theatergoers and critics objected to some of the rougher language of the play, in one instance, to the proximity of the word "prostitute" to the word "mother." When the production was temporarily shut down in Detroit, the controversy was defused by the omission of several of the offending words, although the published version of the play left the original language intact.

When the original production of *A Moon for the Misbegotten* ended its run, its reputation as a disaster was not borne out by the generally mixed reviews it received. Although the Theatre Guild was within its legal rights to bring the production to New York, O'Neill's dissatisfaction prevailed, and the play was withdrawn from the Guild's season. Attempts were made to interest a number of actors and directors in the project, but none of these possibilities materialized. The author himself lost interest in the play, "a play that [he had] come to loathe," as he inscribed a published copy to his wife Carlotta. *A Moon for the Misbegotten* was not produced in New York until 1957, four years after O'Neill's death.

To breathe life into the moribund drama required several major revivals, spanning a period of nearly thirty years. Although British actress Wendy Hiller was offered the part of Josie in 1947, she thought herself "not American enough." Apparently, the actress changed her mind, for a decade later she starred in the first Broadway production, which was followed by an Off Broadway revival in 1968. Thus began the long process of the play's resuscitation. In 1957, *New York Times* critic Brooks Atkinson wrote that "no stage production can solve the problems [of the play]" (21), though Clive Barnes, writing in the same publication in 1968, called the play a "minor-masterpiece," adding that it "may well come to be regarded as the proof of O'Neill's genius" (55).

The arc from disaster to minor masterpiece to proof of O'Neill's genius culminated with the landmark production in 1973. Directed by Jose Quintero, and starring noted O'Neill interpreters Colleen Dewhurst and Jason Robards, the production and the play won resounding praise. Described by critic Harold Clurman as "the best production of the best play of the season" (92), it became the standard by which future productions would be judged.

Frequently performed in regional theaters, the play was again revived on Broadway in 1984, with the diminutive Kate Nelligan as the formidable Josie, and in 2000, with Cherry Jones and Gabriel Byrne in the leading roles: both productions were reviewed in the context of the "definitive" production. With Kevin Spacey's production having made the transfer to

Broadway from London's Old Vic in 2007, the question remains as to whether any production will be allowed to escape the shadow of the 1973 revival, although numerous productions have been intent upon trying. A great play never stops evolving, and with each interpretation, regardless of its level of commercial success, a new drama transpires as a new way of seeing the play emerges. Over the last sixty years, the interpretations of the play have ranged from straightforward realism to the evocation of Irish myth. Yet, the visceral appeal remains unchanged, which helps to account for the enduring appeal of a play that runs approximately three hours and leaves audiences, like the characters, drained by the same despairing vision of life.

Offered as a form of requiem, O'Neill's play attempts to forgive the only member of the Tyrone family who is neither forgiven nor fully understood in the autobiographical *Long Day's Journey Into Night*, set eleven years before *A Moon for the Misbegotten*. Jim Tyrone, the dramatic counterpart of O'Neill's older brother Jamie, appears to be a lost cause. Now a middle-aged alcoholic, he exposes his own appalling behavior at the time of his mother's death in a long and demanding speech, the summit to be ascended by the actor playing him, in the climactic third act of the play. Seeking and receiving forgiveness from his deceased mother through Josie Hogan, his surrogate mother and thwarted lover, the character Jim would seem to be the focal point of the play.

Yet, recent productions have placed Josie in the foreground, presenting her as more than a means to Jim's deliverance, in a role considered to be equal to, or possibly greater than, that of Jim Tyrone. Some have speculated that the play may not belong to Jim Tyrone, or to Josie Hogan, or even to Jamie O'Neill, in whose memory it was written. In fact, the play may have served O'Neill's needs as much as his brother's. Unable to forgive his brother at the time of their mother's death, in writing the play, O'Neill lessens his own guilt while Josie assuages Jim's. In Josie, O'Neill has designed a maternal presence large enough to enfold and infantilize even a grown man, whether that man is Jim Tyrone or his creator, Eugene O'Neill. Josie is a virgin, pure and unspoiled, and at the same time, a sexual presence. With "all kinds of love" to give (*Moon* 927), she is willing to give it, even if it means sacrificing her own desires to save the man in her arms from his tortured past. The gift intended to diminish the suffering of a much loved and hated brother may have reverted to the giver. Finally, the play, as well as the catharsis it creates, may belong to O'Neill himself, with his presence the most pronounced.

The son of a matinee idol forever chained to the melodrama that made him famous, Eugene O'Neill, the reluctant "son of Monte Cristo," wanted no part of his father's theater, at times seeming to dedicate his career to ending drama as his father knew it. In the senior O'Neill's day, the star took center stage, with scant attention paid to the vehicle in which he or she appeared. Eugene O'Neill placed the emphasis on the play, and by extension, the playwright. Whether writing expressionistic dramas or inhabiting the realism that distinguished the early and late periods of his career, O'Neill was determined to create a theater of his own. And yet, the melodrama he found so antithetical made its way into his work with ironic frequency.

A Moon for the Misbegotten borrows its plot from melodrama in which a poor, but virtuous, family, often a father and his daughter, are in danger of losing their home, due to an inability to keep up the payments. Their problems are compounded by an unscrupulous landlord who will accept another form of payment for their debt in the form of the virginal daughter, whose honor will be compromised by the transaction. Even if marriage is promised by the dastardly villain, the family hopes for a last-minute rescue, usually by an upstanding citizen, who is, himself, in love with the innocent daughter, with his own plans to marry her.

While the Hogan family, Josie and Phil, may not entirely share the virtues of their melodramatic counterparts, they are in danger of losing the land they have been working for over twenty years. Following the death of his mother, Jim Tyrone becomes their de-facto landlord. Both landlord and friend to the family, he has promised to sell them the farm at a reduced price. But once the Hogans have humiliated T. Stedman Harder, the millionaire whose land adjoins theirs, their ownership of the farm is in jeopardy. Harder has no real interest in the land and wants only to evict them. Now the Hogans must contend with two layers of land-lord — in Tyrone and Harder.

But Tyrone is also the hoped-for rescuer. Although the Hogans are among the few to see Jim's good points, primarily in his loyalty to them, Phil also knows another side of their friend: "there's a sneering divil in him, and he loves to pick out the weakness in people and say cruel, funny things that flay the hide off them, or play cruel jokes on them" (*Moon* 898). In keeping with this final aspect of his personality, Jim agrees to Harder's terms but has no plans to honor them, in his own way, getting back at the son of Standard Oil, whose unearned affluence he detests. Although the farm and the family are safe from Harder — one villain vanquished — Phil convinces Josie that Jim is about to sell their home out from under them. At first glance, Phil appears to be reprehensible, encouraging his daughter in her seduction of Jim so that she will gain marriage or Jim's money in the bargain. In fact, he is using the scheme to bring the two together, knowing that this might be his daughter's last chance for happiness. Although she boasts of her promiscuity, Josie is the virginal daughter whose honor is intact, but the hoped-for rescue is an impossibility. Jim loves Josie, but he loathes himself more. Entering the play "like a dead man walking slow behind his own coffin" (*Moon* 874), Jim wants nothing more than to die. After a long and painful night of truth-telling, Jim receives forgiveness from Josie and then departs. He will never return, but he has been freed from the guilt that has tormented him.

Josie's realization that the two must part displays more than a touch of melodrama when she pours out her heart to the sleeping Tyrone, saying, "Oh Jim, Jim, maybe my love could still save you, if you want it enough! (*She shakes her head.*) No. That can never be" (*Moon* 934). At Jim's departure, he too speaks the language of melodrama. After pretending that he has no memory of Josie's generous sacrifice the night before, Jim begs her: "Forgive me, Josie. I do remember! I'm glad I remember! I'll never forget your love! (*He kisses her on the lips.*) Never! (*kissing her again*) Never, do you hear! I'll always love you, Josie. (*He kisses her again.*) Good-bye — and God bless you!" (*Moon* 945). The flurry of exclamation points is usually an indication of emotional excess, yet the emotions presented are genuine. In keeping with melodrama, Phil, the wronged father, curses Jim for disappointing his daughter, to which Josie replies, "Don't father! I love him!," a standard declaration in melodrama. Phil retreats from his accusation, admitting, "I didn't mean it. I know whatever happened he meant no harm to you. It was life I was cursing.... Or maybe I was cursing myself for a damned old scheming fool, like I ought to" (*Moon* 945).

The scheming that characterizes the first half of the play is analogous to the plot-driven complications of melodrama. Given that the actions of the three main characters often mask their true intentions, these complications multiply at a rapid pace. But in melodrama, justice often prevails, while in O'Neill's plays, it rarely does. Although the play emphasizes the comic potential of the intrigues in the first half, O'Neill's vision of the world usually finds more of the tragic in life. The play makes its way to tragedy in the second half by way of the bridge provided by the arrival of Jim Tyrone. An unseen listener in the scene with Harder, Jim is part of, and enjoys, the rustic comedy as the slick Harder is routed by the cleverer country folk. But hints are dropped by Jim, both within and outside of the Hogans' hearing, of a terrible secret that will be revealed before the play's end. The revelation of secrets is a staple of melodrama, as in *The Count of Monte Cristo*, when the truth of Albert's paternity is announced at the conclusion of the play by his mother Mercedes to Edmund Dantes, the Count of Monte Cristo and Albert's father. But melodrama ends once the secret is revealed, avoiding the more difficult task of considering the consequences of both the secret and its revelation. O'Neill's play goes beyond Jim's admission to face its outcome. Josie may forgive Jim, but she cannot save him; a night's peace is all that he will enjoy.

According to the plays of Eugene O'Neill, comedy makes life bearable, but tragedy is its essence. In keeping with this view, *A Moon for the Misbegotten* encompasses both. Sometimes accused of a split personality, the play challenges its viewers to reconcile the two as it makes the progression from the comic to the tragic. Without tragedy, the play would be little more than the enactment of a hoax; without comedy, the suffering would be unbearable. Rather than choose between them, O'Neill demonstrates in *A Moon for the Misbegotten* both the fundamental nature of the comic and the tragic, and the necessity of their co-existence.

The Plot

S[haughnessy]. play idea,
based on story told by E[dmund].
in 1st act of "L[ong]. D[ay's]. J[ourney]. I[nto]. N[ight]."
— except here Jamie principal character &
story of play otherwise entirely imaginary,
except J[amie].'s revelation of self.
— Work Diary, 28 October 1941

On a ramshackle farm in Connecticut in 1923, Josie Hogan and her father, Phil, are tenants on land owned by the Tyrone family. The twenty-eight-year-old Josie is an imposing physical presence; a large woman, she is "more powerful than any but an exceptionally strong man, able to do the manual labor of two ordinary men" (*Moon* 857). Without Josie, Phil would not be able to run the farm, especially now that she is helping her youngest brother, Mike, to escape their father and a lifetime of servitude. The only daughter, Josie is also the only one of his four children able to stand up to Phil, using physical force if necessary. Before the self-righteous Mike departs, he takes one last opportunity to lecture his older sister on the error of her ways. Josie has developed a reputation for promiscuity, which has scandalized not only her brother but also the local community. Mike suggests to Josie that she settle down with a decent man, if she can find one, or even an indecent one, someone like their landlord, Jim Tyrone, with whom Josie is secretly in love.

Describing each other as "the damnedest daughter of the damnedest father in Connecticut" (*Moon* 864), Josie and her father have an abiding affection for each other, although it is often masked by insults and a teasing banter. Drawn to the farm by his friendship with both Josie and Phil, Jim Tyrone has promised that that he will sell them the land on easy terms and at a reduced price. With the recent death of his mother, Jim is awaiting the completion of probate on her estate; then, he will return to the only world he really understands, under the bright lights of Broadway. An alcoholic and a third-rate actor, Jim has squandered his life on hard liquor and easy woman. When he arrives at the Hogans' farm, Jim appears to be his usual jovial, if hung-over, self, but privately he is tormented by unnamed wrongs that he has committed, compounded by the self-loathing that defines his character.

Like her father, who always has "a trick hidden behind his tricks" (*Moon* 869), Josie is not above the occasional swindle to sustain the family or to amuse herself. A case in point is the arrival of T. Stedman Harder, the coddled son of a local millionaire. Harder is furious that the Hogans' pigs have escaped through a broken fence to wallow in his ice pond. By birth and breeding, he is certain of his superiority to the Hogans, but Harder is no match for them. Their strategy in verbal battle, according to O'Neill, is "to take the offensive at once and never let an opponent get set to hit back. Also, they use a beautifully co-ordinated, bewildering change of pace, switching suddenly from jarring shouts to low, confidential vituperation" (*Moon* 884). With their quick wit, the Hogans easily subdue Harder by accusing him of attempting to murder their pigs, who have "caught their death of cold" in his pond (*Moon* 888). While Jim, hidden in the house, is convulsed with laughter, Harder retreats, threatening legal action if Phil breaks down the fence again. Jim promises to return later that evening for a moonlit date with Josie.

By eleven o'clock, Josie sits alone on the steps outside the farmhouse, with "an expression on her face that we have not seen before, a look of sadness and loneliness and humiliation" (*Moon* 892), certain that Jim has stood her up. Her father arrives, seemingly drunk after an evening at a nearby inn, with the news that Harder has made an offer to buy the farm at five times the price that the Hogans are able to pay, and that Jim has accepted, reneging on his promise to them. At Hogan's prompting, Josie agrees to the plan, first suggested by her brother Mike, that she seduce Jim in order to get him to marry her, or at least, to pay her off with the estate money in order to avoid the embarrassment of being discovered in her bed.

Despite Josie's reputation, Jim has seen through her disguise and has told Phil that he believes she is a virgin. This admission angers Josie, who agrees to the plan, feeling doubly betrayed by Jim.

When Jim finally arrives and Phil retires to the barn, Josie attempts to ply him and herself with a bottle of her father's best bonded Bourbon. Unused to drinking, Josie chokes on the liquor. Disgusted by her flailing attempts at shamelessness, Jim insists that this night be as different from all his other nights as Josie is as different from all his other women, praising her for being "real and healthy and clean and fine and warm and strong and kind" (*Moon* 915). Physically attracted to her "beautiful eyes and hair, and beautiful strong body" (*Moon* 916), Jim at first stops himself from going beyond a single kiss, making a reference to the "fat blonde pig on the train" (*Moon* 917). To keep him with her, Josie tells Jim that for one night, "everything is far away and doesn't matter — except the moon and its dreams" (*Moon* 917). She cannot convince him, however, for he cannot escape the past, insisting that "there is no present or future — only the past happening over and over again" (*Moon* 920).

A bad actor, Jim believes himself to be an even worse son. He has come to Josie to seek forgiveness for his disgraceful performance on the train carrying his mother's coffin back from the West Coast a year earlier. Before his mother's death, Jim had changed his ways, giving up drinking to please his mother, and serving as her companion after his father's death. With her death, Jim resumes a debauched lifestyle. For the duration of the journey home, he drank and consorted with a prostitute, behavior instigated by his reaction to seeing his mother in her coffin. As Jim confesses, she was "Practically a stranger. To whom I was a stranger. Cold and indifferent. Not worried about me anymore. Free at last. Free from worry. From pain. From me. I stood looking down at her, and something happened to me. I knew I should be heartbroken but I couldn't feel anything. I seemed dead, too" (*Moon* 930). Knowing that a dramatic scene was expected, the actor rose to the challenge and provided a public display of false grief, all the while, privately excoriating himself.

In his mind, Josie is at the same time a mother figure and a virgin, the only person with the purity, love, and understanding to purge him of his sins. Initially, Josie had hoped for a more romantic evening with Jim, which shifts to a desire for revenge once Phil reveals Jim's alleged betrayal.

In fact, Jim lied to Harder, never intending to sell the farm to him, of which Phil is fully aware, and Jim is hurt that Josie believed him capable of this transgression.

Like her father, Jim loves Josie "in his fashion" (*Moon* 915) and knows the truth about her, that she is not the wanton woman she pretends to be. Josie has created this mask to prove to herself that she is attractive, but once any man other than Jim shows an interest, she quickly rejects him. Relieved that the farm has been saved, and still in love with him, Josie offers herself to Jim, who forgets where he is for a moment and treats her like a prostitute. Josie recoils, Jim recovers himself, and then offers to leave. Instead, she takes him in her arms, holding him like the mother figure he desires, and listens to him confess his sins, beginning with the resumption of his drinking at the time of his mother's illness, and followed by the description of his nightly behavior with the blonde prostitute on the train, with his mother's coffin only a few cars away. Jim has created own form of revenge, blaming his mother for leaving him alone, admitting, "I knew I was lost, without any hope left — that all I could do would be drink myself to death, because no one was left who could help me" (*Moon* 932).

Only Josie can help him, but hers is not a permanent cure. She holds him through the night and forgives him, "as *she* forgives ... as *she* loves and understands and forgives" (*Moon* 933). Her own romantic dreams forsaken, Josie chooses instead to give Jim the kind of love he needs, saying, "I have all kinds of love for you — and maybe this is the greatest of all — because it costs so much" (*Moon* 927). As described by O'Neill, "this big sorrowful woman [hugs] a haggard-faced, middle-aged drunkard against her breast, as if he were a sick child" (*Moon* 935). Mocked by the lover's moon overhead, she holds him until the dawn breaks, along with her heart.

When Phil sneaks back the next morning, he admits to his scheme but insists that he did it not for the money but for Josie, to give her a final chance at happiness with Jim, so that the misbegotten pair, "would stop [their] damn pretending and face the truth that [they] loved each other" (*Moon* 944). Like Phil, Josie was mistaken in her belief about Jim: she "thought there was still hope" but now knows that "he'd died already — that it was a damned soul coming to [her] in the moonlight, to confess and be forgiven and find peace for a night" (*Moon* 937). In a *Pieta*-like pose, with the sleeping Tyrone in her arms, Josie declares with mocking irony that a miracle has occurred: "A virgin who bears a dead child in the night, and the dawn finds her still a virgin" (*Moon* 936).

Threatening to leave her father, Josie insists that he hide in the house until Jim has gone. She shakes the sleeping Tyrone, who has enjoyed a rare night of peace, sleeping without nightmares. At first he has no memory of the previous night and is aware only of the beauty of the sunrise, feeling "at peace with [himself] and this lousy life — as if all [his] sins had been forgiven" (*Moon* 942). Another sip of Phil's bourbon reminds him of what he has confessed to Josie, and his disgust returns. Before Jim leaves, Josie reminds him of her love for him, and he responds in kind, although they know that this will be their last meeting. When Phil reappears after Jim's departure, Josie's threat to leave him is rescinded, and they return to their bantering ways; as she says to her father, "living with you has spoilt me for any other man, anyway" (*Moon* 945). In less than twenty-four hours, the lives of Josie and Jim have been radically altered. The play ends with Josie's own form of Irish prayer for the departed Jim: "May you have your wish and die in your sleep soon, Jim, darling. May you rest forever in forgiveness and peace" (*Moon* 946).

1

The Original Production, 1947

Described as "a debacle from start to finish" (Barbara Gelb, "Theater History" iii), the original production of *A Moon for the Misbegotten*, produced by the Theatre Guild in 1947, had its share of problems, from casting difficulties to a controversy over censorship. A study of the production creates a more prismatic rendering, however, as the producers, actors, director, and critics offer an experience of the events that is widely divergent. It would be another twenty-five years before the play would be regarded as great, but the original production of *Moon* was not an outright disaster. A series of circumstances quashed its chance for success, most notably the weight of O'Neill's reputation, which was undeniably an advantage as well as one of the chief impediments to the production.

Eugene O'Neill's long history with the Theatre Guild spanned twenty years. O'Neill's contempt for what he called the "show-shop" of Broadway, combined with the Theatre Guild's reputation for producing the challenging drama that commercial producers usually avoid, made this a logical pairing. Yet, the partnership was not easily realized: the Guild rejected five of O'Neill's plays, including *"Anna Christie,"* before agreeing to produce *Marco Millions* and *Strange Interlude* during the 1927–1928 season. And once the match was made, theirs was a long, and not entirely happy, marriage.

In the early years of the twentieth century, Broadway was no place for serious drama. Producers catered to what they thought the American public wanted, producing mostly melodramas and vaudeville attractions. This left those in search of more challenging fare to create a theatrical home of their own. In 1914, the Washington Square Players were organized, with members including the producer and patent lawyer Lawrence Langner, the actress Helen Westley, and the director Philip Moeller, a trio who would later form the nucleus of the Theatre Guild. The Players presented such daring and difficult plays as Ibsen's *Ghosts* and Shaw's *Mrs. Warren's Profession*, and they were the first to produce Chekhov in New York.

The group disbanded when America entered World War I. In 1918, with the signing of the armistice, Langner, Westley, and Moeller initiated a new enterprise, dropping the name Washington Square Players, in part to avoid some old debts, and setting out to create an art-theatre. As described by Langner, "It must be a little theatre grown up.... It should be a professional theatre, employ professional actors and produce long plays 'which should be great plays'" (115). This emphasis on the professional distanced the Theatre Guild from their early endeavors with the Washington Square Players, and from another creative collective, the Provincetown Players, with whom O'Neill was initially associated. The Theatre Guild regarded the Provincetown Players as amateur in everything except their playwrights, Susan Glaspell and Eugene O'Neill (Langner 229).

The original Board of Managers, in addition to Langner, Westley, and Moeller, were Rollo Peters, designated as director, Helen Freeman, Justus Sheffield, and Lee Simonson, who became the Guild's production designer. Due to policy disputes, Peters and Freeman left the board after the first season, while Sheffield chose to develop his law practice. The stockbroker Maurice Wertheim, who underwrote some of the Guild's financial losses, joined the board after the first production. Theresa Helburn was added as a board member and "play representative," recommending works for the board's consideration. Roy S. Waldau, in *Vintage Years of the Theatre Guild*, notes that "if the Guild's managers had any one thing in common, besides a burning desire to promote worthwhile theater, ... it was their academic background" (8). A number of schools, Harvard and Columbia among them, were represented by the Board. At Harvard, Simonson, Wertheim, and Helburn attended George Pierce Baker's famous "English 47," which O'Neill also sat in on, learning an approach to playwriting, by beginning the process with a detailed scenario, which he employed throughout his career. The managers' meetings were compared to a university faculty meeting by Walter Prichard Eaton, who was commissioned by the Guild to write a history of their first ten, and later fifteen, years.

According to Langner, "it was the function of the Board to select the plays, directors, actors and scenic artists, and to supervise all the details of production, acting and revision of the plays" (158). "Governed absolutely by a committee" that voted on all aspects of production, (Langner 116), the managers' meetings could be contentious, but they were mild in comparison to a ritual unofficially known as the "death watch," when the managers would sit in on a complete run-through of a given production, usually on a Sunday afternoon, and afterwards offer a critique to the director. The managers' collective taste had to be satisfied, and this was usually the toughest audience that the actors had to face. The fact that the Theatre Guild was run as a collective proved to be a distinct advantage in the summer of 1919, when the first major strike of Actors' Equity, the actors union, closed the legitimate theaters in New York. Equity approved of the Guild's cooperative organizational structure, and allowed the production of St. John Ervine's *John Ferguson* to proceed. A tale of poor but virtuous Irish farmers, an unpaid mortgage, and a girl "in trouble," *John Ferguson* became a hit due to the fact that it was the only show open that summer, providing the Theatre Guild with a much-needed financial windfall.

The Guild's often contentious board of directors seemed to agree on only one thing when choosing a production. During the early decades of the twentieth century, the "great plays" were European or anything other than American. According to Langner, "there were no playwrights in America of the stature of Chekhov, Shaw, Galsworthy and Granville-Barker, with the sole exception of Eugene O'Neill" (142). Although not all of their plays were chosen from this distinguished list of playwrights, *John Ferguson* being one example, the Guild aspired to greatness in choosing its authors. Overtures had been made to O'Neill, whose frustration with the Guild was evident in a letter he wrote to Langner, dated 10 January 1921, in which he states, "the whole thing, to my mind, boils down to this: Either you have faith in my plays, or you haven't. If you have, you produce them. If not, not. And you have turned down three of mine already.

In rejections of my work you have a clear lead over any other management" (qtd. in Langner 231).

Nearly all was forgiven when, during their tenth season, the Guild produced two O'Neill's plays, the anti-capitalist *Marco Millions* and the experimental *Strange Interlude*. But this was not achieved without a fight. The board was initially cool to the prospect of the lavish production required by *Marco Millions* and to a nine-act Freudian drama in which a third of the dialogue is spoken as asides. At least one board member said of *Strange Interlude* that the play would be greatly improved if the asides were taken out (Langner 237). On 21 April 1927, Langner wrote what he describes as a "stinging" letter to the board as part of a campaign to secure the production, saying that "in *Strange Interlude* we have probably the bravest and most far-reaching dramatic experiment which has been seen in the theatre since the days of Ibsen.... The play contains in it more deep knowledge of the dark corners of the human mind than anything that has ever been written before. It proclaims O'Neill the great dramatic genius of the age" (234). The hyperbole had the desired effect. The Guild produced both *Marco Millions*, which opened in January 1928 to mixed notices, and *Strange Interlude*, which opened two weeks later, and was both a critical and a financial success. With performances that began at 5:30 in the afternoon, interrupted by a dinner break, followed by a second half that continued past 11 P.M., *Strange Interlude* seemed an unlikely popular success. But the innovative technique of having characters speak their thoughts made *Strange Interlude* the must-see event of the season and a must-read for those outside the immediate viewing area. The production played sold-out performances for a year and a half, even through the un-airconditioned New York summer. It broke all box office records for the Theatre Guild and was followed by a tour that ran for two years and traveled as far as London. Both the Guild and the author benefited; *Strange Interlude* was for O'Neill a great financial success. By 1931, the play in its published version had sold more than 100,000 copies, one reason for the $275,000 windfall that O'Neill earned from the play.

This production seemed to be the beginning of a beautiful friendship. The Guild produced a number of O'Neill plays in the years that followed, beginning with *Dynamo* in 1929, *Mourning Becomes Electra* in 1931, *Ah, Wilderness!* in 1933, *Days Without End* in 1934, and *The Iceman Cometh* in 1946. O'Neill won the 1936 Nobel Prize in Literature for many of the works represented on this list; for similar reasons, the years 1928–1939 are considered the vintage years of the Theatre Guild. The twelve-year break between O'Neill plays produced by the Theatre Guild ended with *A Moon for the Misbegotten*, a play that never made it to New York in its original production.

In the intervening years, from 1934 to 1946, the Theatre Guild had its share of successes, including the musicals *Oklahoma* (1943) and *Carousel* (1945), but had not been able to maintain its status as the prestige producer in New York. Feuding on the Board had forced out two of the most vital members, the designer Lee Simonson and the director Philip Moeller. Several times the Guild nearly folded, saved on one occasion by Philip Barry's *Holiday*, starring Katharine Hepburn, which also saved the career of Hepburn, who had been branded box-office poison. For his part, O'Neill had been absent from Broadway for a full ten years, in part due to a proposed eleven-play cycle, entitled "A Tale of Possessors Self-Dispossessed." O'Neill finished only one of the cycle plays, *A Touch of the Poet*, with *More Stately Mansions* surviving as a revised typescript. The drafts of the other cycle plays were destroyed before his death. O'Neill also wrote several non-cycle plays during this decade, including *The Iceman Cometh, Long Day's Journey Into Night*, and *Hughie. A Moon for the Misbegotten* was the last play that O'Neill completed, the tremor in his hands making it impossible for him to write.*

As his greatest champion at the Theatre Guild, Lawrence Langner was eager to renew the professional acquaintance with O'Neill. The author's third wife, Carlotta Monterey, was less enthusiastic. She, like O'Neill, knew how things stood with the Theatre Guild, and advised her husband not to let the producer read *A Moon for the Misbegotten*. Well aware that the Guild's desire to renew its reputation would work to his advantage, O'Neill gave Langner a copy of the play during the producer's visit to San Francisco in 1944.

---

*Misdiagnosed with Parkinson's disease, O'Neill actually suffered from late-onset cerebellar cortical atrophy, a disease of unknown origin, discovered when his brain was autopsied at his wife's request at Boston's Mass General Hospital after his death in 1953. This affliction was unrelated either to family genetics or to the binge drinking that characterized O'Neill's younger days.

Begun in late October 1941 and completed in 1943, *A Moon for the Misbegotten* serves in some ways as a continuation of O'Neill's autobiographical *Long Day's Journey Into Night* in which the story of the Tyrone family closely follows the pattern of his own. With an aging matinee idol father, a morphine-addicted mother, an alcoholic older brother, and a tubercular younger brother, based on O'Neill himself, *Journey* offers a harrowing look at the family's dynamics. In spite of these circumstances, the play presents a forgiving portrait of the parents, though O'Neill felt that his older brother, Jamie, might have been portrayed too harshly. He wrote *Moon* to rectify this impression. O'Neill stipulated that *Journey* not be made available until twenty-five years after his death, a wish that was not respected, though the play was not performed during his lifetime. When *Moon* was first presented in 1947, it was without the preface of *Journey*.

From the August day in 1912 when *Journey* is set, *A Moon for the Misbegotten* jumps forward to 1923. Jamie Tyrone, now known as Jim, has recently buried his beloved mother and is seeking forgiveness for his sins, real and imagined. Jim looks to Josie Hogan, the daughter of a tenant farmer, for comfort and absolution. Aside from his mother, Josie is the only woman that he has ever loved, and Josie returns his love. Her own romantic intentions must be displaced, however, in order to save Jim from himself. He confesses his deepest secret to Josie, who acts as a mother-substitute and forgives him, sending him off to face the early death he so deeply desires.

In the October 28 entry of his *Work Diary*, O'Neill identifies the events of *Moon* as "entirely imaginary, except for J's revelation of self." The characters were inspired by real people, however. Clearly, Jim Tyrone is based on O'Neill's older brother, and some of the tales the character recounts, such as being expelled from boarding school after bringing a prostitute to the campus and introducing her as his sister, come from his brother's own life. From childhood, Jamie O'Neill had a profound emotional attachment to his mother, Ella. His mother's companion during the long theatrical tours that sustained his father's career, Jamie was stunned when a second son, Edmund, was born, and he was forced to share his mother's attention with a sibling. Left at home with his grandmother and his year-old brother, the seven-year-old Jamie infected the child with measles, which he survived, but his brother did not. Blamed by his mother for the death of Edmund, Jamie was later dispatched to boarding school, not as a punishment, but to receive the education he would not get while his parents traveled, often playing short dates or one-night stands. A popular and successful student, Jamie initially flourished.

His academic promise did not survive the realization that his mother had become addicted to morphine after the birth of her third son, Eugene. With his mother's encouragement, Jamie blamed his father for her condition, and his relationship with James Sr. became increasingly venomous. Jamie's subsequent failure to thrive at a number of academic institutions led to his acceptance into his father's acting company, after which he was often reminded by James of "a thirty-five-thousand-dollar education and a thirty-five-dollar-a-week earning capacity" (qtd. in Gelb, *Life with Monte Cristo* 411). Jamie's behavior onstage at times was erratic; he was known to revise his lines to produce lewd phrases, and to invite a few of the local prostitutes to sit in the boxes next to the stage and cheer his performance.

Following the death of his father in 1920, Jamie resumed the role he most enjoyed, his mother's closest companion. He cleaned up his act, ended his drinking and womanizing, and was happy for a time. In 1922, while traveling in California, his mother suffered a stroke from which she did not recover. Devastated by her illness, Jamie began to drink again. According to Mrs. Libby Drummer, a family friend, in a letter describing Ella's final days, "[Ella] knew he was drinking before she died and realized everything and was helpless" (qtd. in Sheaffer, *Son and Artist* 85; Black 285). Jamie's disgraceful behavior at the time of his mother's death, up to and including an attempt to cut his brother out of an equal division of the property, only added to their growing estrangement. O'Neill was angered by Jamie's inability to attend their mother's funeral, "too broken up" (Sheaffer, *Son and Artist* 87) after his mother's death and the traumatic experience of bringing his mother's coffin home, to pay his final respects to the woman he so dearly loved, and whose loss effectively ended his own life.

By 1923, when *Moon* is set, Jamie O'Neill was living in a sanitarium in Paterson, New Jersey. Prohibition whisky had cost him his sight, and his scurrilous behavior, his brother's affection. Although Jamie made a number of requests, O'Neill refused to visit. By setting the play in September 1923, O'Neill places the events two months before the death of his brother, on November 8, and a year after the death of his mother. In a letter to his friend and attorney Harry Weinberger, dated 28 September 1942, he explains why his daughter Oona, who had previously been named "Debutante No. 1" at the Stork Club in New York, should not go on the stage, thus extending her frivolity in a time of war and also trading on her father's name. O'Neill describes the wasted opportunities that characterized his brother's life: "I had a brother once who took the easy way of going on the stage and trading on his father's name. He became a third-rate actor — a nice, lazy job, when you've got a job, and have someone to support you when you haven't. He ended up in tragedy, embittered, with his life wasted and ruined. The pity of it was, he had a fine brain. I loved him and I can never forget the easy start that murdered the life he might have had" (*Selected Letters* 533). In *A Moon for the Misbegotten*, O'Neill finally permits his brother, and himself, a measure of the peace denied Jamie in life, and which Jamie denied himself.

The character Phil Hogan was inspired by John "Dirty" Dolan, a tenant farmer on one of James O'Neill's properties. Having emigrated in the late 1880's, Dolan, his second wife, two daughters, and two sons, rented a ramshackle farm from James O'Neill, Sr., for the princely sum of $35 dollars per month (Gelb, *Monte Cristo* 203). Dolan, like O'Neill, was a recurrent visitor to New London's Montauk Inn, the model for the offstage barroom frequented by Jim Tyrone in *Moon*. There, the young O'Neill would have heard the account of the feisty Irishman besting his social superiors on the matter of where his pigs would swim. An amusing anecdote in *Journey*, the encounter is central to the plot of *Moon*.

As described by biographer Louis Sheaffer, "[Dolan] was a squarish tree-stump of a man, bandy-legged, with arms like massive branches; ruddy-faced with the sun and all his drinking, he had soft blue eyes and a habitual grin that gave him a deceptive genial look." He came by his nickname honestly: refusing to bathe before he entered a hospital, when a friend proceeded to wash his feet, Dolan howled, "You're taking my toes off!" (qtd. in *Son and Playwright* 260). As the fictional Tyrone says to Phil, when his host offers him water to drink instead of whiskey, "Water? That's something people wash with, isn't it? I mean, some people." Phil replies, "So I've heard. But, like you, I find it hard to believe" (*Moon* 878). The character Phil has also been identified as an homage to O'Neill's father.

Judith Barlow cites a revealing line deleted from the typescript of the play. Jim says, "Your esteemed Old Man would have made a hit on the stage, Josie. He's a natural born actor —." Barlow also notes one of Carlotta's diary entries, dated 11 August 1936, in which she states that her husband wanted to write "a *comedy* of his father! A loveable, *kind* comedy" (qtd. in Barlow 112). A loveable, kind comedy is not what O'Neill wrote, and Carlotta did not feel kindly toward *Moon*, finding some of the play's content in questionable taste, particularly the closeness of life to art in the recreation of O'Neill's own brother.

Josie Hogan comes from a variety of sources as well as from O'Neill's imagination. Her maternal instincts are based in part on O'Neill's governess and surrogate mother, Sarah Sandy. Aspects of Josie's physical and emotional life come from Christine Ell, whom O'Neill met in Greenwich Village. Having previous run the Oaks, a restaurant in Provincetown, Ell, a talented cook, had taken over the restaurant of Louis Hallady, a former roommate of O'Neill's, when Halladay was sent to jail for failing to secure a liquor license. Ell was the illegitimate daughter of a Danish serving girl and a German army officer. When she and her family came to America, she was placed in service by her mother and step-father, then forced into factory work when she was still a child. Seduced by her step-father, a laborer named Lockhoven, Ell left home when she was 14. Her early life would have destroyed a lesser mortal, but by 1915, she was a fixture of the Greenwich Village scene frequented by O'Neill.

Described by her friend Agnes Boulton, as "tall and voluptuous, with the ugliest face ever seen on a woman ... and the most gorgeous, the most wonderful pile of red-gold hair, too heavy and too alive to stay properly on her head" (16), Ell was a sometime artist's model. At nearly six feet tall, she felt deeply the differences in her physical stature from the fashionable women of her day, convinced that she was unattractive. A talented mimic — the Germanic Theodore Dreiser was a specialty — she played the clown to distract from her physical features. Despite having a husband, Lewis B. Ell, whom she loved, Ell engaged in a lively social life, including extramarital affairs with the two O'Neill brothers. In both her size and her generosity of spirit, she served as a model for Josie Hogan.

Dorothy Day also shared an intense friendship with O'Neill during this time, though their relationship was not a sexual one. Before she founded the Catholic Workers Movement, Day spend evenings drinking with O'Neill at a bar called The Golden Swan, nicknamed the "Hell Hole" and located at the corner of Sixth Avenue and Fourth Street. She enjoyed listening to O'Neill recite poetry, most notably Francis Thompson's "The Hound of Heaven," which he knew by heart. Day described to her biographer, William Miller, putting a drunken O'Neill in her bed and holding him until he could sleep, while deflecting his sodden offers to end her virginity (110). According to O'Neill biographer Stephen Black, "Miller believed that Dorothy told him the story to let him know that she considered herself the model for Josie Hogan in *A Moon for the Misbegotten*, the women who holds Jim Tyrone in her arms all night to chase away his devils" (205).

The owner of the ice pond in which the Hogan pigs were reputed to bathe, T. Stedman Harder, was based on two particular plutocrats, both of whom lived on estates in Waterford, Connecticut, near O'Neill's New London home. These sons of Mammon were Edward Stephen Harkness, an heir to the Standard Oil fortune, and Edward Crowninshield Hammond, the actual owner of the ice pond. O'Neill's deep resentment of their type is evident in his initial description of Harder: "Coddled from birth, everything arranged and made easy for him, deferred to because of his wealth, he usually has the self-confident attitude of acknowledged superiority, but assumes a supercilious, insecure air when dealing with people beyond his ken" (*Moon* 884). In the play, the Hogans are clearly beyond his acquaintance or understanding.

Writing of the play, in a letter dated 2 February 1942, from Tao House in Danville, California, O'Neill told his son Eugene: "Last week I finished the first draft of a new play, *A Moon for the Misbegotten*. A good title, eh? I wish I could report the first draft lived up to it, but it does not. Much work to do before it will be anything. A case of too much war on the brain. Pearl Harbor exploded when I was starting the most difficult part. After that I dragged through the rest. It is an extremely simple play with only three characters, and almost plotless from the usual dramatic structure standpoint, so it takes a lot of doing. However, I'm enthusiastic about the idea and eventually I hope to make it what it should be. Just now I'm too sunk in spirit, what with war and rainy season blues and physical ailments, to feel up to it" (*Selected Letters* 526). When producer Lawrence

Langner read the play, he was effusive in his praise, finding it, "one of the greatest plays O'Neill has ever written, and one of the truly great tragedies written in our time. The play has, in its final act, and at the end of the second act, the spiritual uplift which is the characteristic quality of all great tragedy, and along with it is such a profound knowledge of the good and evil in humanity as to raise it head and shoulders above *"Anna Christie,"* which it resembles to some extent in its father-daughter and lover relationship. Indeed, the maturity which 'Gene had reached as a dramatist can well be measured by contrasting these two magnificent plays; the first, *"Anna Christie"* with its partly happy ending (and I am not averse to happy endings), and *A Moon for the Misbegotten* with its ruthless tragic finality" (402). Langner secured this play for the Theatre Guild along with the opportunity to produce *The Iceman Cometh*, though O'Neill preferred to wait a year or two on the latter production, feeling that the play's relentless pessimism would clash with the country's post-war optimism and result in a poor reception. It was determined that *Moon* would open the Guild's 1946–1947 season, and that the O'Neills would move East for the opening.

After a second reading, the producer began to realize some of the play's inherent difficulties. As he stated in his autobiography, *The Magic Lantern*, published in 1951, "the leading woman was to be a veritable giantess — indeed, exactly the kind of woman who, when she comes to see you and asks to advise her whether she should attempt a career in the theatre — you look embarrassed and reply, 'Well, I'm afraid you're a rather big girl — how are we to find a man tall enough to play opposite you?'" (Langner 402). Langner continues, "In addition to the physical requirements of the actress, she must be tremendously experienced in the theatre and must have exactly the kind of emotional acting experience that it would difficult for a girl of her size to obtain" (403). O'Neill's description of Josie Hogan is memorable: "so oversize for a woman that she is almost a freak — five feet eleven in her stockings and weighs about one hundred and eighty." To Mary Welch, the actress who would play her, she was described by the casting officials at the Theatre Guild as "a great earth-mother symbol, and the actress who plays her should have a range from farce to Greek tragedy" (83).

With these descriptions to work with, the casting of Josie posed a formidable problem. The Theatre Guild searched New York, Hollywood, Dublin, and London for an actress to fill the physical and emotional dimensions of the role. A relatively unknown Broadway actress, Mary Welch was the leading candidate, though the playwright was concerned about her somewhat limited acting experience, her "too normal" size, and, most importantly, her degree of Irishness. With parents born in County Cork, Welch passed that part of the audition, and appeared at subsequent readings pounds heavier from a diet of potatoes, bananas, and pies. At the time, a provision known as the "potato clause" was in vogue in Hollywood, stipulating that an actress could not gain weight or substantially alter her appearance. When Welch was finally cast in the role, she signed a contract with a different kind of potato clause, which read, "The artist agrees to gain the necessary weight required for the role." According to the actress, O'Neill's main concern was not her size but that "Miss Welch understands how Josie feels" (Welch 82). This is surprising, given O'Neill's usual insistence that the stage directions be followed to the letter. Subsequent Josies, from Colleen Dewhurst to Kate Nelligan, from Salome Jens to Cherry Jones, have emphasized the emotional amplitude of the character over a misplaced preoccupation with size.

The Theatre Guild attempted to interest a long list of directors in the project, initially contacting Dudley Digges, a Guild regular, about directing the production. John Huston was also approached. Over twenty years before, at age 18, Huston sat in on all of the rehearsals of O'Neill's *Desire Under the Elms*, which was a great success for his father, the character actor Walter Huston, who played the role of the patriarch Ephraim Cabot, and was one of the few actors to live up to O'Neill's original conception of the character; Charles Gilpin, in *The Emperor Jones*, and Louis Wolheim, in *The Hairy Ape*, being the other two. In his autobiography, *The Open Door*, Huston described the lasting effect of this experience: "What I learned there during those weeks of rehearsal would serve me for the rest of my life. Not that I was aware of it at the time. I only knew that I was fascinated" (35). Even before reading the play, Huston responded with an immediate yes. Film commitments at Warner Brothers prevented him from taking on the assignment, a genuine disappointment for Huston, who apologized in person to the playwright and described how meaningful the experience of *Desire Under the Elms* had been for him. Josh

Logan was also offered the chance to direct, but he telegrammed his regrets on 26 November 1946, saying that it was a "tough job for a director" (Theatre Guild Collection). Rouben Mamoulian was approached; better known as a director of films, he had enjoyed successes in several of the Theatre Guild's musical offerings, including *Porgy and Bess*, *Oklahoma*, and *Carousel*, as well as the O'Neill drama *Marco Millions*. In a memo to Mamoulian from Associate Producer Armina Marshall Langner, dated 4 December 1946, with copies sent to Mr. and Mrs. O'Neill, the director was told to consider it "only as a production which would have [the] utmost simplicity and Mr. O'Neill's directions followed to the letter: that there is no opportunities [sic] for a director's 'holiday' since his job is really to get performances from the actors" (Theatre Guild Collection). The offer was retracted after O'Neill insisted on an Irish director — Mamoulian was an Armenian trained in Moscow — though it is difficult to imagine a director known for lavish productions meshing with the character-driven tale of a pig farmer's daughter. Only after the cast was set did the Guild secure the services of director Arthur Shields. Shields was the brother of character actor Barry Fitzgerald, the Guild's first choice for the role of Josie's father, Phil Hogan. A veteran of the Abbey Theatre, Shields was in keeping with the all–Irish imperative that O'Neill had established for the principal players.

If the search for a director and an "overlarge Irish damsel with the acting abilities of a Duse" (Langner 404) was not challenge enough, the casting of the male roles provided its own set of difficulties. Barry Fitzgerald was unavailable due to a lucrative radio contract, and the actor James Dunn, discussed as a possibility for Jim Tyrone, initially had film commitments. Dunn was a song-and-dance man who was signed by Fox Films in 1931, and appeared with Shirley Temple in her first three films. By the late 1930's, musicals were out of fashion, and this, combined with Dunn's alcoholism, made him virtually unemployable. Dunn is best known for his film appearance as the alcoholic father in *A Tree Grows in Brooklyn*, for which he won the Academy Award for Best Supporting Actor in 1945; he was cast in the role of Jim Tyrone based on this performance. As the "name" player in the production, Dunn received a run-of the-play contract and $1,000 per week, compared to the standard contract and $350-a-week salary of Mary Welch. The Irish actor James M. (or J.M.) Kerrigan was cast as Phil Hogan at $750 a week. There was a small flurry of publicity surrounding the casting of Welch's understudy in the role of Josie. A tall blonde actress named Maria Minton, better known as Maria Riva, was cast. She is perhaps best known as the daughter of Marlene Dietrich.

With O'Neill in attendance, the first table reading in New York went reasonably well until the third act, when the tragedy of the play began to overwhelm the cast. According to Langner, "Dunn began to cry. 'I'm sorry,' he said. This is just too much for me.' 'Take a rest,' said Arthur Shields, the director, in his rich Irish voice. 'No,' replied Dunn. 'I'll go right ahead.' He continued to read, but was so overcome by tears that he could not continue. We all decided to take a rest. After a while Mary Welch began to cry and had to stop reading, by which time everybody sitting around the table had tears in their eyes. Said Dunn, 'We're *all* crying now. I guess it will be the management's time to cry later.'" Langner ends the anecdote with "How right he was" (407).

From the first reading, O'Neill had not been happy with the play in rehearsal, but rather than cancel the production — with the scenery built and contracts signed — the Theatre Guild proposed a tryout in several Midwest cities before the Broadway opening. O'Neill reluctantly agreed, and provided a list of preferred cities in which the play could appear. According to Louis Sheaffer, "Where the Guild was doubtful of Miss Welch, the playwright was chiefly dissatisfied with Dunn and complained to Langner that the actor was not making Jamie Tyrone enough of a gentleman. Langner, unaware [at the time] that the character was based on O'Neill's brother, felt that the playwright held an 'idealized' image of the character" (*Son and Artist* 594). O'Neill was too ill to attend all but a few of the rehearsals; Mary Welch describes him at their first meeting as "more bone than flesh" (82). The playwright advised the actors not to forsake the comedy of the first two acts and to wait until the third act to play the tragedy.

While producer Lawrence Langner might not have known that the character Jim Tyrone was based on O'Neill's brother, actor James Dunn was unaware of almost all things O'Neill. Dunn had never seen an O'Neill play, and as he told Louis Sheaffer, "I didn't want to do it (*A Moon for the Misbegotten*). I really didn't like it. I like to do comedy. I love to hear people laugh.... My wife, she's the one, told me to do it — Eugene O'Neill, the Theatre Guild, a big prestige thing" (*Son and Artist* 594). Dunn was not sure that the Guild understood him, and he definitely found the Guild's treatment of O'Neill baffling: "The Guild built a wall around him.... They made an idol out of him. Someone would come dashing into the Guild and say, 'He's just turned in from Fifth Avenue.' A little later, someone announcing, 'O'Neill is coming up the stairs.' One day I got down on my knees and as he walked in, salaamed, 'God O'Neill.' He liked it, I could tell from his face, but the Guild didn't know how to take me" (Sheaffer, "Notes/Dunn" 1).

Due to O'Neill's ill health, the dress rehearsal was performed in New York rather than Columbus, Ohio, the first stop on the tour. The unusual step of a New York dress rehearsal added $5,000 to the budget, an additional 10% to the entire production cost. After the rehearsal, the playwright reassured Mary Welch, telling her, "I know you will play Josie the way I want" (83).

Attended by the Governor of Ohio and his daughter as well as the fashionable Mrs. James Dunn, wreathed in "a halo of roses and a black satin dress" according to *Time* Magazine (47), the opening at the Hartman Theater on 20 February 1947 was the social event of the season and the biggest cultural event that Columbus had seen since before the war. The O'Neills were not in attendance, but the critics were out in force. Samuel T. Wilson, the premier critic in Columbus, wrote in the *Dispatch*: "Developments of narrative, establishment of motivation, [and] definition of character are in the deliberate, painstaking O'Neill tradition. However long [and] drawn-out some of this may have seemed on opening night, the fact remains that none of it is functionally extraneous, nor is the old-time melodramatic plotting and counter-plotting heard in the first and second acts with deliberate, nicely calculated design. The muted beauty and the tremendous emotional impact of the climactic third act would lack much of its effectiveness against any other background." Wilson found Dunn to be "admirably cast" but monotonous in his long speech in the third act; Mary Welch has "all the basic elements the long and taxing role of Josie requires, the stature, the voice, the intelligence, the spiritual awareness. Her comedy playing is, at present, insecure and a bit forced. The emotional side of her performance she has essentially in her grasp" (14A).

Critic Elliot Norton, who traveled from Boston, described the play as "profoundly beautiful," writing: "This is O'Neill at his peak, the O'Neill who has always been fascinated with the idea of stricken human beings who 'belong' to each other.... It is simple romantic tragedy in prose that touches the hem of poetry, written from the heart to move the heart" (Theatre Guild Collection). Norton found the actors nervous in the early scenes but "far more convincing" (Sheaffer, "Notes/Reviews" 1) as the play progressed. He wrote of Mary Welch, whose name he got wrong: "Mary Ward, a hitherto unknown actress who must be close to 6 feet tall, plays the girl in a performance that is not yet perfected. In the early scenes she lacks the hard, sharp tongue, the vigor and quick authority of a girl who could curb or even hit a hard father. In the later scenes, which are far better lighted, she is pictorially and otherwise far more convincing" (Theatre Guild Collection). Writing in the *Boston Post*, on 21 February 1947, he added, "[The play] is not likely to get to Boston" (qtd. in Sheaffer, *Son and Artist* 595).*

At the second stop on the tour, during the week of 24 February 1947, William F. McDermott, who also saw the play in Columbus, wrote in the Cleveland *Plain Dealer*, that the play was "still rough in spots" but also "a harsh, powerful play ... [containing] some of the best and most touching writing of the greatest American playwright." McDermott continued, "the words were not only too numerous but not always chosen with O'Neill's habitual taste and discretion. In striving for frankness and realism he sometimes seemed to achieve mere sensationalism. The play deals with Irish characters, or characters with a strong strain of Irish in them, and the Irish are not dirty talkers. I feel sure that what O'Neill had in mind is not completely realized by the performance of this play" (qtd. in *Time* 47). This objection to the characters as "dirty talkers" would come to haunt the production; apparently, an Irish American writing of Irish Americans should present his characters as models of decorum rather than recognizable human beings. The anonymous reviewer from *Variety* noted that while the

*The same objection to Welch's performance, that she was not rough and tough enough, had been raised by the producers at the Theatre Guild in the rehearsal notes. In fact, supervising producer Theresa Helburn, after executing all the contracts, questioned the choice of Welch in the role, asking Langner in a memo: "Is this really what we want?" (Theatre Guild Collection).

play "still needs more tightening and better tempo, ... none could deny the strange beauty of the "Moon" mood of disillusionment, nor the heart-hitting fervor of the emotional clashes created by the three lead characters as they futilely try to buy their lost dreams" (qtd. in *Time* 48).

At Pittsburgh's Nixon Theatre, the production, which opened on 3 March 1947, was treated to a censorious reaction by both critics and civic leaders. William F. McFall, president of the local chamber of commerce, "admitted he hadn't seen the play ... [but] received an unbiased report on it from reputable business leaders, and was shocked at what they reported" ("Detroit" 7). Mrs. Florence Parry, writing in her column "I Dare Say" in the Pittsburgh *Press*, was equally scandalized "at this evidence of deterioration in a playwright who for over 20 years has maintained an indisputable place as the greatest dramatist of our time" (qtd. in "Detroit" 7). Apparently, the good people of Pittsburgh were not the only ones offended by O'Neill's play. J.M. Kerrigan, who had been well-received by critics in his role as Phil Hogan, chose to leave the production after Pittsburgh, with actor Rhys Williams brought in to complete the run.

There was trouble brewing before Pittsburgh, however. According to the production notes, on the sixth day of rehearsal, Kerrigan walked out. Later, when the cast was interviewed by local papers before the production opened in Columbus, Kerrigan was nowhere to been seen. James Dunn, acting as a sort of master of ceremonies for the event, assured the press that Kerrigan was off enjoying the great art museums of Columbus. Kerrigan's contract called for two weeks notice if he planned to leave the cast. If this clause was invoked, he gave his notice almost immediately after leaving New York. According to *Variety*, in typical *Variety* speak, Kerrigan "has disliked role of boozy, profane Irish farmer from Connecticut, right along, having been skeptical from moment it was offered him, but feeling he might be able to do something with it. Those close to the situation say veteran actor chiefly resented light in which O'Neill had placed the Irish, and furthermore, he's supposed to have told friend, Kerrigan couldn't stomach the profanities he had to mouth, claiming he'd never before cussed on the stage" ("'Moon' Found Anti-Irish" 7). The alleged profanities, mostly variations on the word "damn," would be considered mild today.

But nothing could have prepared the company for the reception in Detroit, where the censor was ready and waiting for them. Expected to open at the Cass Theatre on 10 March 1947, the production was welcomed with a red banner headline in the local *Times*, which read, "O'Neill Play Closed For Obscenity." Police censor Charles Snyder found the play to be "a slander on American motherhood" (qtd. in Sheaffer, *Son and Artist* 595) and insisted that the play be rewritten before the show could go on. Producers Theresa Helburn and Armina Marshall Langner were in Detroit to supervise the engagement, and they met with Snyder to go over his objections. Snyder wanted certain words to be changed: "louse" for "bastard," "tart" for "whore" and the elimination of a reference to a girl as "pig" (Sheaffer, *Son and Artist* 596). Helburn and Marshall were equally appalled at the prospect of a policeman editing the writing of Eugene O'Neill. The Theatre Guild's reverential attitude was lost on the police censor, who was unimpressed by the news that O'Neill had won the Nobel Prize, saying to Marshall, "Lady, I don't care what kind of prize he's won, he can't put on a dirty show in *my* town" (qtd. in Langner 408). The Theatre Guild's tendency to deify the author was superseded by the more immediate need to pacify the censor.

Actor James Dunn had seen the announcement in the morning paper and arrived to see if he could help to quell the controversy. Dunn happened to be friendly with Michigan's assistant secretary of state, whom he contacted. Using this connection as his entrée into the discussion, Dunn met with the censor, who had refused to work with the two women and edited the script with Dunn. Depending upon the version of events, the censor cut eight to thirteen words from the play. For publicity purposes, the Theatre Guild tried to make light of the situation, saying that Mr. O'Neill had been contacted in New York, and that "the changes were so slight that Mr. O'Neill just laughed about the matter and agreed completely" (qtd. in Sheaffer, *Son and Artist* 596).

Director Arthur Shields saw the situation differently. In a transcribed interview with Louis Sheaffer, Shields said: "I had been told that O'Neill wouldn't tolerate any cutting so that it was a great surprise to me when during the last days of rehearsal he asked me if I thought the play should be cut. Truthfully I was floored by the question. My 25 years at the Abbey

Theatre — which was definitely a playwrights theatre — had taught me not to tamper with the work of an established author. It just wasn't done. I truthfully told him that I hadn't thought of it and hoped that no drastic alterations would be made" ("Notes/Arthur Shields" 2). James Dunn and Mary Welch both mention that O'Neill was not averse to making cuts when requested by the actors; according to Welch, "it came about when he realized that we were obviously upset at having just too much to say" (83). Dunn had difficulty remembering lines, and when he wanted to change some lines to make them easier for him to say, O'Neill "didn't make any fuss, just said, 'I don't care what changes you make but don't change the meter.' [Dunn] assured him that he was safe on that" (Sheaffer, "Notes/ Dunn" 1).

The controversy in Detroit was another matter entirely. Shields maintained that more than thirteen words were cut, saying, "I'd expected the Guild to fight that kind of censorship and was surprised when word came that the police officer would be allowed to dictate what could be said. I got the impression that when O'Neill was contacted on the phone by the Guild, he was so fed up that he told them to do what they liked. The whole episode was so distasteful to me that the following morning I left for the Coast" (Sheaffer, *Son and Artist* 596).

O'Neill was no stranger to this kind of controversy; his play *Strange Interlude* was banned in Boston, allegedly because of a veiled reference to abortion. Producer Langner had a slightly different version of the Boston banning of *Strange Interlude*, stating that the real objection came not from the Catholic Church nor from angry Irish Americans, but from certain local political bosses: "we were given a message that the matter could be settled by paying the sum of $10,000 as a legal fee" (Langner 238–39). Instead, the Theatre Guild moved the production to the Wollaston section of Quincy, Massachusetts, and ran buses to the Boston suburb, where the play was an enormous success. (Thanks to the dinner break necessitated by the length of the play, a struggling restaurant near the theater was able to survive: the restaurant was a little place called Howard Johnson's.) In any case, being banned in Boston or anywhere else was a badge of honor for O'Neill. That the original production of *A Moon for the Misbegotten* capitulated so quickly indicates how much things had changed in O'Neill's professional life and in the Theatre Guild's management, which had given in to the author's intractability in casting as well as the decision to tour the production, then submitted to the type of censorship that the Guild previously had challenged or found a way to circumvent.

Despite the controversy and the departure of two key members of the production, the play received its strongest reviews in Detroit. Russell McLaughlin, in the *Detroit News*, described O'Neill as "an Irish poet, for all his unassailed position as America's first dramatist. His present characters, although they use some of the worst modern language ever heard on a stage, are actually dark, eerie, Celtic symbol-folk ... who beat their breasts at the agony of living, battle titanically and drink like Nordic gods, but finally are seen to wear the garb of sainthood and die for love" (qtd. in Sheaffer, *Son and Artist* 596). As McLaughlin continues, "the effect of it all is, frankly, tremendous" (Sheaffer, "Notes/Reviews" 3). Harvey Taylor, in the *Detroit Times*, praised all three of the principals, Williams, Welch, and Dunn, adding, "It's one facet of O'Neill's genius to strip not only his characters but his audience of all protection. *A Moon for the Misbegotten* will make many people feel uncomfortable and vulnerable.... There are profanity, crudeness, and drunkenness in the play, but they are there only because they have to be to lend credence to O'Neill's characters and his theme" (Sheaffer, "Notes/Reviews" 3).

The police censor objected to the language in speeches that are among the most powerful in the play. The first two acts feature a melodramatic plot. Phil Hogan, supposedly fearful that he and Josie will lose the farm, maneuvers to save his home through a ruse that will bring his daughter and Tyrone together. Hogan plans to discover the couple in a compromising position, then force them to marry, knowing that the misbegotten pairing is, in truth, a love match.

Jim, on the other hand, is looking for someone in whom to confide his darkest secret, and it is not until the third act that we learn what that is. On the train ride east, with his mother's coffin in the baggage compartment, Jim resumes his heavy drinking and meets a prostitute whom he describes as "a blonde pig who looked more like a whore than twenty-five whores, with a face like an overgrown doll's and a come-on smile as cold as a polar bear's feet." Every night, for fifty bucks a night, he visited the prostitute "with some mad idea she could make [him] forget — what was in the baggage car ahead" (*Moon* 931).*

Josie is horrified by the tale but forgives him his trespasses. She spends this moonlit night cradling Jim in her arms, allowing him to "[cry] his heart's repentance against her breast" (*Moon* 933). Josie admits that she "has all kinds of love for [him] — and maybe this is the greatest of all — because it costs so much" (*Moon* 927). Thanks to his surrogate mother and her capacity to forgive, Jim, who entered the play "like a dead man walking slow behind his own coffin" (*Moon* 874) ends the play at peace, though "at peace as a death mask is at peace" (*Moon* 927).

In an incident related to Jamie O'Neill's return to New York, Saxe Commins, who began as O'Neill's dentist, then became his chief typist, and finally editor in chief at Random House, describes the evening of 9 March 1922, when O'Neill's play *The Hairy Ape* opened in New York at the Provincetown Playhouse. Commins says that he accompanied the second Mrs. O'Neill, Agnes Boulton, to the opening. O'Neill rarely attended opening nights, but on this evening he was completely unavailable. In a speech written for an event called "Pipe Night at the Players," delivered at the Players Club in Gramercy Park on 10 November 1957, Commins describes how *The Hairy Ape* ended with no fewer than a dozen curtain calls for the members of the cast as well as repeated cries for the author: "Agnes and I sat quietly and sadly through the demonstration, all too aware of the pathetic errand Gene was on at that very moment when the applause and the clamor for his appearance were at their height. He had gone to the Grand Central Station to claim the coffin which contained his mother's body, shipped from California, under the care of his older brother, Jim."

As Commins continues, "The coffin was to be taken, under Jim's direction, from the New York Central baggage car and transferred to a New Haven train for shipment to New London, where burial was to take place. When the train arrived in New York Jim was in a state of catalepsy. He had drowned his grief in whiskey. Gene's efforts to rouse

*Doris Alexander, in *Eugene O'Neill's Last Plays: Separating Art from Autobiography*, disputes this event, citing a letter from Mrs. Drummer, a family friend, describing Jamie's "dreadful condition" when he alighted from the train carrying his mother's coffin as evidence that the drunken Jamie surrounded himself solely with bottles of whiskey, and not with human company, on the journey home.

him failed and he had to abandon them and wander by himself through the catacombs of the Grand Central Station in search of the misplaced body of his mother.

"After groping for almost an hour through the underground mazes he finally came upon the casket and had it placed in the baggage car of the New London train. Then he returned to Jim's berth and shook him to consciousness. One way or another he got Jim and his bags to the hotel, where he promptly passed out on Gene's bed" (Saxe Commins Collection).

Commins wrote out the Player's Club speech in longhand on several sheets of yellow paper, dated 10 November 1954, while he was undergoing tests at Princeton Hospital. He instructed his typist, identified as Mary Q, "the only one who can read his writing," to make four copies for him. The handwritten version has only one word crossed out, so it seems that Commins was certain of what he was writing and completed it with no hesitation. The typed and finished version presented to members of the Players Club is unchanged, as Commins tells the tale of a dramatic offstage night in the life of Eugene O'Neill.

If only it were true. In fact, when Commins and Agnes Boulton returned to the hotel that evening, O'Neill was reticent about what had transpired. He was supposed to meet the train, accompanied by one of his parents' oldest friends, William P. Connor, but when the time came, his nerve failed him. O'Neill was at a loss in a crisis, having begged off traveling to California when his mother first suffered a stroke, using the excuse of his own ill health. Although O'Neill's telegram to his brother claimed he would suffer a "complete nervous collapse" (Sheaffer, *Son and Artist* 82) if he undertook the trip, he was in reasonably good health at the time. Instead, O'Neill sent his brother the name of a specialist to contact in Los Angeles if his mother's condition improved enough to seek further treatment, a physician recommended by his own psychoanalyst, who had diagnosed the author's imminent collapse. Connor, meanwhile, had insisted that O'Neill fulfill his duty and accompany him to the train station, but O'Neill stubbornly refused. Accompanied by his nephew Frank W. Wilder, Connor found the coffin without difficulty and had it removed to the luggage wagon. He then retrieved the drunken Jamie from his compartment, got him into a taxi, and deposited him in a hotel near Times Square.

Disgusted, Connor called O'Neill and filled him in on what had transpired at the station (Sheaffer, *Son and Artist* 86).

Whether the content of Commins' speech is a work of fiction by O'Neill or by Commins's is uncertain; however, everyone seems to agree on what happened next. When O'Neill appeared in the lobby, he asked his friend to take a walk with him in Central Park. They walked from midnight until four in the morning. O'Neill had little interest in what had happened at the theater that evening. According to Commins, "There followed a tormented recital of his mother's struggle against addiction. Gene's speech poured out of him as if at confessional. The Hairy Ape was forgotten. It was not as if it had been played for the first time that night but belonged in another life. His mother now was the central figure of the tragedy. The world most certainly was not hers [an echo of 'The world is mine!' a curtain line from *The Count of Monte Cristo*]. Compassionate as he was toward his mother, so bitter was his denunciation of his brother, Jim. Yet even in his fierce criticism there was a trace of admiration and envy. Jim, in Gene's eyes, was the gifted one, but the one who had committed the great sin against the Holy Ghost; he had wasted his talent, thrown it mockingly away" (Saxe Commins Collection). The conversation with Commins later became the material for both *Long Day's Journey Into Night* and *A Moon for the Misbegotten*.

The original production of *A Moon for the Misbegotten* continued to persevere, but despite positive reviews, the Theatre Guild chose to close the play after two weeks in Detroit and a final week in St. Louis. Critic Myles Standish, of the *St. Louis Post-Dispatch*, was well aware of the drama unfolding offstage, acknowledging that "many decisions as to its ultimate form on Broadway hinge on the way it and the cast shape up here this week" (Sheaffer, "Notes/Reviews" 2). Standish generally liked the play, calling it "a fine play and a moving one, a play that is rough, harsh, almost crude on the surface, but underneath the veneer has tenderness, compassion and a keen psychological insight. In spite of the crudity of some of its language and situations, and the seemingly moral degradation of its characters, 'Moon' is really a highly moral play. The aspirations of the protagonists are toward decency" (Sheaffer, "Notes/Reviews" 2). Standish added that the softening of the dialogue from the original script was not due to the censorship encountered in Detroit; rather, "it was chiefly because some outspoken language had previously caused ill-timed laughter that jangled the serious later mood of the play" (Sheaffer, "Notes/ Reviews" 2).

The Guild had never been entirely satisfied with the casting of the principals, an opinion shared for different reasons by the director Arthur Shields, who was hired after the cast was set: usually, the director is instrumental in making these decisions. Five-and-a-half weeks on the road had done little to change the Guild's opinion. As Lawrence Langner and Theresa Helburn explained in a form letter prepared for investors, "On its own merits, we have always felt that the play is one of genuine quality and importance, and we are gratified that our belief in its basic values is shared by many of the dramatic critics who have seen the performances, [but] recognizing the unusually difficult problems of casting inherent in the play — the burden of the action falling upon the three major characters ... the show has been withdrawn for re-casting" (Hammerman Collection). In a memo dated 27 March 1947, sent to H. William Fitelson, who served as legal counsel to the Theatre Guild, Langner stated, "We are closing MOON at the request of Mr. O'Neill, who does not want the play brought into town with the present cast. You will appreciate, of course, that all the members of the cast were okayed by Mr. O'Neill and that under the Dramatist's Guild contract, we had a perfect right to bring the play in" (Theatre Guild Collection).

The plan was to recast and reopen the play during the following season. But O'Neill's health was uncertain as was his interest in the production. In an inscription to a published copy of the play, dated 22 July 1952, O'Neill dedicates it to his "darling Carlotta," writing that it is "a play she dislikes and I have come to loathe." His wife objected in particular to the scene in which Jim describes sleeping with the "blonde pig" on the train, (Sheaffer, *Son and Artist* 660), but O'Neill refused to change it in order to make the play more palatable to his wife or to a wider audience. O'Neill successfully put off further discussions, stating in the prefatory note to the published text, dated April 1952, that "since [he] cannot presently give it the attention required for appropriate presentation, [he has] decided to make it available in book form." *A Moon for the Misbegotten* was not produced in New York until 1957, four years after O'Neill's death.

For its part, the Theatre Guild continued in the attempt to attract actors and directors, contacting Elia Kazan in January 1949. Kazan was interested in directing and thought Marlon Brando would be excellent in the play, although further discussions were tabled until after the opening of *Death of a Salesman* on the first of February. This casting never materialized, nor did Rosalind Russell, who was suggested for the role of Josie in 1947. British actress Wendy Hiller was also offered the part in December 1947, but didn't think herself "American enough" to do it. She must have changed her mind; ten years later, she starred as Josie in the first Broadway production. The Guild's 1946 production of *The Iceman Cometh* was the last O'Neill play on Broadway during his lifetime.

For about a decade after the initial productions of *The Iceman Cometh* and *A Moon for the Misbegotten*, it became fashionable to bash O'Neill and to find his plays long-winded and out of date. According to O'Neill biographers Arthur and Barbara Gelb, O'Neill himself felt "mortally wounded" by the Theatre Guild's "flawed" production of his final play: "Only another writer of O'Neill's stature could have understood the severity of the blow. Experiencing a similar period of rejection, Tennessee Williams told an interviewer in 1981: 'I'm very conscious of my decline in popularity, but I don't permit it to stop me because I have the example of so many playwrights before me. I know the dreadful notices Ibsen got. And O'Neill — he had to *die* to make *Moon* successful'" (*Life with Monte Cristo* 12).

This may not have been a requirement, but it was not until twenty years after O'Neill's death that the play received its full due. The original production was reviewed through the prism of O'Neill's reputation: O'Neill's name was the main reason that the Theatre Guild had taken on the play in the first place. The production was diminished, if not doomed, by the fact that it was sent out of town for previews, and the cast never had the full confidence of the Theatre Guild. As a result, the troubled production could not measure up to O'Neill's previous successes. As Mary McCarty wrote in her review of the play in book form, "'Casting difficulties' were spoken of, which is generally a theatrical euphemism for loss of interest in a property" (209).

An additional complication was the play itself. What appears to be a melodrama evolves over the course of four acts into what Michael Manheim describes as a transcendence of that form: "The play's interest moves from that associated with melodramatic intrigue to that associated with the total release of pent-up feeling — to a catharsis not unlike that associated with classical tragedy" (155). O'Neill had encouraged the actors not to sacrifice the comedy of the first two acts for the tragedy that followed; audiences were challenged, and, in some cases, confused, by the juxtaposition of the genres. Social attitudes also assisted in the demise of the production; the play's discussion of drunkenness and promiscuity, not to mention the alleged obscenity, shocked the citizens of the midwestern cities in which the play toured. But O'Neill had been teaching audiences to curse for over twenty years. No stranger to the seamier side of life, he often brought them along for the ride, and was likelier to take audiences to a bar for down and outers, as in *The Iceman Cometh*, than to the comforting hearth and home of *Ah, Wilderness!*

Although it is easier simply to blame the actors, it was a combination of circumstances that led to the demise of the original production. Without relying too much on the kindness of out-of-town critics, the original production of *A Moon for the Misbegotten* was not entirely without merit, though it was only an intimation of what the play could and would become. The problems resulted from circumstances not entirely of its own making, and its speedy dismissal as a poorly acted or directed project ignore the larger and more complicated issues that compelled its closing.

2

New York Premiere and Broadway Debut, 1957, and Off Broadway Debut, 1968

Although the rumors about its demise had been greatly exaggerated, after the pre–Broadway closing of *Moon*, a decade passed before there was serious interest in producing the play in New York. In 1954, a group called The Ensemble, headed by Leo Kerz, Joseph Kramm, and Harry Horner, planned to establish a permanent repertory company in New York. Members of The Ensemble included Karl Malden, E.G. Marshall, Maureen Stapleton, Anne Jackson, Eli Wallach, and Eva Marie Saint. The Ensemble initially and ambitiously planned to do five plays per season, alternating weekly. *A Moon for the Misbegotten* was to be the inaugural production. The Bijou Theater, where the production found a home, was leased by an organization called Chapter One, otherwise known as the Greater New York Chapter of ANTA (American National Theatre and Academy), Inc. The theater was then subleased to The Ensemble beginning 1 September 1954. Announced in June 1954 for an October 1955 opening, the play was delayed for two years in order to find a suitable cast, the production finally coalescing in 1957. *Moon* was to follow *The Potting Shed*, a play by Graham Greene, starring Dame Sybil Thorndike, and directed by Carmen Capalbo, who would direct and co-produce *Moon*. Originally scheduled for twelve weeks at the Bijou as part of a three-play subscription series, *The Potting Shed* enjoyed enough popularity to continue beyond its initial run, although the play was moved to the Golden Theater on 22 April to make room for the run of *Moon*.

When approached by the Theater Guild in 1947, Wendy Hiller had deemed herself "not American enough" to play the role of Josie, but ten years later, she would accept the role, although not without some initial hesitation. According to William Peper, writing in the *Telegraph-Sun* on 3 December 1956, "when the young producers [Carmen Capalbo and Stanley Chase] first talked to Miss Hiller, they were in London and she was in Hollywood. She told them, via a transatlantic connection, that it was an interesting play but it was not for her. Weeks later, back in New York, Mr. Capalbo received a phone call from Miss Hiller. 'I must be insane,' she told him, 'but I've just reread the play and you're right. It is for me.' However, when Miss Hiller heard the production was to be presented at the Bijou which has only 614 seats, she said: 'In a theater that small, you can't afford my salary.'

'I know we can't,' Mr. Capalbo blandly replied, and then proceeded to talk her into taking less money for a limited run."

Carmen Capalbo was nothing if not confident of his abilities. At age 31, Capalbo first came to the attention of the New York theater world when he staged Brecht's *Threepenny Opera*, a critical and popular success at Theatre de Lys, with a cast that included Lotte Lenya, Jo Sullivan, and Beatrice Arthur. In 1954, at a time when O'Neill's plays had been deemed too wordy for the theater-going public, Capalbo secured the first option on *Moon* from O'Neill's widow, Carlotta Monterey. Although the play had enjoyed successful productions in Dublin, Berlin, and Stockholm, the widow, still in seclusion after her husband's death in 1953, did not want any of his plays produced in New York after the harsh treatment received by his more recent work.

First approaching Carlotta by letter, Capalbo suggested that withholding the rights to O'Neill's plays would be an injustice both to the American theater and to the reputation of the author, and that a production could not fail to renew interest in O'Neill. Impressed by Capalbo's letter, Carlotta agreed to see him; she was intrigued by the striking appearance of the young director, who sported a Napoleon haircut and a languid manner, invariably with a cigarette between his fingers. After a ten-minute conversation with Capalbo and his co-producer Chase, she agreed to their request. As Capalbo explained to Judith Crist in April 1957, "It looks as if we're trying to cash in — but when we bought the play

O'Neill was really a bad word around New York. Everyone thought of him as cynical and bitter — he was through. Now suddenly, he has emerged as the greatest playwright again" (*New York Hearld Tribune* 1).

O'Neill's reemergence came as a result of the Off Broadway revival of *The Iceman Cometh*, directed by Jose Quintero, with Jason Robards as Hickey, followed in 1956 by the New York premiere of *Long Day's Journey Into Night*, also directed by Quintero, with Fredric March, Florence Eldridge, Jason Robards, and Bradford Dillman as the four haunted Tyrones. In June 1951, O'Neill had written to Bennett Cerf, President of Random House, where O'Neill's plays resided, stating that *Long Day's Journey Into Night* "is to be published twenty-five years after my death — but never produced as a play" (*Selected Letters* 589). Cerf agreed to O'Neill's wishes.

For her birthday in December 1951, O'Neill had given Carlotta full control over all of his writings. Six months previous, he named her his executrix and sole heir, having disinherited Shane and Oona, his two living children. O'Neill was particularly mindful of the feelings of his oldest son, Eugene Jr., who had read the manuscript, but his son's suicide in September 1950 precluded this as an impediment to publication. With the exception of *Journey*, O'Neill's manuscripts were sent from the vault at Random House to Carlotta.

After his son Eugene's suicide, in November 1953, Carlotta requested, via O'Neill's agent Jane Rubin, that O'Neill's remaining scripts, the one-act *Hughie* and *Journey*, be sent to her. Donald Klopfer, an editor at Random House, informed Rubin that *Journey* was under contract for publication in twenty-five years and that they planned to keep the play safe in their vault until that time. In June 1954 Carlotta allowed Bennett Cerf to read the play, "as if he hadn't done it before," as she wrote in her diary on 20 June 1954, hoping that the publisher would change his stance. Cerf had many stipulations if the play were to be published by Random House, including requesting a statement from Carlotta, to be published with the text, explaining her reasons for ignoring her husband's wishes. To this, Carlotta would never agree. Rather than breach O'Neill's trust, Cerf gave up the chance to publish the play, and Carlotta initiated negotiations with Yale University Press, which published the play in February 1956.

As a result of the success of *Journey*, *Moon* was suddenly a hot property, and the right to produce it belonged to Capalbo. Two years after it was first announced, *Moon* made its Broadway debut.

Most critics were quick to point out that Wendy Hiller would not be one's first thought when casting the role of Josie. (One helpful reader of the *New York Times*, Oscar F. Miller, suggested Maureen Stapleton for the role of Josie, finding Stapleton "too fine an actress to waste." The producers did not take him up on his idea.) Writing about the play, Tom Donnelly notes that "When, as Josie Hogan, she says, 'I'm an ugly over-grown lump of a woman,' it is impossible to take her literally." Donnelly also "[doubts] if the actress lives who could meet the physical requirements specified by Eugene O'Neill for the heroine of *A Moon for the Misbegotten*" ("Woman in the 'Moon'" 18). Yet Hiller had made a career of playing plain but strong-willed heroines on the stage in both London and New York and on film. Her West End debut came in 1935 as Sally Hardcastle in the play *Love on the Dole*, written by the playwright Ronald Gow, whom she married in 1937. When the play came to New York, she came to the attention of George Bernard Shaw, who cast her in several of his plays, including *Pygmalion* and *Major Barbara*. Shaw recommended her for the lead in the film adaptations of both plays, and Hiller received her first Academy Award nomination in 1938 for her portrayal of Eliza Doolittle. Previous to her participation in the Broadway debut of *Moon*, Hiller had enjoyed a successful season in classical plays as part of the Old Vic (1955–1956), following triumphs on the London stage in *The Heiress* (1950) and later in *Flowering Cherry* (1958). Hiller won the Academy Award for Best Supporting Actress in 1959 for her performance as Pat Cooper, the lonely hotel manager in *Separate Tables*. In addition to her impressive credentials, the combination of having played plain Catherine Sloper and Shaw's "draggletailed guttersnipe" (16) made Hiller, in the eyes of Capalbo, an ideal candidate to play Josie. In doing so, Hiller would end a ten-year absence from the Broadway stage.

Before contracts had been signed, Lloyd Nolan was announced for the role of James Tyrone, Jr., on 10 January 1957. In fact, he was still in negotiations, and like Hiller, was offered the convenience of a limited run. The actor had made a splash on Broadway in 1955 as Captain Queeg in *The Caine Mutiny*, a role he repeated in London, followed by the filming

Wendy Hiller as Josie Hogan in the 1957 New York premiere and Broadway debut of *A Moon for the Misbegotten*, directed by Carmen Capalbo, at the Bijou Theater. Photograph by Gjon Mili. Billy Rose Theatre Division, The New York Public Library for the Performing Arts, Astor, Lenox, and Tilden Foundations.

of *Hatful of Rain* in 1957, a gritty drama about drug addiction. Nolan was not set in the O'Neill role, however; a blind item in the New York *Mirror*, dated 15 February 1957, quotes him as saying he was in need of a rest: "I'm too tired after a year of non-stop plays and movies abroad.... Besides I have to get my dental work finished."

Capalbo had also been interested in Franchot Tone for the role of Tyrone. Tone made his Broadway debut in October 1927 in Paul Sifton's *The Belt* at the New Playwrights Theatre. Tone would later play Professor Leeds in the 1963 revival of *Strange Interlude*, directed by Jose Quintero, with Geraldine Page as Nina. In 1957, the actor was performing in the New Haven. Their Tyrone was found when Tone willingly left a play called *Hide and Seek*, which opened in New York on 27 April 1957, to dismal reviews and a hasty closing. In appearance, Tone captured the quality of an aging roué; as Jim Tyrone, he would be a man attempting sophistication while struggling with a terrible secret.

For the role of Phil Hogan, the producers chose Irish actor Cyril Cusack. A veteran of the Abbey Players, when the company was under the direction of William Butler Yeats, Cusack would make his Broadway debut in the production of *Moon*. The accent Cusack chose to employ in the production sounded "foreign" to many members of the audience, including the Irish. After the opening, Cusack explained that he had a choice of four Irish accents: north, east, south, and west. He chose that of the north because the O'Neill family has come from County Tyrone, the surname O'Neill gave to his family in the autobiographical *Journey*. The cast was completed by Glenn Cannon as Mike Hogan, and William Woodson as Harder. In the recent revival of *The Iceman Cometh*, Cannon had played Don Parritt, the young informer who betrays his mother, while Woodson had just returned from the national tour of *Inherit the Wind*, where he played the Menckenish reporter. William Pitkin, who had also done the set for *Threepenny Opera*, was engaged to design the Hogans' ramshackle home; Ruth Morley, the costumes; and Lee Wallace, the lighting. With Hiller's safe arrival in New York, via BOAC, on 20 March 1957, rehearsals began on 28 March, with tickets going on sale on April 15 in advance of an April 30th opening, which was pushed back to 2 May 1957. On display in the lounge of the Bijou Theater would be a collection of Eugene O'Neill memorabilia, including paintings, etchings, programs, and mementos selected by the producers in association with May Seymour of the Museum of the City of New York.

With the opening of *Moon*, some critics returned to their plaintive plea regarding the play: the drama is unplayable, the role of Josie, uncastable. In his review, Tom Donnelly describes the play as "something small, with genuine quality, [that] has been inflated and ornamented into something that is bulkily pretentious, or nearly that," pointing to the climactic scene in which Jim Tyrone confesses to Josie, then falls asleep in her arms, as "O'Neill's real story." The critic continues, "What he wants to say, O'Neill gets said, but in the process he comes close to smothering his deepest intention in a massive overlay of tedium" ("A Long Night's Moongazing"). Walter Kerr puts it more bluntly: "The work of these two people in this third-act dance of death is superb, and should be seen. The rest of the play does not yet exist on the stage."

On the other hand, Richard Watts Jr., in the *New York Post*, admitting that "the only possible current rivals to one of his dramas are a couple of [O'Neill's] other works," the recently revived *Journey* and *Iceman*, adds that "There is no way of avoiding, or reason for denying, that his final play is the least satisfying of the three.... But this has little to do with the fact that, after 'A Moon for the Misbegotten' has managed its occasionally tedious beginning, it is overwhelming" ("Another Moving O'Neill Tragedy"). Brooks Atkinson, in *The New York Times*, describes the play "not so much an ascent into tragedy as a descent into squalor," viewing *Moon* as "only an echo of the major O'Neill dramas." Despite his largely negative review of the play, Atkinson thanks director Capalbo for "realizing that even a minor O'Neill play deserves a beautiful production and an admirable performance" ("O'Neill's Last" 21).*

Whatever their reservations about the play, critics were in general agreement about the performances, particularly Hiller's. Noting that the

---

*After reading Brooks Atkinson's review, playwright Sean O'Casey, whose work is often identified as analogous to the comic-tragic *Moon*, offered his own take on the play, writing in a letter to Atkinson: "A sad history of a self-lost brother. Eugene was inclined to be too compassionate, too inclined to torture himself by the sin of omission in others who were near and dear to him. Frailty thy name is man as well as woman, and all that Eugene could do about it was nothing; and so it was futile for him to grieve. I've seen over the years great talents in my own brothers, not one, but three, wasted either through drink or vanity; but it availeth nothing to go into perpetual mourning about it. Well, Brooks, there's me for you."

play called for "a female behemoth, 'weighing around 180 pounds,'" John McClain grants that "Wendy Hiller, who plays the part, carries no such weight but by sheer force of animal vigor and some ingenious pads is able to create the desired effect," calling her performance "tender, earthy, and primitively proud" (18). Although the *Saturday Review* describes Hiller as "[working] frantically at contorting her face, walking in grotesque postures, and speaking in a slightly cockney accent that cannot help but remind us of her Liza Doolittle in the film, 'Pygmalion'" (Hewes 34), most critics were favorably impressed. All acknowledged the obvious, that physically, she did not measure up to the dimensions specified by O'Neill in the stage directions, but, as John McClain put it, "her strength and her size are within her" in a performance that the critic calls "magnificent" (18).

Tom Donnelly, in a second review of the play two weeks after its opening, describes how Hiller, as Josie, "can extinguish a lighted cigarette butt against her bare foot with an indifference that powerfully implies a long acquaintance with the soil of a mangy Connecticut tenant farm." Although O'Neill describes the soles of Josie's feet as "earth-stained and tough as leather" (*Moon* 857), Hiller's probably were not, making this move alone worth the price of admission, which, in this case, ranged from $2.30 to a top price of $5.25 for an orchestra seat. Donnelly continues by saying that "Josie is worth knowing, and Miss Hiller lets us know her, completely" ("Woman in the 'Moon'" 18). According to Richard Watts, "Wendy Hiller, who plays the girl, may not meet O'Neill's demands for physical bulk in the role, but she plays so beautifully that this soon becomes unimportant" ("Another Moving O'Neill Tragedy"). As Kerr puts it, "the image of Miss Hiller — arms folded in a battle for self-control, head hunched low to keep her from betraying all that she feels, eyes alert to every move of the stumbling man near her — is one you won't soon forget or want to." For her performance in *Moon*, Hiller received a nomination for the Antoniette Perry (Tony) Award as Best Actress in a Play in 1958. The Tony went to Helen Hayes, in her role as the Duchess of Pont-au-Bronc in an English translation of Jean Anouilh's *Time Remembered*.

Both Franchot Tone and Cyril Cusack came in for their share of praise. Watts calls Tone "brilliant" as the "lost alcoholic" Tyrone, and Cusack "splendid" as the father, a performance McClain calls "superb" (18). Atkinson describes Cusack as giving "a tight-jawed, purse-lipped, immensely enjoyable performance that is comic in its swagger moments and pathetically crushed at the end," while Tone "is at the top of his bent in character portraiture — the braggart on the surface, the lonely child at heart, the baffling mixture of good and bad influences, a man doomed to kill the things he loves" (21). The critics' primary interest was in the three main characters, but William Woodson, as Harder, was acknowledged as "a properly stuffy landowner," and Glenn Cannon's "brief moment" as Mike Hogan was "a good one" (McClain 18).

Although many critics discuss the play as if there were no director, John McClain finds the director's work "always forthright and never intrusive" (18), though Walter Kerr insists that "Carmen Capalbo has apparently found no rhythms, no lights or shade, no relieving rests to give weight and light to O'Neill's opening movements." Woolcott Gibbs, in *The New Yorker*, states that "Carmen Capalbo's direction did all that could be expected with an interminable and dismayingly static script, adding that "[set designer] William Pitkin's ruined farmhouse is ... just a little too much. Even Jeeter Lester lived more fashionably" (86). The *Saturday Review* wrongly attributes "some excellent morning sky effects" (34) to Pitkin rather than lighting designer Lee Watson, whom Brooks Atkinson praises for his "sensitive lighting" as well as acknowledging that Pitkin "has filled the stage with a ramshackle house that has a bleak power of its own ... and the costumes by Ruth Morley are a beggar's symphony of rags and tattered decency" (21). Unfortunately, despite the mixed to positive critical response to the play, it closed after sixty-eight performances, the producers blaming its hasty demise on an unusually warm spring and early summer in the New York area.

Yet the Broadway debut in 1957 brought to light several features of the play: first and foremost, that it was playable and that it could be done with a degree of success. The reviews of the original production, produced by the Theatre Guild in 1947, had focused primarily on one aspect of the production: O'Neill's name and reputation, both of which seemed to overwhelm the production. In 1957, critics like Tom Donnelly, who alluded to the fact that this was O'Neill's last completed work, also added a word of caution: "The serious theatergoer is warned: seeing it must largely be a labor of love" ("A Long Night's Moongazing"). Similar to the out-of-town critics in 1947, Richard Watts observes that the play suffers from "[O'Neill's] characteristic failings of excessive length and insufficient eloquence, but," Watts adds, "whatever its incidental weaknesses may be, it is a moving, beautiful and shattering play" ("Another Moving O'Neill Tragedy"). The play may have suffered by comparison to the recent revivals of *Journey* and *Iceman*, but, for the most part, the production managed to hold its own.

While the cachet of O'Neill's name carried the original production, ten years later, the career of Wendy Hiller was a major selling point for the Broadway production. The acting of Hiller, Tone, and Cusack was singled out for praise, in the eyes of some, saving the play. According to the critic in *Theatre Arts*, "the remarkable intensity which Wendy Hiller and Franchot Tone brought to the roles also did a great deal to shore up the scenes, and almost made one forget the looseness of the structure and the downright tedium of the first two acts, in which a certain lusty humor fights a losing battle with clumsily handled exposition." The critic also states that "if everything about this work were as good as the last forty-five minutes of its ample playing time, it would rank with O'Neill's best" (*Theatre Arts* 67).

Another complaint about the original production, repeated by a number of the critics in the Midwestern cities in which it played, centered on the play's content and language, which was considered offensive. A play set on a squalid pig farm was bad enough; the portrayal of the daughter as "a terrible wanton woman" (*Moon* 866) was offensive to many. Perhaps because a decade had passed, or because the Broadway audience did not share the same attitudes as their Midwestern counterparts, the New York reviewers did not object to the language or content of the play, only to its length. The short run of the play, blamed on uncooperative weather, did not bode well for its commercial prospects, but even the limited success of the Broadway premiere demonstrated that the play, despite its difficult past, did have a future.

Off Broadway Debut, 1968

The play's next major revival was in 1968, at a time when the Off Broadway movement was alive and well, due in no small part to the efforts of Theodore (Ted) Mann and Jose Quintero at the Circle in the Square. Years before, they had converted the AMATO Opera House at 159 Bleecker Street into a three-sided arena theater, after leaving their original base of operations at 5 Sheridan Square, when it was demolished to make room for apartments. Established in 1951, The Circle in the Square made its name by reviving plays that had failed on Broadway. According to *The Saturday Review*, "Circle in the Square has built a reputation on its ability to revive Broadway's distinguished failures in such a way that they become more effective than the original" ("Sweetest Music").

With the 299 audience members seated on three sides of the stage, the aptly named Circle in the Square was run as a non-profit; like most Off Broadway theaters, it was subsidized by the low pay of all involved. As Sheila Hickey Garvey notes in her history of Circle in the Square, "...an actor's pay [in 1959] was $5.00 per week during rehearsals and $25.00 per week during performances. If a show was successful, the weekly pay could rise to between $40 and $70 per week. But a $70 a week paycheck was rare" ("Not for Profit" 212). The use of apprentice labor, paid at below union scale, was also a financial necessity, as were the modest and inexpensive sets that would serve the play without distracting from it.

Under Quintero's direction, the revival of Tennessee Williams's *Summer and Smoke* in 1952, starring a then unknown Geraldine Page, was a pivotal moment in the history of Off Broadway. As Brooks Atkinson wrote in the *New York Times*, "Nothing has happened for quite a long time as admirable as the new production at the Circle in the Square" ("Tennessee Williams"19). Suddenly, critics from major news outlets were finding their way to small, out-of-the-way venues. Off Broadway had became a theatrical destination.

In 1963, due to a variety of conflicts, Quintero left Circle in the Square. As he told Mel Gussow in an interview in 1974, "There was a difference of opinion of what the destiny of the Circle should be. I wanted to make it a theater that belonged to theater people, who would be invited to work there if they had something they wanted to do. Ted wanted to do — exactly as he's done. Two ideas and two different people. I left of my own volition" ("Jose Quintero's Long Road Back" 34). Before Quintero's departure, he and Mann had been instrumental in reviving interest in the plays of Eugene O'Neill. "We practically rescued [O'Neill] from oblivion," said Mann to Lewis Funke in a remark that the interviewer deemed "neither egotistical nor hyperbolic." As Mann continued, "They were saying that O'Neill had been greatly overrated, that he was corny and passé. Even worse, his plays were being ignored — no one in the United States wanted to produce them" (19). Having rejected multiple requests from Quintero and Mann, O'Neill's agent Jane Rubin and his widow Carlotta finally acquiesced to their request to produce an O'Neill drama. Although Circle was $10,000 in debt at the time, they jumped at the chance to produce *Iceman* in 1956, which Quintero directed, in a production that brought attention to an unknown actor named Jason Robards, and played to sold-out houses for almost two years. Mann produced and Quintero directed the Broadway premiere of *Long Day's Journey Into Night* in 1956, the revival of *Desire Under the Elms* in 1962, and a 1963 revival of *Strange Interlude*, directed by Quintero and produced in arrangement with Circle in the Square. The theater continued under the artistic management of Ted Mann and the business management of Paul Libin, who had come to New York from Chicago in 1951 to pursue an acting career, moved into stage managing, and then served as the president of the League of Off Broadway Theaters and as manager of the Martinique Theatre.

Ted Mann's route to the 1968 revival of *Moon* was more indirect. Following two years in the armed services (1944–1946) stationed in Carmel, California, Mann passed the New York bar as a 1950 graduate of Brooklyn Law School. A native New Yorker, he might have joined his father's law firm, but a stint with the Loft Players, a summer stock company in Woodstock, New York, where he first met Jose Quintero, changed the direction of his life. As Garvey writes, "[Mann] held down numerous jobs from building sets to counting cans of food in the kitchen pantry. Eventually, he became the group's business manager" ("Not for Profit" 38). When the Loft Players moved to New York and created the Circle in the Square, Mann continued to fight their financial battles.

Better known as a producer, Mann gained some directing experience with Brecht's *Drums in the Night*, produced at Circle during the 1967 season. Having planned the production of *Moon* for over a year, he wrote that "Because all the critics had considered it almost impossible to produce and because it had not had a successful major production, we did a considerable amount of research into the history of those past productions, into Eugene O'Neill's attitude towards the play, into Jamie's historical character, and so on. This research, as well as intensive study of the play, convinced us that it was not meant to be performed as three hours of unrelenting tragic gloom." Mann insisted that "the movement from farce to tragedy is the underlying structure of the play and of its meaning. For Mr. O'Neill, comedy is the way in which we defend ourselves

64

Salome Jens as Josie Hogan and Mitchell Ryan as James Tyrone, Jr., in the 1968 Off Broadway debut of *A Moon for the Misbegotten*, directed by Theodore Mann, at the Circle in the Square. Photograph by Friedman/Abeles. Billy Rose Theatre Division, The New York Public Library for the Performing Arts, Astor, Lenox, and Tilden Foundations.

against the unbearable in life, comedy permits us to go on living..... As the play moves through the comedy to its final stages of tragedy, the focus shifts from the living to the dying man who no longer finds life's pain bearable" ("'Moon for Misbegotten' Planned For Year").

In an interview with John Dempsey of *The Baltimore Sun*, Mann provides his take on Jim Tyrone as "a complicated character — he's a boozer, [a]cutely intelligent, and very sensitive, and all these elements of his personality are crashing together.... But he's self-destructive in that he's afraid of expressing his true feelings. He tells Josie he loves her and then seems to take it back in the next breath.... Then he proceeds to shame her into admitting that her vaunted sexual prowess is nothing but a sham. In short, these passionate avowals are truly sterile because they never lead to anything except renewed withdrawal and further evasion." Mann concludes by saying, "All of us are like James Tyrone — we're afraid of our deepest feelings. Instead of telling someone 'I love you,' we'll say, 'I love you a lot.' That way, it seems we're making a joke out of it — nobody can then accuse us of being sentimental or corny" (Dempsey D1).

In casting the revival, Mann challenged O'Neill's instructions stated in the stage directions. As Josie, Mann cast Salome Jens, who performed in the Circle's production of Jean Genet's *The Balcony*, directed by Jose Quintero. Jens studied with Lee Strasberg and was a charter member of Lincoln Center's early repertory company, where she performed in Elia Kazan's premiere of Arthur Miller's *After the Fall* as well as Kazan's production of *Tartuffe*. An actress with a distinctive voice, Jens seemed to share only Josie's height; at first glance, as George Oppenheimer indicated in the title of his piece in *Newsday*, "Miss Jens Too Lovely for Earthy O'Neill Role."

Mitchell Ryan, who was cast as Jim Tyrone, and who would become known as a supporting actor in film and television, seemed a little closer to type. His interest in acting grew when he was assigned in 1951 to the Navy's Special Services. By 1966, Ryan was an original cast member in the Broadway production of *Wait Until Dark*, playing the role of Mike Talman, and of television's *Dark Shadows* in the role of Burke Devlin, from which he was fired due to problems with alcohol. At the Circle in the Square, Ryan had just completed a six-month run as Agamemnon in a highly successful production of *Iphigenia at Aulis*. W.B. Brydon, a British-born Canadian cast as Phil Hogan, had previously appeared in Peter Ustinov's *The Unknown Soldier and his Wife*, which opened at Lincoln Center in 1967 and moved briefly to Broadway. The cast was completed by Garry Mitchell as T. Stedman Harder and Jack Kehoe as Mike Hogan.

The unusual floor plan of the Circle in the Square Theater, with the audience seated on three sides of the thrust stage, created a unique challenge for set designer Marsha Eck. As William A. Raidy noted in the *Long Island Press*, "Marsha Eck has produced an ingenious setting of a slatternly farmhouse, which is a credit to her imagination. A farmhouse in theater-in-the-almost-round is a designer's nightmare and she has done very well, creating the mood without overpowering it" (26). The mood was enhanced by Jules Fisher's lighting design, which Edward Sothern Hipp, in the *Newark Sunday News*, called "the most credible dawn this side of nature's" (E2). Most, though not all, critics felt that the production "[lent] a final luster to the now flickering season" (Barnes 55), when it opened on 12 June 1968, following previews that began on 31 May. Ticket prices ranged from $3.50 to $4.50.

Among those who chose to praise the production was Clive Barnes in the *New York Times*. Having previously described the 1957 production as a "a minor O'Neill play" (21), Barnes now saw the play as a "minor-masterpiece" and "a most distinguished play ... in a production that does it glorious justice." Barnes praised Mann, who "clearly has a feel for the play. He plays the first scene like an O'Casey farce, and then builds up tension and tragedy as the play moves along into the later phases of its pain." Describing Ecks's setting as "wonderfully evocative," Barnes also admired the performances, finding W. B. Brydon "superb" as Phil, "the playboy of Connecticut, roistering and besotted." Barnes acknowledges that "Mitchell Ryan has the more difficult task in portraying Tyrone, but he fulfills it splendidly ... this Tyrone courted and sought forgiveness with such a touchingly muzzy gallantry, making O'Neill's self-pity not so much self pitying as agonized." Describing Salome Jens as "gawky and yet beautiful," Barnes admits, "She has the play at her fingertips, and every movement, every vocal inflection, seems right, just and proper." Barnes even manages some begrudging words of praise for the playwright: "[O'Neill] is a clumsy, awkward writer, but here the development of his plot, unfolding like a tidal wave, is masterly, and the play's ending, in the muted minor key of distant tragedy, comes with the inevitability of a final sigh" (55).

Whitney Bolton, in the *Morning Telegraph*, also praises Jens's performance, saying, "Miss Jens pleases me enormously as Josie, she has the meaning of the character, the depths that existed in a Josie who wanted to comfort the world and ended with Jamie in her lap." Bolton calls *Moon* "a disturbing play and meant to be so." Remarking on the previous production on Broadway a decade earlier, Bolton states, "... the off Broadway production is the better of the two from the point of view of both performances and direction." William A. Raidy, in the *Long Island Press*, concurs, finding Mann's direction of the play "splendid," adding, "while it remains a 'minor' play of O'Neill, it is still well worth seeing, primarily for the stunning performance of Salome Jens, who plays Josie Hogan with a positive passion. Believe me, she far surpasses Miss Hiller's interpretation" (26). Bernard Drew, of the *Hartford Times*, had his "most moving experience ever" at an O'Neill play, stating that "All his career, O'Neill aimed and failed at the poetry he finally achieves in the eloquent moments of 'A Moon for the Misbegotten'" (E4).

In *The Villager*, Leota Diesel called the production "stunning" and agreed with those who found this production far more moving than the production on Broadway in 1957. As she states, "That is one of the joys of seeing a revival — when the play is good — experiencing a sense of rediscovery, experiencing a profounder impact the second time." Diesel praises the acting, first and foremost that of Salome Jens, "who is almost too beautiful for the part, [but] plays her beautifully. The acting of the others is faultless." Diesel describes Brydon as "magnificent," Ryan, "very fine," and Garry Mitchell and Jack Kehoe in their minor roles "excellent" in a production that Mann "directed superbly." Diesel adds that "Theodore Mann again merits the acclaim of O'Neill addicts (not to mention literate playgoers in general) for salvaging an important work from the Broadway dustbin...."

A more measured response came from Richard Watts, Jr., in the *New York Post*, who feels that "[The play] is too long, it approaches its climactic scenes too leisurely, and the earthbound prose style that was [O'Neill's] besetting weakness is frequently evident in it. Yet, seeing it revived ... I was convinced once more that it is one of the saddest and most beautiful plays he ever wrote." Watts also praises the work of Jens: "The role of Josie calls for a huge and unattractive actress, which Salome Jens emphatically isn't. Indeed, she looks handsomer than ever. But for all this unusual handicap, she gives a fine, honest performance" ("In Memory of a Doomed Brother" 57).

Not all the commentary was as positive, however. Martin Gottfried, in *Women's Wear Daily*, writes that "it is difficult to believe that a man who could write a play as staggering as *Long Day's Journey* could also write such near trash as *More Stately Mansions* or *Marco Millions* or *Strange Interlude* or *A Touch of the Poet*. Or that the writing of the powerful *The Iceman Cometh* could be followed so shortly by the really awful *Moon for the Misbegotten*.... O'Neill never was much of a writer — a language artist — nor a story teller. What he had going for him was a naked power that bled through no matter how much he tried to cover it with pretensions to classical tragedy or poetry" (37). Gottfried admits that he walked out before the third act, generally acknowledged as the greatest of the play. The critic did manage to sit through the entire play when it was revived again in 1973.

Of those who preferred to bury the play, most notable was A.D. Coleman in the *Village Voice*, who found the production "disappointingly pedestrian and strangely askew." As Coleman elaborates, "For some reason, Theodore Mann has chosen to interpret this play — a bitterly tender portrait of his brother Jamie and of a woman who loved him — far more lightly than the work itself permits. Since the play is somber, almost tragic in mood, this results in a serious distortion; Mann's interpretation seems constantly in conflict with O'Neill's vision, a directorial red herring leading the audience farther and farther away from the core of the play's truth." Citing the approach as "a serious mistake," Coleman goes on to say that using Salome Jens in the role of Josie is "a miscasting so major and so obvious as to be well-nigh incredible." Noting that O'Neill's Josie "was drawn as a big, awkward, overgrown cow of a woman," Coleman states that "Miss Jens is so far from that physicality that not even a great performance could make her credible, and her portrayal of Josie is neither credible nor creditable." The other actors were not spared: According to Coleman, "Mitchell Ryan, as James Tyrone, walks as if hewn from petrified wood." On the other hand, Coleman found W.B. Brydon, "a rip-snorting actor with talent to burn, but the false premises on which the production is built, and the uninspiring work of his cohorts, manage to dim even his fire" (62).

To defend his approach to the play, Mann took the unusual step of writing a long letter to the editor, published in the *Village Voice*, taking exception to what he referred to as Coleman's "irresponsible and uninformed" review. In reply to Coleman's objection that the play was performed "far too lightly than the work itself permits," Mann quotes Mary Welch, the original Josie, in her article in *Theatre Arts*: "'Mr. O'Neill gave us some notes that really helped us. One of them was that we were playing the tragedy of the play too soon. He felt that it should be played almost for farce in the first act and develop into tragic stature in the fourth.'" Mann also quotes O'Neill in a statement to biographer Barrett Clark: "'Moon' was a simple play which starts as farce and ends as tragedy." Another note of O'Neill's to Arthur Shields, director of the 1947 production of *Moon*, that the play should have a minimum of stage movement, directed Mann to do the same, and "was of great help to us in establishing a mood of intro-spection and self-revelation and in evoking that calm which is the lowest depth of despair...." Finally, to Coleman's attack on the casting of Salome Jens "on physical grounds," Mann countered: "To feel that one is 'an ugly duckling' it is not necessary to actually be one, and the words that Mr. Cole-man uses to describe 'O'Neill's Josie' are actually Josie's hurt description of herself, not O'Neill's character description of his heroine which is much more flattering." As Mann continues, "Salome Jens is far from conventional prettiness, but she is beautiful in O'Neill's sense.... That is what we were looking for in an actress and what we, and what the other critics, who sen-sibly overlooked the fact that Miss Jens is not as large as O'Neill's suggested dimensions for his heroine, found so moving in Miss Jens's performance" ("Letter" 6). With that, Mann's letter, and the discussion, effectively ended.

On the strength of the generally positive reviews of the production, *Moon* ran for five and a half months, closing on 30 November 1968. Fol-lowing its Off Broadway run, the production played Ford's Theater, where Mann and Libin served as artistic managers from 1968 to 1971. Opening in Washington, DC, on 29 January 1969, the production began a national tour with stops in Los Angeles, Boston, Baltimore, and Chicago. Stefan Gierasch replaced W.B. Brydon as Phil, with John Tremaine as Mike Hogan and Richard McKenzie as T. Stedman Harder.

At Los Angeles's Lindy Opera House, the production was generally well received after its May 14 opening. John Goff, in *The Hollywood Reporter*, described Jens as a "consummately beautiful Josie" and her per-formance "magnificent." "Mitchell Ryan does to perfection the self-destructive and haunted James Tyrone, Jr.," according to Goff, and Stefan Gierasch "captures [Phil's] rough Irish temper and humor and combines it with an unsung love of his daughter to provide a complete dimensional portrait of the Connecticut farmer." Although the critic feared that a challenging O'Neill drama might not find an audience in Los Angeles, "artistically, [the production] would have pleased even O'Neill himself" (6).

Dan Sullivan, in the *Los Angeles Times*, also found much to praise in the production, describing the play as "clearly near the top of the O'Neill canon." The critic was pleased to see that "it is refreshingly free of the smoggy grandiloquence that O'Neill so readily assumed when he was talking about Life, with a big tragic capital 'L.'" Sullivan describes Jens as "not, physically, the lady titan that O'Neill had in mind for Josie. But, enraged or moonstruck, she is every inch a woman and the voice is wonderful: a voice with backbone in it." More measured in his praise of Mitchell Ryan, Sullivan suggests that the actor "too often translates Jamie's inner deadness into an outer flatness." Yet, he praises the production "that redeemed 'Moon for the Misbegotten' in 1968 after two previous companies had failed to bring it off" (10).

When the production left Los Angeles, moving to its next stop in Boston, it left behind its leading man. With the offer of a film role, Mitchell Ryan dropped out of the production, leaving the producers to rush in a substitute, Jack Davidson, who had replaced Garry Mitchell in the role of T. Stedman Harder at Circle in the Square, and had played the role of James Tyrone, Jr., three years earlier at the Theater-on-the-Wharf in Provincetown. The Theater-on-the-Wharf seats 100 people; Boston's Colonial Theater seats over 1700. According to critic Elliot Norton, in the *Record American*, Davidson failed to be accommodate the additional 1600 patrons: "he was good, though slow, in Jamie's tender moments, when the embittered alcoholic tells the truth to Josie. But he missed the brashness, the flash, the swagger of the old ham actor, the Broadway guy of the twenties. He was in period costume, but never in period." Given that Davidson occasionally had to be prompted from the wings, "under the circumstances he is to be commended for his achievement," although Norton also admits that "the play suffers." The critic acknowledges that Jens's performance "had been admired by others," but what he saw was "no more than an ingenue in an old-fashioned romantic melodrama." He hopes that the play "will be more effectively acted day by day as the new actor begins to understand Jamie Tyrone a little more and the others become accustomed to his style" ("Leading Actors Out of 'Moon'" 32).

Kevin Kelly, in the *Boston Globe*, was not as optimistic. In a review titled "'A Moon for the Misbegotten' — You'll Hope Dawn Is Early," Kelly writes, "Although it is touched with moments of power and eloquence, Eugene O'Neill's play is like 'Tobacco Road' with a brogue," with Gierasch's Phil Hogan described as "Jeeter Lester as a derelict leprechaun." Kelly identifies the play as the "somber, essentially static story of two misguided persons reaching out for love," insisting that "O'Neill's lyricism is allowed to get the better of him and the clear beauty of the language ... ends in a thick fog of rolling words and repetitive attitudes." Kelly does acknowledge the "lovely" performance by a "miscast" Salome Jens, who "singlehandedly holds the play together" (21).

By mid–June, when the play opened in Chicago for a month-long stay at the Studebaker Theatre, the production had a new James Tyrone, Jr., in Morgan Sterne. The critical response to the production was mixed. As his jumping-off point, Richard Christiansen, in the *Chicago Daily News*, quotes O'Neill's inscription to his wife Carlotta, which described *Moon* as "a play I have come to loathe"; the critic states that "a lot of the people who had come to the Chicago premiere of 'Moon' shared the playwright's sentiments." Finding the play wordy and overlong, Christiansen still acknowledges that "such is the intensity of O'Neill's agony and the depth of his despair, that in the end, the play, for all its muddling, becomes touched with the genius of a great dramatist." Christiansen continues, "It is a play of dark and elemental emotions, and to work it must be played with a brilliant vehemence." The critic found only Salome Jens up to the challenge: "she creates the illusion of size with a magnificent control of body and voice. Not a pretty woman, she is nevertheless beautiful, creating a stage radiance of immense presence." Christiansen thought Morgan Sterne too new to the role and simply inadequate to the task of playing Tyrone: "Sterne never creates his character and as a consequence his bitter and pathetic cry of desolation in the second act lacks any kind of depth and perspective." All in all, Christiansen finds that "O'Neill is still there, plodding through rough-house comedy and soaring into theatrical poetry to create for us that excruciating vision of the inner depths that he carried with him through his life" ("O'Neill Play Bores Through to Tragedy" 33).

William Leonard, in the *Chicago Tribune*, begins with the standard critique of O'Neill's plays, that they could be mawkish and repetitive, but adds, " he could and did turn out plays that knocked you right out of your seat and left you brooding about them for days after you left the theater." Leonard described *Moon* as "a tale that deserves the telling, like so many of Eugene O'Neill's threnodies, no matter how awkwardly he told them." Leonard praised the acting of Jens: "Hers is a sensitive performance, with humor just under the surface and a sense of direction that is unerring." As Tyrone, Morgan Sterne gives "a moving performance," while Stefan Gierasch "wallow[s] in the plump role of a Hibernian Jeeter Lester." According to Leonard, "O'Neill's psychology may be superficial and his pessimism may be too pervasive, but the strength of his writing is not to be denied."

Kathleen Morner, in the *Chicago Sun-Times*, called the production a triumph, adding, "Salome Jens is that singular kind of actress who, when she gazes out at the dawn after the strangest, saddest, most hopeless and yet the most wonderful night in Josie's life, makes you feel that you are seeing with her eyes. You are not quite as you were when the play began, and when the play is over, still it is not over." Morner describes it as "a great performance. But greatness infects the whole production." She praises the performances of both Sterne and Gierasch, adding that "Theodore Mann has directed the three of them in a lyrical performance that makes O'Neill's language seem more poetic than I have remembered it and makes it completely incredible to think that critics once considered 'A Moon for the Misbegotten' impossible on the stage."

Opening in July 1969 for a three-week run at the Morris Mechanic Theater in Baltimore, the production was again greeted with a mixed critical response. Lou Cedrone, in the *Evening Sun*, called O'Neill's later plays "both long-winded and powerful," and stated: "If Shakespeare can be cut, so can O'Neill, and 'Moon for the Misbegotten' would be less trying than it is if the scenes were shortened here and there." Cedrone describes Jens as "not the visual 'cow' her father brands her, [though] she very easily projects this quality." Though suffering from vocal strain, Stefan Gierasch is commended for a "most authentic" Irish brogue; to Morgan Sterne, a kind of compliment is paid: "he manages to make a basically tedious character (particularly in the second act drunk scene) a sympathetic one." Cedrone's final assessment is that *Moon* is "solid but overdone theater" (A6).

On the other hand, David Kearse, of the *Baltimore Sun*, praises

Mann's ability to take O'Neill's "intensely personal" biographical drama and "make it communicate with an audience and give it a life that perhaps it never has had before." For Kearse, the production succeeds "because of the evenly balanced and reasonably fast-paced touch of the director and because of the sheer power and force of the principals." According to Kearse, "Salome Jens plays Josie with considerable strength and stature.... Hers is a marvelous voice, face, and body, and she plays upon them all as if they were a musical instrument." Noting that "Morgan Sterne brings to the role of Jamie a certain brittleness and world-weariness," Kearse praises the actor for his lengthy monologue in the second half: "This Mr. Sterne does with searing skill." Identifying Stefan Gierasch as "the key to the comedy," the critic also acknowledges the contribution of Richard McKenzie and John Tremaine in minor roles. Director Mann's previously disputed approach is favored by Kearse: "Mr. Mann's approach to the drama is wise in that he plays the first act for pure [f]arce and eases into the tragedy that follows." Finally, Kearse praises the playwright himself: "O'Neill's dialogue is at its most lyrical in the final scenes and here we glimpse the greatness of the playwright" (B4).

With the 1968 revival, the fortunes of the play continued to improve. From the negative to mixed reviews of the original production, to the mixed to positive reviews of its Broadway debut, *Moon* found its largest audience to date in its Off Broadway incarnation. In fact, the type of praise usually associated with the 1973 production had already found its way to the 1968 revival. For example, John J. O'Connor, in the *Wall Street Journal*, insists that "This excellent production has the good fortune of near flawless performances" (C74). Ads for the production trumpeted its success: Norman Nadel, the critic for the Scripps-Howard newspapers, is quoted as saying, "It has taken 21 years for 'A Moon for the Misbegotten' to find a production which lets us see O'Neill's boisterous and delicate tragedy as the master work it is." Although it would take another five years, the play was well on its way to achieving greatness.

3

Broadway Revivals,
1973 and 1984

The original production of *A Moon for the Misbegotten* may have died on the road, but the play was resurrected there in 1973. In fact, the enterprise was named the Resurrection Company, referring not only to the play but also to the careers of the major players, several of whom were overcoming serious problems. The shifting of social mores over twenty-five years made the language and behavior presented in the play, condemned by some as obscene in 1947, more to be pitied than censored. Jim's tale of his journey homeward with his mother's coffin is still a searing indictment, but of Jim's behavior, not of American motherhood. The censors were not called in when the play debuted at the Academy Theater in Lake Forest, Illinois, outside of Chicago, when the play at last achieved greatness in a legendary production described as brilliant in its acting and direction.

In the summer of 1973, the Resurrection Company, made up of Colleen Dewhurst, Jason Robards, and Jose Quintero, was put together, or, more precisely, put back together. Colleen Dewhurst had first been directed by Quintero in *Children of Darkness* in 1958 at Circle in the Square. Previous to *Moon*, Dewhurst's O'Neillography included *Desire Under the Elms* (1962), directed by Harold Clurman at the ANTA Playhouse; *More Stately Mansions* (1967), directed by Jose Quintero at the Broadhurst Theater; and *Mourning Becomes Electra* (1972), directed by Ted Mann at Circle in the Square. Known for her "whiskey voice," the result of tubercular glands of the neck, which were surgically remedied when she was young,

Dewhurst was often cast as a sensual Earth Mother. She had twice played Josie Hogan in productions directed by Quintero: in Spoleto, Italy, in 1958, at the opening of Gian Carlo Menotti's Festival of Two Worlds, and in Buffalo, New York, in 1965, for the opening of the Studio Arena Theatre.* In 1968, director Ted Mann had wanted Dewhurst to play Josie at the Circle in the Square, but she would not do it without Quintero. In 1973 Dewhurst, who had recently divorced the actor George C. Scott for the second time, was unengaged professionally, and, like Quintero, broke.

Dewhurst suggested to Quintero that they put together a package to tour on the summer-stock circuit. Quintero suggested *Moon*, although the play is far from the usual summer fare, usually light comedy or musicals populated with familiar faces from television and movies. The director also called Jason Robards, who was eager to join them. Although the two actors are now so closely identified and had met before, this was the first shared working experience for Dewhurst and Robards.

Robards, who had been directed by Quintero in both *The Iceman Cometh* and *Long Day's Journey* in 1956, shared much with the character he played in *Moon* and its creator. Robards came from a theatrical family. Similar to O'Neill's father, Jason Robards senior was an actor: matinee-idol handsome, often out on tour, and a hard drinker. Of the two sons, Robards was the one who chose to follow his father into the acting profession. While serving in the Navy, Robards discovered O'Neill in the form of a copy of *Strange Interlude* in the ship's library. Indifferent to the screenplays in which his father often performed, Robards was impressed by the complexity of the O'Neill drama, and began to consider a life on the stage. After a discharge from the Navy following World War II, he enrolled at the American Academy of Dramatic Arts in New York. It was at this time that he attended his first O'Neill drama, the production of *Iceman* by the Theatre Guild in 1946. Although unmoved by the production's Hickey, James Barton, Robards later admitted, "I saw part of myself standing there in Hickey" (qtd. in Barbara Gelb, "Jason Jamie Robards Tyrone" 57). In ten years, he would be.

---

*Though Dewhurst full appreciated what the role of Josie had meant to her life and career, in an interview with Michael Buckley in *TheaterWeek* in 1989, she admitted that although it was diffiicult to pick a favorite role, O'Neill or otherwise, she chose the role of Abbie Putnam in *Desire Under the Elms*, which she played in 1963 under Quintero's direction at Circle in the Square.

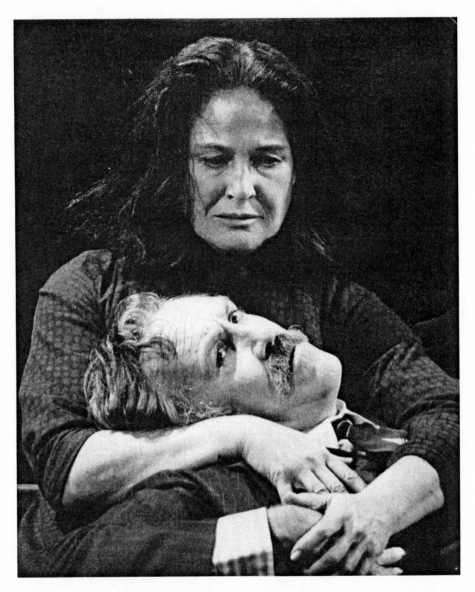

Colleen Dewhurst as Josie Hogan and Jason Robards as James Tyrone, Jr., in the 1973 production of *A Moon for the Misbegotten*, directed by Jose Quintero, at the Morosco Theater. Photograph by Martha Swope. Billy Rose Theatre Division, The New York Public Library for the Performing Arts, Astor, Lenox, and Tilden Foundations.

The quintessential O'Neill actor, "Robards even looks like O'Neill," noted T.E. Kalem in *Time* Magazine: "He has the same brooding deep-set eyes that look out from O'Neill's photographs with such searing gravity" (42). Throughout most of his adult life, like many of O'Neill's characters, and like the author himself, Robards fought an own uneven battle with alcohol, which, in 1973, he nearly lost. The actor learned that he would not repeat his stage triumph as Hickey in the film version of *The Iceman Cometh*—Lee Marvin was cast in the role. Film director John Frankenheimer wanted to do his own version of *Iceman*; to avoid copying someone else's production, he had never considered using Robards. The actor resented this and was furious that the director never called to explain his choice, though Frankenheimer felt that the actor was not owed an explanation. In response to the director's decision, Robards took a ride down the Pacific Coast Highway, suffering an accident that came close to disfiguring his face and destroying his voice, and thus, ending his career. Rehearsals for the Chicago production of *Moon* had to be held in Los Angeles, in rehearsal space supplied by Gordon Davidson at the Mark Taper Forum, to accommodate Robards's schedule of surgeries: in the accident, the actor had broken every bone in his face and needed to have his upper lip reattached.

Jose Quintero had his own mystical connection to O'Neill, seeing the playwright as his "spiritual father." As Quintero told the *Wall Street Journal*, "O'Neill's life so paralleled my own life and feelings that it was as if he had a hand in my upbringing. When I read him, there is nothing strange about him. It is all so painfully familiar" (Phyllis Funke 20). Groomed for failure from birth, Quintero disappointed the father who disdained and ultimately disowned him, first, by not being a girl; then, by having darker skin than the other members of his Panamanian family; and later, by failing to become a doctor according to the future that had been mapped out for him. When his younger sister Carmen attended the Broadway premiere of *Journey*, she said to her brother: "Jose, how could you? With just a few changes, it could be our family" (qtd. in Barbara Gelb, "Touch of the Tragic" 43).

In a series of lectures delivered at the Provincetown Playhouse in New York in August 1998, at a point in his life when he relied on esophageal speech to communicate after surgery in 1987 to remove a cancerous larynx, Quintero impressed upon his audience the need to be *vulnerable* to

O'Neill's material, the syllables of the word extended by the robotic yet hypnotic quality of his speech. In his own life, he may have made himself too vulnerable to the material, suffering from acute alcoholism, at times so severe that he was unable to work, admitting, "the drinking increased to the point where I lost a desire to do anything" (qtd. in Gussow, "Jose Quintero's Long Road Back" 34). As a director, Quintero was described by Ed Flanders as "one of the most sensitive, most vulnerable persons I've ever met.... Jose listens, and then he just drops a line, and pow! It all falls right into place" (qtd. in Gent 20). And as Dewhurst insists in her autobiography, "I would rather be directed by Jose Quintero drunk than most directors stone cold sober" (216). By 1973, Quintero was on the wagon and remained there for the rest of his career.

While most bookers turned down the chance to play O'Neill in the summer, Lake Forest theater producer Marshall Migatz was eager to proceed and engaged the company for a three-week run as part of his summer season. This was a real show of confidence, given that the usual summer stock engagement is one week. Tragically, the day before rehearsals were to start, Migatz was killed in an automobile accident. Although the production could have been cancelled due to an "act of God" clause in the contracts, out of respect for the producer, the theater's board of directors decided that the show must go on. The production would be a tribute to Marshall Migatz.

Added to the triumvirate of Dewhurst, Robards, and Quintero was the actor Ed Flanders, ten years younger than Dewhurst, to play her father. Although his favorite role up to and including this point in his career was the Rev. Daniel Berrigan in *The Trial of the Catonsville Nine*, Flanders is probably best known for playing the kindly Dr. Westphal on the television series *St. Elsewhere* from 1982 to 1988. Luckily, Flanders was an immediate fit into the group of Dewhurst, Robards, and Quintero, who often rehearsed in a whispered shorthand that had evolved over decades of working with the director. As a seasoned professional, Flanders savored the opportunity of "working with supertalented people who don't have to talk each other to death about the motivation behind every word and action." Describing his approach to the role, and displaying his dry wit, Flanders insisted, "The ear is extremely important to the actor, almost as much as overcoming advice on acting. You have to learn to listen while talking. The play's real difficulty — and it's O'Neill's problem for us — is conveying the love Phil has for Josie under the comic lines. Played too broadly, Phil could be a stage Irishman, a caricature" (qtd. in Gent 20). Dewhurst describes Flanders's performance as "having a wonderful tree to lean against, knowing it would always support me" (217). Rounding out the cast were Chicago-based actors Ned Schmidtke as Harder and Don Modie as Mike Hogan.

As Dewhurst describes the rehearsal period, "O'Neill makes a demand for commitment from an actor unlike any other playwright.... With Jason, I could also make the commitment to O'Neill that allowed me, as Josie Hogan, to step off the edge of the cliff and into an abyss with the firm conviction that there was solid ground around me, in the words, in the actors onstage with me and, of course, in our director, Jose.... Jose allowed Jason and me to be transparent with each other. He gave us moments of absolute breathing, where everything we were playing became one thought: Eugene O'Neill's" (218). Both Dewhurst and Schmidtke describe the three-week rehearsal period in Los Angeles as an enthusiastic time, imbued with a feeling of "Let's put on a show" (Dewhurst 218; qtd. in McDonough 172). This was due, in part, to the fact that money was so tight. For example, most of the costumes came from Hollywood thrift shops or the actors' own closets. Robards, at age 51, and Dewhurst, at 49, were attempting to portray characters in their early forties and 28, respectively. Dissipation had aged Tyrone prematurely, but Dewhurst was particularly concerned about her age in comparison to that of her character. According to Schmidtke, who spent most of the rehearsal period watching the events unfold: "She thought she should be younger. She was therefore concerned that they pick just the right clothing. They took a long time choosing what she was going to wear and how it was going to look" (qtd. in McDonough 172).

Of the 1968 revival of *Moon*, critic Lou Cedrone wrote, "If Shakespeare can be cut, so can O'Neill" (A6). Apparently, Quintero agreed. Although he had directed two previous productions of the play, Quintero began with an uncut script, which he proceeded to edit. In her autobiography, Dewhurst insists, "Only Jose knows how to cut O'Neill. He knows when O'Neill had given all the lessons in his play, what he wants repeated over and over again. Like many great playwrights who are, in some ways, terrible writers but wonderful playwrights, he overwrites because he's afraid; he forgets the actor, so the actor has to sit up there and talk it to death instead of the playwright, but Jose knows when to let the repetition come in and when to take away 40 pages because it can be done with a look" (qtd. in McDonough 173). But as Schmidtke also notes, "The problem in cutting is that O'Neill has repeated the idea to introduce it in a slightly different context; the leitmotif has a different contrapuntal effect because of the other elements going on in the scene. If you cut one of them, the idea is still there, but you have it in only one context. It does not reverberate as O'Neill intended" (qtd. in McDonough 173). The cutting proceeded in the same manner as the rehearsals: as a director, Quintero was notable for not saying much. Although Schmidtke had planned to watch the rehearsal process, he found that Quintero said so little and that "the conversation went on at such a low level or in a kind of shorthand that I couldn't begin to pick up on that I thought, 'I've seen this. I saw this yesterday and the day before,' because the salient element was the way people related" (qtd. in McDonough 174). Schmidtke gave up attending rehearsals of scenes that did not include him. When the production moved to Chicago, the stage manager, Jane E. Neufield, acknowledged similar difficulties while attempting to listen in on the rehearsal process; for those who were not part of the conversation, there appeared to be little or nothing to hear.

When the show opened in Lake Forest, it was an immediate success, playing to sold-out houses and enthusiastic audiences, even during a hot Chicago summer. Quintero told the cast he was certain that "we will all be together in New York in the fall" (qtd. in McDonough 176). In fact, the production had no immediate future. Dan Isaac, of the *Village Voice*, made the journey to Lake Forest and wrote a positive review, which is acknowledged as one reason for the production's move to Broadway. As Isaac wrote of the play, "Was it worth traveling to the Midwest to see? Yes, yes, 1000 times yes. At every point I had the feeling that I was watching a classic." Even at this early stage, Issac felt that he has seeing the "definitive production ... brilliantly directed and beautifully acted" (53).

To extend the life of the production, Quintero, Robards, and Dewhurst tried to arrange financing themselves, but the rights had been purchased by producer Elliot Martin as a vehicle for Jack Lemmon. When Lemmon decided against the project, Martin could not raise the capital and yielded controlling interest to producer Lester Osterman, who wanted it to play his then-dark Morosco Theater for five weeks, to be followed by a national tour. Certain that investors would not be interested, Osterman put up the money himself.

By late fall 1973, the company was in New York, as Quintero had predicted, rehearsing for eight days, beginning the Friday after Thanksgiving. Coincidentally, the date, November 27, was the twentieth anniversary of O'Neill's death. A few changes had been made before the New York opening. Edwin J. McDonough, who went on to write *Quintero Directs O'Neill*, a study of the director's work from 1956 to 1988, joined the cast as Mike Hogan, with John O'Leary as Harder, a role he had previously played under Quintero's direction in the Buffalo production. Along with Jane Greenwood on costumes, Ben Edwards was brought in to design the sets and lighting. The set design in Lake Forest was influenced by the unusually wide stage at the Academy Theater, approximately fifty feet. At the Morosco, Quintero wanted a "freedom of space," so, unlike the set in Lake Forest, Edwards took the façade off the house by creating "a skeletal house. You could walk in and out. When you were outside, you lit outside and dimmed the inside. You change the lights when they went inside." As Edwards describes his more expressionistic design: "It was a very simple set. One, it *was* simple and two, there was no money. If we wanted anything more complicated, we would never have gotten it" (qtd. in McDonough 177). On the frame of the Hogan home, only the back wall and half of the roof were suggested by widely-spaced slats, with the side walls left open. Two trees, perhaps O'Neillian elms, hung over the house but did not block the sky. With the façade taken off, the house served as a metaphor for the drama that unfolded. The house was built on a foundation of flat rocks, with the flat-top boulder described by O'Neill in the foreground.

Before its Broadway opening, the production played a three-week stint prior to Christmas at the 1100-seat Eisenhower Theater at the Kennedy Center in Washington, DC, where the reviews were positive but not overwhelming. David Richards, writing for the *Washington Star-News*, focused primarily on the performances of the two leads, writing, "Miss Dewhurst's performance is as uncluttered as a Matisse drawing, at the very same time it suggests the multiple depths of Josie. And therein lies its remarkable beauty." (What is also remarkable is how often critics would point to the beauty as well as the power of Dewhurst in her performance of a self-described "great ugly cow of a woman.") About Robards, Richards is more circumspect: "the role of the comforted is certainly less engaging than the role of the comforter. But he offers an impressive physical portrait of James Tyrone — looking like waste itself, reeling under the onslaught of too many drinks too early, and fumbling with cigarettes as if they might provide a steadying influence.... And yet that, to my mind, is the shortcoming. He appears haunted from the outside, not the inside" (17).

In December, the production moved to the 1009-seat Morosco Theater in New York, also the site of O'Neill's first Broadway production, *Beyond the Horizon*, which played there in 1920. After five sold-out preview performances, beginning the day after Christmas, *Moon* opened on 29 December 1973, with a top ticket price of nine dollars, and a limited engagement planned of four to six weeks. Although the producers had not arranged for an opening-night party — Robards and Dewhurst hosted their own gathering, to which the producers were not invited, but attended anyway — there were plenty of reasons to celebrate. The raves cascaded in, recognizing the work of all those involved.

Clive Barnes, who reviewed the production during its second performance, when the cast, due to exhaustion, was experiencing vocal trouble, raved about what he saw. Having previously deemed the play a "minor-masterpiece" in 1968, Barnes begins his awestruck review: "There are some performances in the theater, just a few, that surge along as if they were holding the whole world on a tidal wave. I felt that surge, that excitement, that special truth revealed while watching Eugene O'Neill's 'A Moon for the Misbegotten.'" Describing what he saw as "a landmark production that people are going to be talking about for years," and O'Neill as "one of the great playwrights of the modern theater," Barnes continues: "His best plays enclose you within the dimensions of their own world. You believe that you are listening to life, yet at the end, you have intimations of something beyond naturalism." Praising the director, Barnes states that "Quintero plays his cards unerringly. You could take a temperature chart of his staging, and it would be the same as the play itself." Moving on to the actors, Barnes asks, "how can you write about performances you are going to talk about for years?" Of Dewhurst as Josie, he writes, "She spoke O'Neill as if it were being spoken for the first time — and not the first time in a theater (you always hope for that) but for the first time in a certain New England farm, on a certain September night in 1923." Moving on to Jason Robards in the "whirlpool role" of James Tyrone, Barnes asserts, "with his diffidently cocky stance, his map-lined face a stark report of suffering, and yet also an odd recollection of pictures of O'Neill himself, [Robards] lays bare the simple secret of the Tyrones." Of Ed Flanders as Phil Hogan, he adds, "This is O'Neill at his most Irish, and Mr. Flanders is a nimble, loving rogue of Abbey Theater vintage." Barnes also praised the "very decent conviction" of Edwin J. McDonough and John O'Leary in their "contrived cameo sketches" ("A Landmark 'Moon'" 22). A rave in the *Times* is a rave in the *Times*, and as Dewhurst knew, "We'll get a few more weeks out of this review, regardless of what anybody else says" (qtd. in Chase 1). When the rest of the reviews had been read, the New York engagement was extended indefinitely.

Quintero writes in his autobiography: "It took O'Neill to write a woman as strong and large as nature.... A woman 'more powerful than any but an exceptionally strong man' but with 'no mannish quality about her.' A woman who is 'all woman' for Colleen to feel at last that she was properly cast" (193). Walter Kerr, also writing in the *New York Times*, concurs: "Colleen Dewhurst is a beautiful woman giving a beautiful performance in the newest revival of Eugene O'Neill's *A Moon for the Misbegotten* (which also happens to be a beautiful play, possibly O'Neill's best)...." Kerr was of two minds when he reviewed *Moon* in 1957, saying, "The work of these two people [Hiller and Tone] in this third-act dance of death is superb, and should be seen. The rest of the play does not yet exist on the stage." In 1973, Kerr writes, "It is difficult to take your eyes off Miss Dewhurst, whether she is smiling or in fury.... Her face actually seems to brighten under the hint of pain, a sense of unruly merriment tries hard to assert itself, a vixen gaiety becomes permanent companion of disaster." Speaking of her permanent companion in disaster, Kerr describes Robards as "[beginning] brilliantly, self conscious not only about his natty 1923 clothes but about his need for a drink, his need for a woman who will not turn out to be a whore, his need for nothing so much as an impossible forgiveness. The shaking hand with which he lights a cigarette as their tryst together is to begin establishes its outcome; the succulent surrender to a first taste of a drink she brings him outlines precisely the one comfort this doomed man can know."

While Kerr praises Robards's physicality in the role as "conscientiously arrived at, intelligently used," he admits to "one important reservation and feels like an ingrate bringing it up." As he continues, "the terrifying 'almost' of the third act — the teasing possibility that against all odds two rattled, emotionally starved, yearning and yet distrustful misfits will somehow find a crooked way to an ultimate meeting — simply didn't happen." Kerr faults Robards for this, saying that he "continually aborts that promised rhythm, lurching away in self-disgust and trying to spit from his mouth the venom of lost years so often that the design becomes fragmented, the contrast stalemated.... there were times when I wanted to collar the man and order him to stay with the scene, stay with the woman, until O'Neill's play could come as close as it dared to a psychic embrace. *Then* it might be shattered, letting us see the remorse-ridden figure as truly dead." Missing "the crest of the wave, before it collapses on the beach" left Kerr with "slightly fonder memories of the 1968 production at the downtown Circle in the Square." In summation, he calls this play "O'Neill's richest work for the theater," as opposed to the autobiographical *Journey*, because in *Moon*, "the creative impulse is allowed more play ... life is made on the wing rather than painstakingly remembered" ("Rich Play, Richly Performed" 1).

Finding the production even more praiseworthy was T.E. Kalem, in *Time* Magazine, who writes, "Broadway is a noble word again. Power, beauty, passions and truth command the stage of the Morosco Theater where *A Moon for the Misbegotten* has been revived in unmitigated triumph. We owe it all to the sensitive direction of Jose Quintero, the matchless performances of Jason Robards, Colleen Dewhurst, and Ed Flanders, and the piercing vision of Eugene O'Neill." Kalem continues, "[Jason Robards'] performance will remain a touchstone for all actors to measure themselves by. Similarly, Colleen Dewhurst is ideally cast. No woman has been big enough for the part before, not only physically but in that generosity of heart, mind, and spirit which Josie must convey" (42). In a similar vein, Brendan Gill, in *The New Yorker*, asserts that "Colleen Dewhurst gives the performance of her life as Josie; in my mind the part is hers forever" (58). Albert Bermel, in the *New Leader*, insists that "Ed Flanders ... creates a characterization that would have made O'Neill weep with pleasure" (28). Richard Watts, who reviewed *Moon* in 1957 and 1968, had been a fan of the play, though with some reservations, finding it initially tedious but finally overwhelming, too long and yet "one of the saddest and most beautiful plays [O'Neill] ever wrote." Writing in the *New York Post*, he was more succinct in 1973, calling *Moon* "A Superb Play, Superbly Done." He also finds Flanders "quite wonderful," with Dewhurst's performance "truly magnificent" and Robards "perfect in all phases of Tyrone's complex character" (9). Douglas Watt, in the *Daily News*, described Robards as "devastatingly real" under Quintero's "inspired" direction (25). In *Newsweek*, Jack Kroll praises Robards for "one of the best performances I've ever seen. His Jamie is a frayed gentleman, a spoiled poet and polluted idealist. In the climactic scene Robards gives an amazingly clear, detailed, subtle and powerful portrayal of a man in the fourth dimension of an alcoholic fog, lurching between past and present, being wrenched about by his agonized memories" ("Bottled in Bondage" 62).

George Melloan, in the *Wall Street Journal*, explains why he thinks it all works: "the brilliance of the performances in this production goes deeper than mere discussions of 'presence' or 'talent.' Part of it comes from technique; Mr. Robards, Miss Dewhurst, and Mr. Flanders are masters of the acting craft, the subtle movement of the shoulders, or the mouth or the eyes, the inflections of the voice. They also have an intelligent instinct for what the lines really mean and how they should be said.... All the elements coalesce into something larger than the individual parts, an Irish wedding that has its own synergistic energy" (16). Like most critics, he saw greatness in the individuals and in the play as a whole.

Writing in *The Nation,* Harold Clurman, with whom Dewhurst had studied acting in the early stages of her career, described the play as "the best production of the best play of the season" (92). Clurman's review is memorable for his short tirade on the failure of the original production, blaming its author and producers. Alluding to O'Neill's description of Josie Hogan, "*almost a freak—five foot eleven in her stockings and weighs about one hundred eighty,*" and the infamous clause that required actress Mary Welch to gain weight for the role, Clurman went on to say, "This stupid and horrible clause may very well have led to the actress's death shortly after the play's production" (92).

Sadly, Mary Welch had died in 1958 at the age of 35. The cause of death was an internal hemorrhage that occurred during the late stages of her second pregnancy. In the ensuing years, Welch had played Stella in the national tour of *A Streetcar Named Desire* in 1948–1949 and originated the role of Missy LeHand in the Broadway production of *Sunrise at Campobello* in 1958. While a significant, if temporary, weight gain is not beneficial to one's health, it is unlikely that this played a role in her untimely death over ten years after playing the role of Josie Hogan. And the attachment to the stage directions originated with the author and not the producers at the Theatre Guild. The "author-worshipping" tendencies that enabled O'Neill to demand a literal translation of his words belonged to the Theatre Guild, however, "where all O'Neill's faults were presented to the public with careful reverence" (333), as Eric Bentley wrote of the Theatre Guild's production of *The Iceman Cometh*, which ran concurrently with the original *Moon for the Misbegotten*.

While most critics were generating superlatives for the 1973 production, not all were in agreement. Martin Gottfried, writing in *Women's Wear Daily*, objects to "[the] shameless use of the past reputations of its director and actors, rather than their present talent" in a "manufactured attempt to imitate that past." Though praising the performances of Dewhurst and Flanders, Gottfried contends that under Quintero's "listless" direction, "Robards goes through the motions of the thousands of times he has played the same role in various O'Neill plays" (17). This opinion was very much in the minority, however; the only other negative review came from Kevin Sanders at WABC-TV, who described the play as "one of those bleak, dismal stories of miserable people and their self-inflicted sorrows." Sanders notes that *Moon* is not only O'Neill's last play, "It's widely regarded by his admirers as being his greatest. That's why I hesitate to say it was one of the most wretched ways one could imagine of spending a good Saturday night." Identifying Dewhurst and Robards as "two of Broadway's best talents," Sanders still found the play "a dispiriting experience to sit through," the comedy of the first half apparently lost on him. Although he thought Dewhurst "a most alluring and comely woman in a mother earth sort of way," Sanders describes Robards "in one of those noisy, tiresome, drunken O'Neill speeches ... wallowing in absurdly operatic and indulgent self pity." Most, however, agreed with Julius Novick in the *Village Voice*, who stated that there would "probably never be a better production of *A Moon for the Misbegotten* than the one Jose Quintero has directed at the Morosco" (67).

When the 1974 award season rolled around, the work of the Resurrection Company was amply rewarded. Dewhurst, Robards, Flanders, and director Quintero received Drama Desk Awards for their outstanding work. When the Tony nominations were announced, all four received nominations along with Ben Edwards for Lighting Design, although Jules Fischer took home the award that year for the lighting design of *Ulysses in Nighttown*. In a highly competitive field that included Zero Mostel, in *Ulysses in Nighttown*, and George C. Scott and Nicol Williamson in *Uncle Vanya*, the award went not to Jason Robard but to Michael Moriarity, in *Find Your Way Home*. In his review of *Moon*, John Simon had said, somewhat dismissively, that "Jose Quintero's direction seems minimal, but, with these actors, that is enough" ("A Great Compassion" 53). Apparently, the Tony voters agreed. Along with Jose Quintero as Best Director of a Play, both Flanders and Dewhurst were recipients of the award. In her acceptance speech, after thanking her family and telling her young sons to go to bed, Dewhurst said, "I know that what I hold in my hand is for *Moon*, for the total. What has been most fantasy-like, I guess, is that it was us all, it was the theater.... Most of all I want to thank you all for a joy you may never know you have given me, the joy that theater is alive and well and living inside of us all" (222). Producers Elliot Martin, Lester Osterman, and Richard Horner also received a special Tony Award for the production in addition to an Outer Critics Circle Award. After a total of 313 performances, *Moon* closing on 17 November 1974, and was later filmed as a television play and broadcast for the first time on ABC-TV on May 27, 1975. Thus far, this is the only production of *Moon* available on video.

Although the 1968 production in some areas equaled the achievement of the 1973 revival, as Walter Kerr notes, "the event took place Off Broadway, where revivals that run six months or so do not necessarily establish themselves indelibly on the popular mind" ("Playwrights, Take Heed" 1). The tremendous success of the 1973 revival made believers of almost all who had undervalued the play in its earlier incarnations. And yet, as Harold Clurman wondered, "One might ask why it has taken so long for the reviewers and the public to recognize its unique distinction in O'Neill's work" (92). The felicitous reunion of Colleen Dewhurst, Jason Robards, and Jose Quintero, with the fortunate addition of Ed Flanders, made for a thrilling evening in the theater, but this does fully explain the appeal of material that had never been fully accepted by the theater-going public.

It was still the same play, if slightly edited, a "strange combination comic-tragic" work, as O'Neill had described it in his Work Diary, even if, according to some critics, overwritten.

Yet, even those who had derided O'Neill's writing also acknowledged that his writing does work on the stage. At best, it speaks in an almost subliminal language that makes the audience hear what the author intended, whether or not it has actually been said. As Michael Billington stated in the London *Guardian*, "As a dramatist, O'Neill may commit every sin in the book, but when you watch him in the theatre ... your senses tell you that you are in the presence of a master." At worst, as Benedict Nightingale has written, "Sitting through [an O'Neill play] can be like standing beneath a landslide, with rock after rock bouncing painfully off your head. And yet the paradox is, that it often, very often, seems a privilege to endure the onslaught, and for more than masochistic reasons. One is, after all, being battered into a level of consciousness where one sees and feels things no other playwright has confronted" ("A Flawed Masterpiece" 5). In any case, the audience appeared in droves: similar to the debut of *Strange Interlude* in 1928, the heaviest drama of the 1973–1974 Broadway season also became the hottest ticket. From its humble beginnings as an out-of-town failure, *Moon* was finally a critical and a commercial success. Even O'Neill's children benefited. No one had renewed the copyright to the play after Carlotta, the chief beneficiary, died in 1970, and the original (1945) copyright expired. Although disinherited by their father, his offspring had the right to renew the lapsed copyright, becoming the sole owners of the play due to a legal technicality. In 1973, *Moon* brought in $3,200 per week to the estate, including returns from domestic and foreign stage revivals of the play, future movie and television adaptations, and the published versions of the play (Barbara Gelb, "A Mint for the Misbegotten" 43). The play that was published "so we can eat," as Carlotta wrote to Bennett Cerf in 1952, had become the estate's biggest financial success to date.

The combined appeal of O'Neill, a small cast, and a single set have made *Moon* the most frequently revived work in the O'Neill canon. Comparisons between productions are inevitable, and, in this instance, invariable. Revivals of the play mounted on Broadway in 1984, 2000, and 2007, as well as on numerous regional stages, have been reviewed in the context of the 1973 production, which is regarded as definitive. The myth has grown to the point where it frames all productions before or since. Clearly, this production would be a tough act to follow.

Broadway Revival, 1984

It was over a decade before the next major revival of *Moon* on Broadway. After the complicated history of the previous revival, the 1984 revival was refreshing in the simplicity of its start. According to the British director David Leveaux, the play literally fell into his hands — from the high shelf of a Manhattan bookstore, during his first visit to New York in January 1983. Returning to London, he was determined to direct the play. As associate director of Riverside Studios, he was able to make this happen, although the Riverside usually presents classic or experimental work.

The young director, only twenty-six at the time, envisioned a musical structure for *Moon*: "it was a musical preoccupation that led me to the play," he admitted to interviewer Ellen Levene, fueled by a desire to work on a play "that demanded an extreme passion, that had a language that had to be wielded, that was in every sense not urbane, that, despite the fact that it was prose, demanded of us, in our style of production and the means of the delivery, the music of the play." In *Moon*, Leveaux identified "a symphonic structure: four clear movements," beginning with "allegro, where the major themes and linguistic landscape are established. There were one or two pulses in a kind of minor key which were hinting at something to come." This is followed by the second act/movement, "extraordinary and beautiful"; the third act, "an adagio duet"; and the fourth, "a little coda" (qtd. in Levene 13). According to Leveaux, the musical structure is also a way to manage what he sees as one of O'Neill's prime difficulties — repetition — provided that the returning phrases, to borrow Mahler's term, are played in a slightly different context and weight each time they reappear. Leveaux's approach was also to treat *Moon* as an Irish play, "O'Neill's most Irish play" (qtd. in Freedman, "Ghosts Haunt the Stage" 1), stressing the poetry of O'Neill's language as something more akin to Synge or O'Casey.

To the Riverside production Leveaux was able to bring the British stage actress Frances de la Tour. Tall, but without the girth associated with

Josie Hogan, de la Tour appeared as Mrs. Lintott in the 2006 Broadway production of Alan Bennett's *The History Boys*, for which she received the Tony Award for Best Featured Actress in a Play. In the 1960s, at the beginning of her career, de la Tour asked the director Peter Hall if she could play Juliet, to which Hall replied that "it would never happen because she was far too tall and gangly and didn't fit the public's perception of how Juliet should look" (Gardner 12). Although the actress had enjoyed success in her career, going on to play Cleopatra at the Royal Shakespeare Company, such Josie-like moments might have caused her to rethink her theatrical calling. At the time of the *Moon* revival in 1983, the actress was returning from a self-imposed exile from the theater. She later admitted that playing Josie had cured her of the anxiety attacks that had plagued her for years: "I really wrestled with that part. I was really ashamed of my voice and I tried to compensate by acting big. It was only when I stopped and was myself that it all fell into place. It was like a revelation" (qtd. in Gardner 12). Ian Bannen, enjoying a successful career in film (*Gandhi*) and on television (*Tinker, Tailor, Soldier, Spy*), was also making a return to the stage to play James Tyrone, Jr., having performed the role of the older brother in *Journey* twenty-five years earlier. The cast was completed by Alan Devlin as Phil Hogan, Ronald Fernee as Harder, and Piers Ibbotson as Mike Hogan.

When the production opened at the Riverside Studio in June 1983, the greatest praise went to de la Tour's performance as Josie. "She is the kind of actress who can make you feel that she is fat, ungainly, fatally ugly, if she wants to," as James Fenton wrote in the *London Times*: "The extraordinary availability of her emotions, the variousness of her manner and the richness of her voice give her a unique access to the sympathies of the audience, sympathies with which she will never trifle." The production ran at Riverside from 18 June through 1 July 1983, followed by a transfer to London's West End. At the same time, Robert Brustein, artistic director of the American Repertory Theatre, the sister operation to the Riverside Studios, invited Leveaux to bring the production to Cambridge, Massachusetts, outside of Boston. Having recently escaped the threat of foreclosure, Riverside Studios could not afford to send its actors; only Leveaux arrived in the Fall of 1983, to begin the task of choosing an American cast.

His first choice surprised many. Leveaux decided to approach Kate Nelligan to play the role of Josie Hogan. The two had never met, although it would quickly become apparent that the director and the actress shared an exacting set of professional standards. The previous season, Nelligan had been nominated for a Tony Award for her portrayal of the sleek and sophisticated Susan Traherne, the disillusioned wife of a British diplomat, in David Hare's *Plenty*. The Toronto-born actress was educated at the Central School of Speech and Drama in London, paid for by wealthy patrons of the arts in Canada whom the determined young actress had petitioned for financial support. Nelligan began her career in repertory at the Old Vic, playing thirteen parts in her first year, from Shakespeare to Neil Simon. Certainly, the O'Neill role would require all of her transformative skill. Yet Nelligan padded only her chest to emphasize the "big, beautiful breasts" (*Moon* 878) that Jim Tyrone so admires, if only to lay his head upon. As to the role of Josie, Nelligan is quoted as saying, "Playing Josie is like being O'Neill's emotional whore.... He'll pick this specific shape, this specific emotional texture and that's the only woman who can please him. That's his hang-up about Josie's size. Only if she's that big will O'Neill be smaller than her and can be held like a child." Nelligan insisted that "it's not a play about a fat girl, it's a play about Eugene O'Neill's — and Jim Tyrone's — emotional needs.... For a modern woman to take up this role, you feel like Atlas. There's this drunken father and this drunken, dark-eyed Irishman and she holds them both up" (qtd. in Freedman, "Ghosts Haunt the Stage" 1).

Originally inspired by the photographs of Walker Evans, capturing impoverished woman during the Depression, Nelligan's Josie had the look of a feral child; her hair was long and matted, her eyebrows busy. Her level of hygiene was one of the more naturalistic details on the set. In keeping with life on a pig farm, she actually was dirty. The actress even searched for a dress that was destitute, finding just the thing: "It was in the bottom of a basket of clothes that no one was buying.... It was trying so hard

Opposite: Ian Bannen as James Tyrone, Jr., and Kate Nelligan as Josie Hogan in the 1983 A.R.T. production of *A Moon for the Misbegotten*, directed by David Leveaux. Photograph by Richard Feldman, courtesy of the American Repertory Theatre.

to be something it couldn't be," not unlike Josie early in her date with Jim Tyrone in Act III, when she tries to act the loose woman. To complete her outfit and to create the feeling of being "absolutely defeated" (qtd. in Freedman "Ghosts Haunt the Stage" 1), Nelligan found shoes two sizes too big, for feet unused to wearing shoes.

Nelligan even viewed a videotape of the 1973 revival so that she would know exactly what she was taking on. Although this might defeat some, Nelligan benefited, realizing that she and Dewhurst had little in common. As she said, "There was so little connection between her persona and mine that I wasn't frightened.... I knew Josie had to be new minted" (qtd. in Kakutani 1). One difference between these two performances occurs when Josie wakes the sleeping Tyrone; with a beautiful dawn on the horizon, she shakes him vigorously, complaining of her stiffness after sitting in the same position by saying, "I'll never be the same" (*Moon* 940). No Josie is the same after this evening, but the statement might be most true of Nelligan's Josie at the end of the play, who "heaves and sobs with the recognition that her life's only moment of truth and communion is over" (Rich C21). Unlike Nelligan's Josie, who is emotionally devastated, Dewhurst's Josie, though deeply saddened by the events of the evening, quickly regains her jocularity, "well content" with the prospect of a future of living with her father, telling him, "Sure, living with you has spoilt me for any other man" (*Moon* 945).

Previous Josies had been criticized for being tall but not big enough, not beautiful but too pretty for the role. Given these criteria, Nelligan failed on all fronts: she was small, thin, and attractive. Instead, she chose to create the character through an intense physical and vocal transformation. Nelligan's transformation was so radical that during the Boston run, her vocal cords hemorrhaged, requiring a visit to a throat specialist, who photographed her vocal cords as she spoke her lines. This was followed by Nelligan working with a vocal coach to protect her voice against permanent damage. During the time of her injury, Nelligan missed a week of performances, but the show must go on, so Bannen played opposite Nelligan's understudy, Marianne Owen, who read the lines from a script.

In the role of Jim Tyrone, Jason Miller was cast, best known as the author of the Pulitzer-Prize–winning play *That Championship Season*, and for his Oscar-nominated turn as the tortured Father Karras in *The*

Exorcist. A recalcitrant Catholic, like the character he played, Miller was a little closer to type. As a high school athlete at St. Patrick's High School, in Scranton, Pennsylvania, Miller was neither a model student nor a model citizen. The intervention of Sister Celine, a teacher of public speaking and debate, changed the direction of his life. She encouraged Miller to study elocution and to develop his powerful voice. Coached by Sister Celine, Miller won local public speaking contests, and went on to graduate from Scranton University and then from Catholic University in Washington, DC, with degrees in theater and playwriting.

Jerome Kilty would appear as Phil Hogan. A playwright as well as an actor, Kilty is the author of *Dear Liar*, which follows the forty-year correspondence of George Bernard Shaw and Mrs. Patrick Campbell. Kilty cheerfully admitted to not really liking O'Neill before his experience with this production of *Moon*: "I found him boring and repetitious. And when I started working on this play, I found that the director's intention was almost 180 degrees away from the intentions and stage directions indicated in the play. I felt that a naturalistic rhythm was indicated, but David Leveaux wanted it to go like a train with no stops." Also an experienced director, Kilty worried about his working relationship with Leveaux but accepted the director's way of doing things: "I realized Leveaux was right to play O'Neill like that, and that, indeed, it was like peeling an onion — each slight variation on a theme or idea that might seem repetitious if one did it more slowly ... seems to achieve a lifelike quality. In real life people actually do say the same thing over and over again. I found it a revelation" (qtd. in Bennetts C3). Also cast in Cambridge were Thomas Derrah, a founding member of the American Repertory Theatre, as T. Stedman Harder, and John Bellucci as Mike Hogan.

Leveaux had no lack of what the British call "cheek," although his personal style, even at twenty six, was not characterized by the ebullience of youth but a calm and collected presence. To follow the landmark production of *Moon* was indicative of this. Although Leveaux was a mere 15 and living in Surrey, England, at the time of the 1973 revival, he was well aware of its existence: "Any production as good as that will grow to an almost metaphysical stature once it's closed. And we're inevitably going to invite comparisons." But he was certain of his own vision of *Moon*. According to the director, "'Moon' has a symphonic and poetic life that almost supercedes its autobiographical life. The very sound of the language, the length of the lines, contains a kind of expression that goes beyond what we know about Jim Tyrone or James O'Neill or the archetype of Josie. Our production is probably more romantic in the vigorous sense of the word, in that it's a play of expansiveness rather than withdrawal." It was a vision that Nelligan shared: "what we're doing is so different, so radically different. Our version is far less naturalistic. We're not pretending these people are sitting outside a real shack. These people's language is not naturalistic. So the play becomes a huge, rather clumsy, beautiful thing, hewn out of the ground. If it's a painting, it's broad brush strokes, not something pointillist" (qtd. in Freedman, "Ghosts Haunt the Stage" 1).

As a director Leveaux had a clear plan; in fact, the cast began to call him "Twyla," after choreographer Twyla Tharp, for the precision of his blocking (Freedman, "Revisionist 'Mooon'" C17). Leveaux also suggested the stylized aspect of the set design by Brien Vahey, the designer in residence at Riverside Studios. On a bare circular platform, a realistic shanty was placed. In addition, the façade of the Hogans' shanty home could open and fold shut, similar to an accordion. On Vahey's uncluttered set, the rocks were limited to a lone boulder in front of the house and a few scattered at the back, giving the impression, as opposed to the reality, of the New England terrain. When Tyrone makes his first entrance into the play, he quotes Latin, which he roughly translates as "Ain't you the lucky bastard to have this beautiful farm, if it is full of nude rocks." Phil replies, "If the cows could eat them this place would make a grand dairy farm" (*Moon* 875). On this farm, the cows would starve.

Leveaux had impressed most of the cast members with his personal calm, but this was quickly put to the test when Jason Miller left the cast after only one week of rehearsal — due to what Artistic Director Robert Brustein politely described as "incompatibility" with Leveaux's vision of the play. With three weeks left until the opening, Leveaux brought in Ian Bannen, who had played the role in the Riverside production. Bannen was ill at the time, which delayed his arrival for nine days, and the opening, three times. But when the play did open, just before Christmas in December 1983, most of the Boston critics sang its praises. One of the most striking reviews is that of Kevin Kelly, of the *Boston Globe*. On the basis of this production alone, Kelly, he who had wanted the dawn to come early in his negative review of the 1968 revival, admits that he was "forced to reevaluate Eugene O'Neill's play which, on more than one occasion, [he] had severely discounted." Still finding the comedy "rough and tumble," the romance "sentimental and stretched," and the play "over full of O'Neill's poetic brand of high articulation," Kelly also finds the production "poignant, honest and very moving," primarily due to the "beautiful" acting of the three principals. Kelly calls Ian Bannen "wonderful as James Tyrone, Jr., brilliantly passing in and out of his drunken reveries, then wandering into the torture of his most shattering memory and taking us with him." Jerome Kilty successfully avoids turning Phil into a stage Irishman, but plays him with "bourbon-soaked charm." Kelly has particular praise for the performance of Kate Nelligan, which he describes as "indelible." Although not physically imposing, Nelligan "commands an intensity that reaches the essence of Josie's character. She becomes Josie Hogan to the center of her noble heart." This is achieved "by moving in awkward ways, by raising rude elbows, by a loping, flat-footed run. She uses a low, rusty register in her brogue-ish voice. If all that doesn't erase her beauty, it does, at the least, create the impression of a rowdy, feisty, ungovernable woman" (Kelly, "O'Neill's 'Moon'" 8).

Writing in the *Boston Herald*, Arthur Friedman had his reservations about the play itself, including "the relentless use of slang ('Nix on the rough stuff, Josie')" and what he refers to as "O'Neill's 'Ah, Wordiness!' syndrome (his chronic inability to say anything once) [which] turn the climactic moonlit confession into an exhausting endurance test." But as Friedman continues, "the A.R.T. production is just about the best 'Moon' we earthbound New Englanders can expect to find — although casting the attractive Kate Nelligan, in smudged fashion frocks yet, as the titanic Josie seems peculiar if not perverse." Friedman describes Nelligan's Josie as "spunky, growling, yet deeply moving," and Ian Bannen's Jim, "as insightful and gentlemanly a portrait of a devil-driven sot as you could hope for." Friedman acknowledges the "raw melodramatic power that churns through the play" as well as its essential humanity: "in a long moonlit tryst with the tormented, gravebound James, [Josie] realizes that the way to give him at least one night of peace is to offer him maternal understanding and forgiveness, not sex. In aborting her father's scheme and suppressing her own desires, Josie knows she will lose James forever, but her sacrifice proves how deep her love really is" (28).

Carolyn Clay, writing for the *Boston Phoenix*, and insisting that the Dewhurst/Robard *Moon* is "still transfixed in [her] memory," attends the production with an open mind, finding the play "a strange mixture of the Aristotelian and the mischievous." Clay agrees with Leveaux's decision to move the play at a faster pace, so "its lyrical prose could be made to sing like Shakespeare with the meter running." Clay acknowledges what the actors already knew: "[Leveaux's] staging approaches choreography in its sleekness," finally "a blend of naturalism and ballet." She applauds Nelligan's performance, "informed by intelligence and technique," particularly in a moment near the end of the play: "when the loss is complete and she has watched her love amble off toward his inevitable and blessed demise, Nelligan's small body is wrenched backward and then forward in a spectacular movement that suggests Greek tragedy. The cries seem to come up from her toes." Yet the critic feels that the production really belongs to Ian Bannen as Jim, a less romantic figure than Robards, "as indeed he should be," and "also frightening — as ghosts are supposed to be." As Tyrone, Bannen "exposes the man's muling babyishness without a flicker of embarrassment. This is a man who has died; only the infant and the actor in him are still twitching" (Clay, "Moonlight Sonata" 2).

Continuing in this vein, Jack Kroll, writing in *Newsweek*, states that "where Jason Robards's 1974 performance was terrifying in its psychic dislocation, Bannen's equally strong one is a shattering rhapsody of poisoned sweetness" ("Courage of their Convictions" 69). When the script calls for Tyrone simply to knock a drink out of Josie's hand, Bannen's Tyrone had been directed to hurl her to the floor. Similarly, when Josie threatens to leave her father at the end of the play, Kilty's head drops to his chest, as if "the very thought had broken him" (Clay,"Moonlight Sonata" 2). Phil Hogan recovers, but Jim, and in this production, Josie, do not. In performances that were "at once haunted, gravelly, and beatific" (Clay, "Moonlight Sonata" 2), the production aspired to the mythic, as opposed to a realistic portrayal of events. And it succeeded in at least one sense, accord-

Opposite: John Bellucci as Mike Hogan and Kate Nelligan as Josie Hogan in the 1983 A.R.T. production of *A Moon for the Misbegotten*, directed by David Leveaux. Set Design by Brien Vahey. Photograph by Richard Feldman, courtesy of American Repertory Theatre.

ing to Joan Lautman, writing in the *Brookline Chronicle*: "Once in every generation, it seems, a definitive production of an important work takes place. This current production of O'Neill's celebrated play is such a production ... [it] rips through your sense and strips your soul bare, leaving you to examine your own emotional commitments" (1). Jon Lehman, of the Quincy *Patriot Ledger*, concurred, writing that "the marvel of the play, and of this production, is that behind these seemingly cardboard cutouts are truly heroic human beings," describing the production as "a magnificent, nearly flawless rendering of a first-rank play" (33).

The positive critical response in Boston prompted the Shubert Organization and Emanuel Azenberg, an independent producer, to invest $400,000 to bring the production to New York. Previews began on 9 April 1984 at the 1,009-seat Cort Theatre, a little over twice the size of the 499-seat American Repertory Theatre. Thomas Derrah chose to honor his contract with the A.R.T. and stay in Cambridge, and he was replaced by Michael Tolaydo as T. Stedman Harder. The demands of the play were taking a toll on the other players, however. Ian Bannen fell ill with a bronchial infection and missed ten days of performances. Then, Kate Nelligan developed laryngitis and missed four performances. After her throat injury, Nelligan never played eight performances a week, performing six times a week for the first five weeks and seven times a week thereafter. The hemorrhaging continued, this time in the form of money: the production was losing $40,000 a week as rumors swirled that it would never open. But open it did, on 1 May 1984. After the praise the Leveaux production had received in London and in Boston, the New York producers undoubtedly hoped for more of the same. Unfortunately for them, the New York critics were far more mixed in their response.

In the make-or-break review in the *New York Times*, Frank Rich focuses his attention on the "startling" transformation achieved by Nelligan. The critic is less impressed by the actress's ability to transform herself: "Miss Nelligan's stunning achievement in the play at the Cort is not the relatively straightforward matter of disguising herself as O'Neill's 'great, ugly cow' of a woman." The critic is more impressed "when Miss Nelligan must tear away her disguise [and] we confront the seething heart of her performance — and the crushing primal force of O'Neill's masterpiece." Describing the play as "a straight, bottomless drop into the agonizing, solitary pit of existence," Rich also points to a moment of salvation, "a brief, peaceful way-station on their intersecting paths to separate graves ... a selfless and sexless consummation of love ... so real it makes the earth move." In the inevitable debate as to whether this production matches the 1973 revival, Rich is certain that Nelligan's "overwhelming" performance can withstand the scrutiny and "will be talked about as long as the debate goes on."

Finding the production "imaginative" and "laced with fresh insights into the play," Rich praises Leveaux's decision to free the play from naturalism, viewing it instead as a timeless drama. With the Hogans' farmhouse set on a tilted oval against a nearly blank cyclorama, the drama is located both on a pig farm and in a "dreamy, abstract realm of consciousness." Seeking the lyricism of the language, "the grave poetry of the text," Leveaux also locates a brute intensity, as when Jim "knocks [Josie] clear across the stage." Rich finally suggests that the young British director "be quarantined in New York until we've seen him direct more American plays." Leveaux was not quite quarantined, but he has enjoyed a successful career, directing both plays and musicals on Broadway. He led a well-received production of "*Anna Christie*" in 1993, bringing together the talents of Natasha Richardson and Liam Neeson, followed by a range of productions, including *The Real Thing* and *Betrayal* in 2000, *Nine* in 2003, *Fiddler on the Roof* and *Jumpers* in 2004, and *The Glass Menagerie* in 2005.

Rich finds much to praise in Leveaux's energetic direction and Nelligan's compelling performance, but even more to criticize in Ian Bannen's Tyrone, "a major casting error," according to Rich, with Bannen not in the league or at the level of Jason Robards. Bannen's performance had been praised by critics in London and in Boston, but Rich asserts that the actor is "too silkenly actorish ... he fails to embody the dissipation that defines Jim as the walking ruin of the sensitive artist he might have been." Rich acknowledges that Mr. Bannen does capture the "ghostliness of a living 'dead man who is walking behind his own coffin,'" but his self-lacerating monologue falls short ... the expiation of guilt seems too sonorous and practiced. " In fact, according to Rich, this speech is saved by Nelligan, "whose intense concentration pulls like a chain at our necks throughout, makes us hear the speech as Josie hears it, rather than how it is delivered" (C21).

Benedict Nightingale, writing for the same publication, saw a different play. Describing *Moon* as "a flawed masterpiece," the critic asks the question: "How many plays can you name which touch greatness without actually managing to be good?." Yet, for all the cumbersome repetition that he attributes to the play, Nightingale acknowledges its power, although he feels that this revival is not as powerful as it could be, describing the play as "lopsided" in its attempts to balance the "gallumphing rustic comedy" with its bumper crop of "theatrical corn" and the scene of expiation that follows: "Somehow a journey that began among country bumpkins has ended in the heart, the intestines, the very bowels of human existence." Equally unbalanced, according to Nightingale, are the weight and importance, as well as the success, of the two leads, with "the less important protagonist scoring the hits, the more important one accumulating the misses." In discussing the performances, Nightingale writes, "Ian Bannen's Jim, whose tortured feelings are the reason O'Neill wrote the play, turns out to be a far less arresting stage presence than Kate Nelligan's Josie, who has a less vital emotional contribution to make.... Somehow, we're left feeling that there's more depth to the farmer's daughter than to Jim Tyrone himself; that it's more difficult, painful and momentous to admit one is chaste than to confess that one has wronged the ghost of one's mother.... " ("O'Neill's 'Moon' 5). Certainly, his brother's tortured feelings, as well as his own, are the reasons O'Neill wrote the play, but that does not diminish the essential and difficult emotional contribution made by Josie Hogan. Many, myself included, would argue that Josie and Jim are equally important to the play, with Josie making the longer and more compelling journey as a character, admitting not only that she is chaste but also that she loves Jim Tyrone, and that her love for him is so great that she is willing to sacrifice it in order to save him, if only for the duration of the evening, from himself.

Although Nightingale was willing to attribute some of Bannen's "lack of authentic intensity" to the actor's recent throat troubles, he has praise enough for Nelligan, who "can't convince us that she's the 'ugly, overgrown lump of a woman' she's said to be. But who cares? Miss Nelligan has the magnetism and the technique to make us forget what she isn't and accept what she is; and she's a woman whose surface harshness and rancor hide thwarted feelings of great strength and surprising subtlety. Her face can crumple, sobs can wrack her body, and it seems true." Despite what

Nightingale sees as the distortion, or only partial fulfillment, of the play's intentions, "enough remains at the climax for us to know we're in the presence of something exceptional" ("O'Neill's 'Moon'" 8).

Other critics echoed some of the negatives on Bannen's performance and added a few of their own. In the *New Yorker*, Brendan Gill, who insists that "[O'Neill's] Swedes and his Irishmen speak in accents unknown to history," finds Bannen "totally at sea as James Tyrone, Jr., ... we believe in neither his alcoholism nor his sexual prowess." Identifying O'Neill as a "second-rate writer," with the notable exception of *Journey*, Gill sees no masterpiece here but a "fustian, ill-plotted melodrama ... the characters [owing] more to such bookish sources as Boucicault, Synge, O'Casey, and the unavoidable Dowson than they do to the individuals whom O'Neill encountered in real life and whom his biographers have been at pains to identify" (130). Edwin Wilson, writing in the *Wall Street Journal*, depicts Bannen's acting as "about as stiff as a wooden fence pole on the Hogan farm — there is none of the anguish, self-revulsion and longing for love that Tyrone must project." Douglas Watt, in the *New York Post*, also feels that "as keen and commanding an actor as Ian Bannen is, he lacks the haunted quality without which any account of Tyrone loses its magic." On the plus side, Watt is impressed by both Nelligan and Kilty : "Kate Nelligan gives an impassioned, quicksilver performance as Josie Hogan.... And Jerome Kilty, as unkempt in his own way as Phil's barefoot daughter is in hers, is marvelously funny and real as the father" ('Moon' is Back" 25). Kilty's performance was generally well-reviewed, with Frank Rich describing Kilty's character as "an impish leprechaun, a wise Puck, and, finally, an aged loving parent" (C21).

Bannen was not entirely without his champions. Howard Kissel, in *Women's Wear Daily*, insists that "Ian Bannen gives a performance remarkable for the lyricism he injects into what is usually an exercise in agonizing." Kissell is also impressed by Marc B. Weiss's "deeply, beautifully dramatic lighting" and by "the tempo at which the play is, so to speak, conducted by director David Leveaux." Although her performance was generally praised, Nelligan was not without her harsher critics, Kissel among them, who declared: "Kate Nelligan must devote much of her energy to compensating for her physical inappropriateness to the part.... She brings tremendous intensity to the part but lacks the earthiness and warmth that might give it emotional impact" (23). Alisa Solomon, in the *Village Voice*, also took note of Brien Vahey's set and costumes, "completely convincing down to the rusty junk stuffed under the porch and Jim's shiny cufflinks," noting also that Marc Weiss produces "a final dawn truly worthy of Belasco, beautifully passing through pinks, reds, oranges, and yellows." Finally, Solomon adds, "The production achieves a loveliness all its own, never once invoking a comparison to the Robards/ Dewhurst version" (79).

Dan Isaac, the author of the first major review of *Moon* in 1973, written while the production was still in Chicago, continues to identify the Quintero, Dewhurst, Robards production as the touchstone, but endorses this revival, calling it "important and worth seeing." This is primarily due to Nelligan's performance and Leveaux's directing: "What Nelligan lacks in bulk is more than compensated for by a portrayal that captures all the raucous, raw sluttiness of this Irish pig-wench." Writing in the *Chelsea Clinton News*, he concurs with those who find Jerome Kilty "wonderfully funny without sacrificing the brooding humanity that O'Neill artfully managed to keep mostly out of sight." Isaac describes Leveaux's direction of the production as "hugely perceptive, sensitive to the many underground rivers that course beneath the surface of this play," specifying one instance among many: "the way Josie and Tyrone address each other on their first meeting, each in turn sinking to their knees in what is a beautifully ritualized gesture of love sanctified by honor." Isaac notes that Bannen failed to capture "either the complex contradictions or the depth of self-loathing that O'Neill wrote into this tortured portrait of his older brother. Too frequently, Bannen croons key lines in a melody that suggests the conventional stage Irishman filled with booze and blarney" (14).

Clive Barnes, whose opinion of *Moon* had gradually improved over almost two decades, offers the most contradictory assessment of the play and its author. Describing O'Neill as "indisputably one of the great playwrights of the 20th century" and "a giant talent [whose] plays all but crush us in their superhuman efforts to relate to the human condition," Barnes also insists that "[O'Neill] wrote very badly. His sentences often hang in the air like clods of empty earth trying to get down. It is not a pretty sight or sound." (Neither, it seems, is that simile.) Yet, Barnes concludes, despite the fact that it begins with unsubtle and overextended exposition, the play "gathers it own momentum ... we capture the essence of O'Neill's sincerity, and the play carries us like a muddy whirlpool to the vortex of our feelings.... So far, so O'Neill." But Barnes also sees a new *Moon* rising, "a moon rising with a difference that perhaps O'Neill never envisaged."

This new *Moon* is not the American O'Neill that audiences were used to, "rough and articulately inarticulate ... full of introspection and swallowed lines." In what Barnes identifies as a revisionist *English* version of the O'Neill classic, blessed with a brilliant young director, who has only a passing connection to the American O'Neill tradition, the end result is "different. Remarkably different," thus renewing the play by offering "new insight into an old poet." No lines were swallowed in the course of this performance, certainly not by Ian Bannen, "in a blazing, white-hot and charred performance, [who] gives us Tyrone as a burnt-out case, an ashcan of a man." Instead of the required Earth Mother, "Kate Nelligan is an earth-daughter — technically she is too beautiful for the role, but conscientiously tries gawky on for size — and with Bannen she creates an arc of ashen poetry that sustains, invigorates, and renews O'Neill's vision. They are also far more erotic, or, if you like, passionate." Following Leveaux's direction, "his strange actors [catch] the play's force and [place] an unexpectedly new stamp of sensual naturalism on O'Neill." Barnes encourages audiences to see the play, for "O'Neill will never seem quite the same again" ("'Moon' Rises Over Broadway, British Style"). This, he seems to suggest, is a good thing.

Leveaux's revisionist approach to the play, along with Nelligan's performance, were viewed by most as the strength of the production, proving that an approach to the play that was not strictly naturalistic or, for that matter, strictly American, was indeed possible and possibly even successful. The production moved at a faster rate of speed than the more stately pace associated with presentations of O'Neill's work, particularly the later plays, when delving into unspoken truths can be both painful and painstaking. The heightened level of physicality was another alteration, with the hurling of actors in the place of drinking glasses, for example, enacted by a Josie who was severely undersized when compared to the original physical dimensions specified by O'Neill. Some critics accused Nelligan of having to expend too much of her energy compensating for her lack of size, but this seeming disadvantage may have proven advantageous. Following Colleen Dewhurst, whose iconic performance was now a part of the O'Neill mythology, Nelligan was absolutely nothing like her predecessor. The significant adjustments Nelligan made to the role, in keeping with Leveaux's rethinking of the play, made it clear that the play could be revived, in every sense of the word, by a revised perspective and an unconventional choice of leading lady. A significant portion of the critical and theatergoing audience was able to accept what was there on the stage as opposed to what was not, and despite mixed reviews, the production did have its supporters. The question remained as to whether there would be enough of them to sustain a run on Broadway.

Awards season followed closely after the play's opening, and the work of the actors and the director was recognized. A Drama Desk nominee for her performance, Kate Nelligan also received a Tony Award nomination, as did David Leveaux, for Best Direction of a Play, and Marc B. Weiss, for Best Lighting Design. The producers of the play, the Shubert Organization (Gerald Schoenfeld, Chairman, and Bernard B. Jacobs, President) and independent producer Emanuel Azenberg also received a nomination for best revival, at this time called the Best Reproduction of a Play, in a production that worked hard not to reproduce what had gone before. Unfortunately, none of the nominees received awards, which might have boosted the flagging box office sales. The production closed on 9 June 1984, after only 40 performances, following 19 previews. The 1984 revival proved it possible to escape, if not erase, the shadow of the landmark 1973 production, but it also had the dubious distinction of having the shortest run on Broadway, even fewer than the 68 performances of the play's Broadway debut in 1957. Although short-lived, the production still managed to make its own ineffaceable contribution to the life and history of *Moon*.

4

Broadway Revival, 2000, and Regional Productions

In the decade before the 2000 revival, several of the main players in the 1973 production had died: Colleen Dewhurst in 1991, Ed Flanders in 1995, and Jose Quintero in 1999, followed by Jason Robards in December 2000. Their presence was still deeply felt, however. The 1984 revival, while intriguing, lasted only a month. The 1973 revival still took precedence, seemingly inscribed in the memories of all who had seen it, with its reputation in no danger of diminishing.

Against these odds, producer Elliot Martin is credited with moving the 2000 revival forward. Martin has enjoyed a long and distinguished connection with productions of O'Neill, beginning as stage manager of the Broadway debut of *Long Day's Journey Into Night* in 1956 and the Broadway debut of *A Moon for the Misbegotten* the following year. As a producer, Martin has worked with Jose Quintero on *More Stately Mansions* (1967), *A Moon for the Misbegotten* (1973), and *A Touch of the Poet* (1977), followed by the 2007 Old Vic and Broadway revival of *A Moon for the Misbegotten*, directed by Howard Davies and starring Kevin Spacey. Forced in 1973 to relinquish controlling interest to producer Lester Osterman, Martin was determined not to repeat that experience in 2000, although he would need to find financial backing before this production could proceed. To gain financing, he would need a name player to commit to the production. The first name he thought of was Cherry Jones. By 2000, the Tennessee-born Jones had become a Broadway, if not a household, name. Jones was

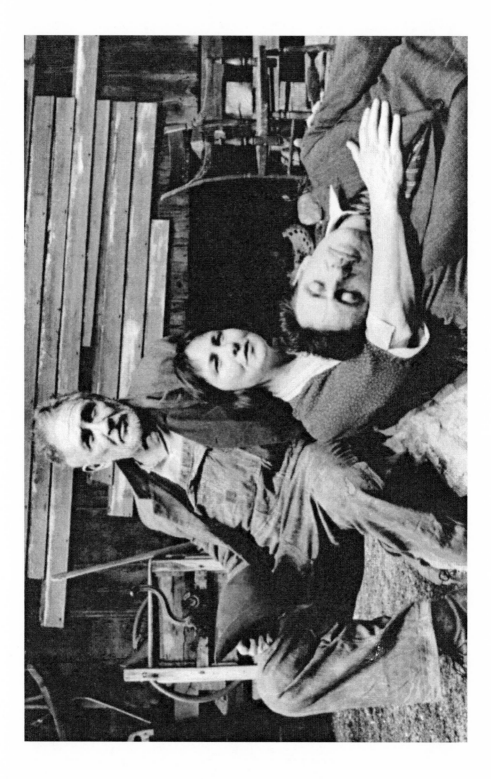

a founding member of the American Repertory Theatre, coincidentally, where the 1984 revival, originating in London, had begun its American run. A company member from 1980 to 1991, during one stretch at the A.R.T., Jones played 25 roles in six seasons, including Rosalind in *As You Like It*, Irina in *The Three Sisters*, and Grusha in *Caucasian Chalk Circle*. Leaving in 1991 to try her luck in New York, she quickly gained recognition with a Tony nomination for Timberlake Wertenbaker's *Our Country's Good*, and an Obie nomination for her performance Off Broadway in Paula Vogel's *The Baltimore Waltz*. Jones had previously played Josie Hogan at Baltimore's Center Stage in 1993, a safe distance from Dewhurst's performance, and only after the actress's death. Her major breakthrough came with the revival of *The Heiress*, directed by Gerald Gutierrez, for which she won the Tony Award for Best Actress in 1995. Similar to Wendy Hiller, the first Josie on Broadway, Jones made the transition from *The Heiress* to the pig farmer's daughter. More recently, Jones created an indelible impression as Sister Aloysius in John Patrick Shanley's Pulitzer-Prize–winning play, *Doubt*, for which Jones received the 2005 Tony Award as Best Actress. In 1999, producer Elliot Martin saw Jones in Tina Howe's play *Pride's Crossing*, playing Mabel Bigelow, a woman who swam the English Channel in record time, and a character who ages from 10 to 90 without benefit of make-up. Martin immediately offered Jones the role of Josie. The actress suggested that Gutierrez direct her in the O'Neill drama.

With Jones and Gutierrez on board, Martin approached Jujamcyn Theatres. Jujamcyn enjoys a varied producing career, balancing the commercial money-makers, including musicals such as *Jersey Boys* and *The Wedding Singer* (2006), *The Producers* (2001), and a revival of *Guys and Dolls* (1991), with less commercial fare, such August Wilson's *Gem of the Ocean* (2005), Arthur Miller's *The Crucible* (2002), and Tony Kushner's *Angels in America* (1991). Occasionally, even their prestige productions made money, as was the case with the 1999 revival of *Death of*

Opposite: Roy Dotrice as Phil Hogan, Cherry Jones as Josie Hogan, and Gabriel Byrne as James Tyrone, Jr., in the 2000 production of *A Moon for the Misbegotten*, directed by Daniel Sullivan, at the Goodman Theatre, Chicago, Illinois. Photograph by Eric Y. Exit. Billy Rose Theatre Division, The New York Public Library for the Performing Arts, Astor, Lenox, and Tilden Foundations.

a Salesman, starring Brian Dennehy, which not only won awards but made a profit.

In addition, Jujamcyn had its own connection to O'Neill theater history in Paul Libin, the Producing Director; in 2000, he was one of the organization's vice presidents. As Managing Director of Circle in the Square from 1964 to 1990, Libin had an extensive O'Neill resume and was involved in producing the 1968 revival of *A Moon for the Misbegotten* as well as *Ah, Wilderness!* (1969, 1975), *Mourning Becomes Electra* (1972), *The Iceman Cometh* (1973), *All God's Chillun Got Wings* (1975), and *Hughie* (1996), in a production that brought Al Pacino back to the Broadway stage. Libin also co-produced the 1964 revival of *Hughie* with Jason Robards, which managed to recoup its losses only after it went on tour. Well versed in the risky demands that an O'Neill drama makes not only on the actors but also on the investors, Libin, with Jujamcyn, provided the financing for the revival of *Moon*, along with a group of co-producers including Chase Mishkin, Max Cooper, Anita Waxman, Elizabeth Williams, and the Goodman Theatre in Chicago. The production would try out at the Chicago theater, away from the prying eyes of New York audiences and critics.

Director Gutierrez was not as big a fan of Chicago as Jujamcyn, stating, "They have bad audiences" (qtd. in Garvey "New Myths for Old" 124). This did nothing to endear him to Libin, who hailed from Chicago and had begun his theatrical career there. Additionally, Jones had spent a significant portion of her career performing in regional theaters; in fact, she had performed at the Goodman in 1997 in *The Good Woman of Setzuan*, winning Chicago's Jefferson Award for Best Actress. Gutierrez's tenure with the production would seem to be tenuous, and things did not improve when the director himself attempted to secure the rights to *Moon*. After his experience in 1973, Martin had made certain that his rights to the play were unassailable as long as he could arrange the financing. With Jones, but without Gutierrez, the production would make its way to Chicago.

Gutierrez was replaced as director by Daniel Sullivan. Having served as Artistic Director of the Seattle Repertory Theatre from 1981 to 1997, Sullivan first came to the attention of New York audiences in 1989, when he staged Wendy Wasserstein's *The Heidi Chronicles*. Since then, Sullivan has had a busy Broadway career, most recently directing David Lindsay-Abaire's *Rabbit Hole* in 2006, for which Sullivan received the Tony Award for Best Director. Previous to the *Moon* revival, Sullivan directed a successful revival of *Ah, Wilderness!* in 1998 at Lincoln Center.

It was Sullivan who suggested the Dublin-born Gabriel Byrne for the role of Jim Tyrone (Garvey, "New Myths for Old" 124). Although he had not been seen onstage since 1982, Byrne had extensive stage credits in Ireland, beginning at Dublin's Project Theatre, which also launched the careers of Liam Neeson, Stephen Rea, and Neil Jordan. This was followed by work at the Abbey Theatre, and in London at the Royal Court and National Theatres. In America, Byrne is known as a movie star, in films as varied as the Coen brothers' *Miller's Crossing* (1990) and the more commercial *The Usual Suspects* (1995). One of Byrne's earliest film roles was as Lord Byron in Ken Russell's *Gothic* (1986). Of Byron, Lady Caroline Lamb famously said that he was "mad, bad, and dangerous to know." Ruggedly handsome, with the bearing of a matinee idol, Byrne could bring a dangerous quality to the role. Byrne was also a name that audiences, beyond the Broadway cognoscente, would recognize, which would help to bring audiences to an O'Neill drama.

Although movies have made Byrne the better known name, Jones had to approve this casting choice, as did the producers at Jujamcyn. They all were in agreement, and Byrne was offered the role. Byrne, himself, seemed less convinced. Having seen Ian Bannen in London in 1983, the 49-year-old actor was well aware of the emotional demands of playing Jim Tyrone, later describing the role as "a man-eater, a ball-breaking role" (qtd. in Senior 74). Byrne would agree only to a limited run, ending 18 June 2000. The Broadway run would, in all likelihood, end 13 weeks after it had begun. Unless Byrne agreed to re-sign, it was unlikely that the producers would be able to recoup their 1.5-million-dollar investment in so short a time. But in theater, hope springs eternal, and the producers agreed to his terms.

The distinguished British actor Roy Dotrice was cast as Phil Hogan. At 77, Dotrice looked decades younger; dapper offstage, he bore no resemblance to the pig farmer he played. The first line of the actor's biography in the playbill certainly grabbed the reader's attention: "Roy Dotrice began his acting career in a German prisoner-of-war camp in 1942, having been shot down after flying with the Royal Air Force Bomber Command." Dotrice played Shakespeare at the five POW camps in which he resided

until the end of the war. This was followed by a more conventional acting career, beginning with work in repertory, finally leading to the Royal
Shakespeare Company in 1957. American audiences would be more familiar with Dotrice's illustrious performance as John Aubrey, the seventeenth-
century British antiquary and diarist, in *Brief Lives*, or perhaps as the
monster Vincent's "Father" in television's *Beauty and the Beast*, popular in
the 1980s. Having seen *Moon* twice before, Dotrice disagreed with previous interpretations he had seen of "a crusty, bad-tempered moneygrub-
ber," saying that "Hogan is full of regret at the end of the play, there's no
belligerence left. I try to make it as moving as possible" (qtd. in Gubernick 13C). Completing the cast were Irish-American actor Tuck Milligan
as the millionaire Harder, and Paul Hewitt as Mike Hogan.

With the cast set, it was time to create some backstage drama with
which to feed the press's interest in the production. The 1973 revival was
replete with tales of personal and professional associations with O'Neill
and his drama, often painful, sometimes life-threatening. The members
of the Resurrection Company collectively served up tales of alcoholism,
shattered marriages, and near-death experiences, all to reinforce their connection to the broken dreams in the play. The 2000 revival had consid-
erably less to offer in this department.

Cherry Jones wisely diverted questions comparing her performance
to that of Colleen Dewhurst by praising her predecessor as "more the
Mother Earth woman, and I'm sort of the Child-woman, I suppose" (qtd.
in Phillips F1). She gave credit to Dewhurst for inspiring her own career
choice, as it did many actresses of Jones's generation. In 1973, while a
drama student in a theater summer school at Northwestern University, the
16-year-old Jones saw a performance of *Moon* during its run in Lake Forest. As Jones later told an interviewer, "She was my idol ... she knocked
me out. Right then, I knew what I wanted to do" (qtd. in O'Haire 11).
Early in her career, fresh out of the acting program at Carnegie Mellon,
Jones saw herself as a "huge girl," not quite Josie-like, but "convinced that
[she] would never get an acting job until [she] was thirty-five years old"
(qtd. in Feinberg). The actress would later admit that playing Josie
had been "a rough go" for her (qtd. in Drake). In addition to following
in Dewhurst's footsteps — "Now, every night, when I play her role, I wres-
tle with her ghost" (qtd. in O'Haire 11) — Jones confessed to a crisis of

confidence exacerbated by "encroaching middle age, the questioning of her own success, and a series of depressing roles back to back" (Cummings). Jones also admitted that in order to play Josie, "You really have to make yourself an emotional mess.... And you are about as exposed as you can be in this play. That can really effect your sense of yourself" (qtd. in Dezell C4).

But at the time of the pre–Broadway interviews, the 43-year-old Jones tried to emphasize the positive, including her professional rapport with Gabriel Byrne, and how they were "growing together and supporting each other," describing Byrne as "the dearest, sweetest, gentlest, most articulate man." Having already been open about the fact that she is a lesbian, Jones circumvented any question of romance with praise for Byrne's gentlemanly qualities: "It's an Old World quality, something from another era. He's so full of contradictions because he does have that movie industry savvy — he's nobody's fool. At the same time, there's something about the man that is so naively sweet" (qtd. in Pogrebin L45). Whatever else Byrne brought to the character, it was a gentlemanly quality that O'Neill had originally sought, complaining to the Theatre Guild's Lawrence Langner that James Dunn, the original Jim Tyrone, was not making the character enough of a gentleman to suit him. And for the record, Byrne and Dotrice got along famously, with Byrne casting Dotrice as his father in the short-lived television series *Madigan Men*, which followed the run of *Moon*.

The press was determined to trawl the lives of the players for sources of personal pain to connect them to their characters, but with limited success. For example, Dotrice and his wife of fifty-three years, the parents of three daughters, lived a quiet offstage life. Byrne appeared to the press to be the cast member most likely to be haunted by his own ghosts, his life story yielding a few promising leads. Courtesy of his friend Brian Dennehy, Byrne's ex-girlfriend, Big Annie, who had recently died of cancer, was introduced into the conversation. As described by Dennehy, "she *was* Josie Hogan. Tall and beautiful and smart and very tough in a way that Irish women can be." As far as Dennehy was concerned, "There's a big relationship between Annie and Josie. You ask yourself why he took the part" (qtd. in Senior 74). Having encouraged Byrne to perform O'Neill, Annie was also the woman Byrne left to marry the actress Ellen Barkin, the mother of his two children, from whom Byrne was divorced. Although Dennehy hinted at the need for forgiveness on the part of Byrne, the actor was preoccupied simply with getting through the performances. At the end of the run, Byrne admitted, "In five months I went through terror, doubt, regret, exhilaration, stretching myself as an actor every night to get that emotional peak that you have to hit," referring to Tyrone's epic monologue in the third act. When asked by interviewer Robin Pogrebin, "what demons of his own he might be summoning that makes their release seem so real," Byrne responded: "If you live sufficiently long enough, you have enough things in your life that make you, when you think about them, sad. What I think about when I'm doing that monologue is something very personal and private.... It's a tough place to go every night ... but I'm now permanently in touch with that place" (qtd. in Pogrebin L45).

With the cast and their backstory in place, the show could go on. Describing the process of working on the play, Daniel Sullivan was quoted as saying, "You keep making discoveries about the play on a daily basis.... Just when you think you've come to the end of O'Neill, you find a word or a moment in a play that, like a secret chamber, springs open to the touch. Revealed is a whole new corridor of meanings and associations, of harrowing epiphanies" (qtd. in Keller 1). Similar to the Quintero production, director Sullivan cut the script in order to avoid repetition and to keep the play moving. Unlike the Quintero production, the set on which the actors performed would be realistic, rather than the expressionistic structure designed by Ben Edwards in 1973. Qunitero had said that the 1973 production was inspired by Van Gogh's painting "Starry Night" (Gussow, "Saving O'Neill and Himself" E1); clearly a starry night could be seen through the open roof on Edwards' set. In 2000, Eugene Lee, a designer often associated with musicals, including *Showboat* (1997), *Ragtime* (2000), and most recently, *Wicked* (2003), would create the single set for *Moon*, a farmhouse described by O'Neill as a disharmonious addition to the landscape, "an old boxlike, clapboarded affair, with a shingled roof and brick chimney," and "a big boulder with a flat-top" in front (*Moon* 856). In fact, Lee left no stone unturned on the Hogan property, opting for an extremely realistic shanty surrounded by huge boulders, with smaller rocks decorating the ground in front. O'Neill describes how "[the house] has been moved to its present site and looks it" (*Moon* 856). Lee also moved the

Hogans' home, this time, downstage. This effectively limited the acting space and left the actors to play many scenes downstage center. Closer to the audience, they would not have to work quite as hard to project their voices to the 947 seats of the Walter Kerr Theatre.

First, the production had to fill the 683 seats of the Goodman Theatre, which it did, from 14 January through 19 February 2000. Like the 1973 revival, this production of *Moon* would begin its run in Chicago, a coincidence not lost on the cast or on the critics, who frequently mentioned it in their reviews. At the opening on 24 January, the audience was enthusiastic, the critics, somewhat less so. Chris Jones, in *Daily Variety*, writes: "Since neither new textual revelation nor a revisionist directorial concept is in evidence, Daniel Sullivan's Broadway-bound revival of "A Moon for the Misbegotten" will live or die based on how audiences and critics respond to the three actors in the fiendishly difficult central roles.... Cherry Jones, Gabriel Byrne, and Roy Dotrice are together capable of offering a whopping emotional payoff in possibly the greatest final act in American drama. But unless Sullivan elicits a consistent and connected style from his talented but currently widely disparate trio, it will be rough going for the audience." Jones thought the performances were "valid, striking, highly competent and intriguing. But they each seem to be in a different production of the play." In fact, the critic thought the play a little unbalanced: "At this point, the extroverted, funny and extraordinarily charming Dotrice thoroughly dominates his daughter, their alcoholic landlord and the entire show. Although that's a credit to this actor's exquisitely developed comic and dramatic technique, that's not the way it should be." Jones found Byrne's character "at first so introverted and disconnected that he rebuffs sympathy.... Byrne sends Tyrone down the path to utter darkness earlier than the script really demands." The critic thought "the beautiful, radiant Jones," even "bulked up," an unusual casting choice, but he was more troubled by the emotive dimensions of her portrayal: "Jones's Josie is an emotional dam ready to burst from the moment the curtain rises. As a result, her ultimate vulnerability is not the desperate surprise it really needs to be." The critic felt that Jones and Byrne rose to the occasion in the final scenes, describing the ending as "extraordinarily powerful": in O'Neill's "most powerful" monologue, Byrne "catches its poignancy beautifully." Before the production reaches New York, however, the critic advices that "Jones needs to toughen up, and Byrne let loose, especially in the first half. Most importantly, Sullivan must stretch this potentially rich and complex canvas over a single cohesive frame" (25).

Writing of the Chicago production, Joel Henning, in the *Wall Street Journal,* is more impressed by Jones's performance of "perhaps O'Neill's supreme female character": "Jones is an ample woman but does not literally fit O'Neill's specifications. Yet she is altogether believable as the thoughtful virgin who pretends to be a slut, the nurturing woman who pretends to be a female thug," suggesting that "Ms. Jones can almost make us forget Colleen Dewhurst's powerful performance as Josie in the 1973 production." Henning was less impressed by Byrne's Tyrone: "Gabriel Byrne's Jim Tyrone is pallid compared to that of Jason Robards, Jr., in the earlier revival." But the critic agrees with those who find Roy Dotrice "hugely successful here as Josie's conniving father, Phil Hogan. How wonderful to see this enormously skilled old actor use every bit of his voice, his body and brain to beguile family, friends, and the audience" (A24).

Richard Christiansen, in the *Chicago Tribune,* agrees that "at this stage, the production, though worthy, does not deliver the overwhelming emotional force that O'Neill's story of tormented souls should possess." Christiansen acknowledges that Byrne, although "a little stiff in his first few moments ... has the right seedy swagger from the start, and as the play proceeds, his handling of Jim's deep despair and longing takes on a fiery intensity." On the other hand, according to Christiansen, "Jones, a formidable presence as well as a radiant actress, is almost too sweet and good in her early scenes.... The change and softening she goes through as she turns Earth Mother for Jim is much less effective when she seems to be a fairly soft person to begin with." He also finds that Jones' Josie "appears curiously blank in her volcanic passions and all-encompassing compassion. That throws off the balance of the play, and Josie's act of loving kindness seems less monumental than it should." As for Roy Dotrice's Phil, Christiansen describes the actor as playing "the bantam rascal Hogan with gleeful mischief, using all sorts of vocal and physical tricks to suggest what a reprobate he is." Finally, according to Christiansen, "all the elements of an important production are here. At the moment, however, they've not come together" ("A Masterful 'Moon' in the Making" D1). Given that the same critic had begun his 1968 review of the play quoting O'Neill's description of *Moon* as "a play I have come to loathe," stating that many Chicagoans "shared the playwright's sentiments," the play would seem to have improved in his estimation. The critic appeared confident that the production would gel by the time it opened on Broadway.

After a sold-out month in Chicago, the production moved to New York, with preview performances beginning on 7 March 2000 for a 19 March opening. Although Cherry Jones was suffering from the flu, noted in a few of the reviews, the show did go on. In the extensive coverage of this much-anticipated theatrical event, there was a wide range of critical opinion.

Ben Brantley, in the *New York Times*, issued a glowing tribute to the production, entitled "A Love Story to Stop the Heart." As Brantley insists, "Every time Cherry Jones and Gabriel Byrne make physical contact ... the flood gates open to a tide of clashing emotions," including "exaltation and disgust, hunger and resignation and, most acutely, a sorrow that is all the more profound for the faint sparks of hope it lets shine through." After a brief history of the previous incarnations of *Moon*, including the 1973 revival "regarded as definitive," Brantley asserts that "Masterpieces, it seems, never stop growing, and the current production emanates both a springtime freshness and autumnal mellowness."

Describing Roy Dotrice's Phil Hogan initially as "a Gaelic Pappy Yokum," Brantley notes that each character "dexterously suggests a slightly exaggerated, slightly bogus persona on first appearance." While Jones's Josie has "the air of a roguish Rabelaisian giant, tough-tongued and intimidatingly large of gesture ... there is evidence of an uncertain girlishness behind the bravado." As Brantley notes, "Byrne has the wry papery voice and stylized mannerisms of the wastrel actor.... Then there are those truly shocking moments when his face goes blank as a cadaver's, and you realize that those fancy finger waves with which he punctuates the lighting of a cigarette are used to camouflage delirium tremens." As the characters are unmasked, "Each is brought to a painfully wrought climax of self-revelation." Brantley has particular praise for Byrne in this regard, describing his wrenching confession as "a self-administered surgery, etched in escalating degrees of pain. It is, in a word, brilliant, itself the stuff of theatrical legend." As previously noted, recent Josies have tended to dominate their respective Tyrones, when it was, in fact, the character Tyrone, based on O'Neill's older brother, for whom the play was written. According to Brantley, this is not the case here, nor does the critic see it as a problem, suggesting that although Jones is a quiet presence during Jim's long speech, she does not disappear, instead "[becoming] almost an elemental presence, embodying the radiant spirit of acceptance and forgiveness that makes 'Moon' unlike anything else O'Neill wrote." A rave in the *Times* is certainly a promising start, but it would not be the last word written on the production.

While Brantley was fully convinced, John Simon, in *New York* Magazine, saw only a "Three-Quarter *Moon*." Simon identifies Josie as the protagonist of the piece, "a woman Eugene would have wanted for himself but invented for his brother James: part virgin, part whore; part big-breasted earth goddess, part tenderhearted mother surrogate; recognizably a figment too good to be true." Simon rehearses the difficulties of finding an actress to play the part, dismissing Hiller and Nelligan, with Jens and Dewhurst coming closest to being "the right actress." As for Cherry Jones, Simon praises her as an actress, calling her "transcendent"; in this part, however, "she is tomboyish, powerful, and luminous, but there is also a girlish refinement, a lack of rough-hewnness." (Jones being "somewhat miscast" would seem to account for the missing 25% in the title of the review.) According to Simon, Byrne "gives a complementarily moving performance as a lost soul in a dying body, whom we watch superbly enact the painful rites of a redemption as his flesh visibly wastes away." Simon finds "the wonderful Roy Dotrice ... a shade too leprechaunish, but who can quarrel with a performance so vibrant with venal roguery and sheepish love?" Certainly not the often contrary Simon, who praises Daniel Sullivan's "detailed yet unfussy direction," finding Eugene Lee's set "a bit boulder-happy," but Pat Collins' lighting "moon-drunk," a term of praise for a production to which he attributes "a meatiness, a tenacity of grip, and, finally, a grandeur" (56).

Although the production had been endorsed by two of New York's toughest critics, it did not avoid some harsher appraisals. In the *Village Voice*, Michael Feingold, after acknowledging that Jones was performing with the flu, describes a "tenderer, more soft-spoken version of Josie than we're used to," her "sweet and girlish side" taking precedence. As the critic explains, "The forgiving smile comes early. The bold and bawdy gestures are gentled down or made less convincing; in two intense scenes with Jamie, the soft voice often catches Byrne's pitch and comes in under his volume. These qualities, too, belong to the role, and when Josie can pour them out openly, Jones is stunning." With time, or a return to good health, Jones might capture the necessary roughness in the role, but Feingold disapproved of Dotrice's turning the role of Hogan into "an Irish-dialect music-hall act," and of director Daniel Sullivan's giving the actor "free rein" to do so. Similarly, according to Feingold, from Gabriel Byrne, "we get a different phase of show biz, a dashing actorish leading man, exquisite of profile, who can evoke many of Jamie's emotions — he caught my heart three or four times — but doesn't create Jamie, neither the dissipated exterior nor the deadness at the core, for more than a few minutes." Feingold found excessive both Dan Sullivan's commitment to "old style naturalism" and Eugene Lee's commitment to adding "rocks and foliage" to the set design until "there's no glimpse of the Connecticut sky, though moon and sunrise are important reference points." For a variety of reasons, Feingold anticipates that it would take a return visit to *Moon* before he could speak well of it.

In a similar vein, Amy Gamerman, in the *Wall Street Journal*, found little to praise in the production, save Eugene Lee's set, "with the kind of loving detail calculated to win a round of applause from the audience the moment the curtain comes up. Smoke curls from the stovepipe chimney of the weather-beaten clapboard house, and there's even a muddy puddle near the (fully functioning) water pump." Most of Gamerman's praise went to Roy Dotrice as "a cantankerous billy goat in patched denim overalls," injecting a note of burlesque that Gamerman, unlike Feingold, welcomed. Gamerman was unconvinced of the purported sexual chemistry between Josie and Jim Tyrone, attributing to Byrne "enough sex appeal for both of them": "This Jim exudes a boozy allure even when he's supposed to look like a man who's sitting in on his own funeral. Speaking in a soft voice just this side of a moan, he tells the bullying Josie, 'Mother me, Josie, I love it.' Many actors would give this line a sarcastic spin, but Mr. Byrne is plaintively earnest. His Jim doesn't have a sardonic edge — in fact, all the edges seem to have been rubbed off him" (A20). In her review, Gamerman undercuts even that which she admires.

The critical consensus continued to bounce back and forth, some preferring Jones' work, and some finding Byrne's the superior perform-ance. Charles Isherwood, writing in *Variety*, states that "Broadway's new revival of Eugene O'Neill's 'A Moon for the Misbegotten' offers reason to celebrate, but also much to mourn." Celebration comes in the form of Gabriel Byrne's "devastatingly beautiful performance ... perfectly [embody-ing] the aching soul of the play." Isherwood praises the "breathtaking emo-tional transparency" of Byrne's third act aria: "It's a speech that descends to the soul's darkest places, and a false note or stagy gesture can be disas-trous," asserting that Byrne "rises to its challenges magnificently." Accord-ing to Isherwood, "a hush descends upon the theater in this exquisitely written scene, broken only by sobs of sympathy erupting from the audi-ence." The critic also approves of Dotrice's "antic, sensationally funny turn as the wily Phil."

Isherwood saves his censure for Jones' performance as Josie, although he sees things differently from most of the critics, who found her Josie too soft. According to Isherwood, "[Jones] accentuates the most superficial aspects of Josie's character — her truculent toughness — without sufficiently communicating the presence of the deeply loving woman beneath the tough hide." In the climactic scene, Jones "has a soft, self-effacing sym-pathy" (32), but, as Isherwood notes, "a vital quality of tender grace, of spiritual power, is missing from most of the performance, which must qualify as the saddest, most surprising disappointment of the theater sea-son." Isherwood sees the lack of warmth in Jones' performance as emblem-atic of the production as a whole, which was missing "a vital energy." He adds, "While hardly misbegotten, then, this 'Moon' is nonetheless not what it might have been" (38).

Like Isherwood, Elyse Sommers, writing for *Curtain Up*, initially was not convinced by Jones' "softer, less aggressive" Josie, put off by her phys-ical features — "it takes a bit to get past the All-American girl, snub-nosed prettiness"— as well as the choice of stylish blunt haircut "seen on some of the smartest-looking woman about town." (In fact, the hairstyle, while it may be the actress' own, was more Louise Brooks than Josie Hogan, a curious choice in a production noted for its attention to physical detail.) Sommers could see that "little signs of vulnerability beneath the back-woodsy tough banter between [Jim] and Josie point the way to the shat-tering finale. When she cradles him against her bosom ... the love and sadness that light up her face break your heart." Although like Feingold, Sommers chastised director Daniel Sullivan for allowing Roy Dotrice "leeway to overdo the Irish roughhouse jocularity," she also notes that "Dotrice is good enough to make us see his Irish cutup as part of a triple portrait of ordinary people as actors on the stage of life." With Byrne as the third member of the trio, "this *Moon* shines brightly indeed," his final monologue, described as "an incredible feat of self-revelation." According to Sommers, "The pull between these two lost souls ... is what acting that doesn't look and feel like acting is all about."

The out-of-town critics were also heard from. Michael Phillips, in the *Los Angeles Times*, submits that the production was "a good, solid, granite-like revival ... [but] it's granite that could benefit from a crack or two, a little roughing up, some distinguishing characteristics beyond solidity and respect." In its physicality, this production "goes further than you're expecting it to: Byrne slams Jones up against the clapboard house, and in its aftermath, Jones' face reveals all the shock and rage and pity of a woman who isn't sure what to forgive and what to forget." And as Phillips notes, "Jones and Byrne don't lack for a strong third point to this play's triangle," with Roy Dotrice "like a wizened old Puck ... wonderfully, almost shamelessly entertaining," and even the minor roles played by Tuck Milligan and Paul Hewitt "nicely handled." With this cast, as Phillips points out, "greatness wouldn't be out of the question." The production does not achieve greatness, however; Phillips feels that the production would benefit from "a more imposing directorial presence ... within the space allowed by scenic designer Eugene Lee's claustrophobic, tumbledown farmhouse setting."

According to Phillips, Jones' performance lacked "a distinctive voice, as well as the kind of ferocity that can only come from loneliness," while Dotrice's was not quite a performance but "a turn (a terrific one) ... and it throws the play's triangle out of whack." "Though Byrne's intonations tend toward low-keyed introspection," Phillips writes, "he comes through in James' most desperate moments. Mourning becomes this actor, and when he lets his guard down and the tears fall, it's unusually affecting." Although he expected to see more, Phillips judges the production to be "worth seeing" ("Unspoken Passions" F3).

Writing for the *San Francisco Chronicle*, Steven Winn admired the "carefully crafted" performance of Cherry Jones but felt that "Jones' Josie never comes together as a rounded character. The component parts shift in and out of view — the vigor and vulnerability, the surges of love and wary misgivings — without creating a bigger picture." According to Winn, "the great acting in this show — the heart-shattering, spontaneous glory of this 'Moon'— comes from the two male leads, Roy Dotrice and especially Gabriel Byrne," with Byrne "[revealing] the acrid self-loathing and raw, unreachable pain of the character." Winn describes Dotrice as "a perfect scoundrel ... with a clockwork sense of comic timing," but identifies Byrne's performance as "[giving] *Moon* its glowing center." As he writes, "Cradled in Josie's arms, his body pooled there in exhaustion and relief as he confesses his sins to her, Byrne carries the audience along with James to the bottom. It's an astonishing, soul-scouring feat." Winn concludes by saying that the theater-going audience may have come to see Cherry Jones, but they would leave "with Byrne's James Tyrone, Jr., burned into their memories" ("Gabriel Byrne Outshines Cherry Jones" El). Conversely, according to Brendan Lemon, in the *Financial Times* (London), it is Gabriel Byrne's portrayal of Tyrone that "keeps us all too earthbound.... Byrne insufficiently conveys the character's struggle to shed his core weakness." According to Lemon, although the interpretation "seriously mars" the production, it does not destroy it, thanks to Cherry Jones, "[bathing] the audience in her not-to-be-taken-for-granted radiance. With an aptly moon-shaped face and a voice whose emphatic essence could make an advert for breakfast cereal persuasive, the actress makes us believe that Tyrone is pardonable." While Lemon identifies Roy Dotrice's performance as "an extended jig" ("In vino — or whiskey — veritas" 40), there were those who thought Dotrice's Phil Hogan better suited for selling cereal, in his case, Lucky Charms.

Nearly a month after the production opened, Robert Brustein, in *The New Republic*, wrote an analysis of the production, which was notable for the range of experience he brought to the discussion. Many critics tried to flex their expertise when discussing the O'Neill drama, but Brustein knew whereof he spoke, having seen all of the major revivals of *Moon*. In 1957, he was "blown away" by "an inscrutable Wendy Hiller ... out of her element as a lusty American Irish girl" and "a sardonic Franchot Tone ... in a ferocious, lacerating performance." Needless to say, he had seen

Dewhurst and Robards, and was also one of those guiding the 1984 revival with Kate Nelligan, which transferred from the American Repertory Theatre, where Brustein was Artistic Director and where he had first hired Cherry Jones as a member of the company.

According to Brustein, although Jones had "eaten her way into the part ... she gives the impression of being a slender person in a fat suit." Brustein also objected to the choice of a page-boy haircut "more appropriate to Shakespeare's Rosalind [which Jones had played at the A.R.T.] than to the gamey daughter of a pig farmer." But the performance is the thing, and he felt that while the actress was "a little subdued and tenative at first, Jones eventually develops the size and fullness necessary for the part, reaching a fourth-act climax that will knock your socks off." Brustein blames Roy Dotrice for part of Jones' initial failure, forced as she is to play against "one of the most shameless and engaging instances of scene-stealing in recent theater history," in a performance "right out of Synge or O'Casey" (64).

Yet, even with good actors and a powerful play, the critic was less than satisfied with the production, blaming, again in part, Gabriel Byrne's Tyrone. Although Byrne "promises much" on his first entrance, with his dark intensity, "all sharp angles with a febrile glow in his eyes," and while the actor "takes no short cuts" and "does not trade indecently on his screen persona," Byrne "failed to tap into the life experience needed to exhume the inner soul of this tormented man." According to Brustein, "his Jamie does not seem to be feeling his anguish as much as whining it." Until the powerful climax, with Tyrone in the comforting arms of his mother substitute, "nothing seems to be binding these two people together." Brustein describes Sullivan's direction as "perfectly competent without being penetrating." Brustein hopes that the play "will soon be revived again in a more consuming, more unsettling production" (66).

Brustein's review appeared three weeks into the run of the production as did that of John Heilpern, in the *New York Observer*, unusual for a weekly paper. This may also account for Heilpern's positive assessment of the production, which had a few weeks to settle in, and for the cast to recover from the opening and anything else that ailed them. As Heilpern writes, "This is, quite simply, one of those nights of theater that we live for." Calling the production in all respects "magnificent," Heilpern asserts that it "[brings] honor to O'Neill's last drama that amounts to a Miracle

Play in its pain and compassion and absolution." Heilpern is particularly impressed by the performances of Byrne and Jones. According to the critic, "Gabriel Byrne's tormented James Tyrone, Jr., touches such greatness in the strength of his dark emotional honesty that I cannot imagine a different Tyrone, let alone a better one," finally identifying Byrne's "restrained, amazing performance" as "one for the ages." Many critics had preferred either Byrne's performance or Jones', but Heilpern had praise enough for both: "Cherry Jones' resonant notes of deep, quiet, compassionate strength and yearning for a love that will never be are stunning. A coarse earthiness might not yet have come fully to boil in her Josie, but everything else about this impossible role, including the transcendent love, is in place in her beautiful performance." Heilpbern admits to not understanding how O'Neill's plays work, asking "How do they achieve greatness when most everything he does seems to fly in the face of it? He repeats messages *ad nauseum*; his plotting is clumsy; the texts are long and overwritten, as if daring cuts." Heilpern comes to the conclusion that a play that appears overwritten on the page can work on the stage, but "O'Neill lives only in the company of great actors [who] make it truly alive" (20). Similarly, Clive Barnes, in the *New York Post*, who had bandied about the word *landmark* in his 1973 review of *Moon*, tries to quell the inevitable comparisons by stating, "Like all great plays it will never, happily, receive a definitive production," calling the 2000 production "exquisitely done" (11).

Any play on Broadway, even one with plenty of pedigree, has a challenge in filling the seats. As two of the previous Broadway outings had shown, O'Neill can be a hard sell despite, or perhaps because of, the weight, and by extension, the heaviness ascribed to his work. Although the reviews for the 2000 production of *Moon* had been mixed, the highly anticipated, and in many cases, highly touted, revival still had much that worked in its favor. Gabriel Byrne's Broadway debut had been distinguished, and he was sharing the stage with Cherry Jones, an actress who previously could do no wrong. Both the director Daniel Sullivan and the set designer Eugene Lee favored a naturalistic approach, in keeping with the conventional wisdom about how an O'Neill drama should be played. And at the third point of the acting triangle, Roy Dotrice was receiving the best reviews of his career. Even those who described his performance as shameless scene-stealing also found it engaging.

124

But the production would need more to sustain box office sales, and it was hoped that their efforts would be recognized with a number of significant prizes. The Outer Critics Circle Awards, bestowed by those who review New York theater for out-of-town publications, voted *Moon* the best revival of a play, with Roy Dotrice as Best Featured Actor in a Play; and Daniel Sullivan, Best Director, but for the Off Broadway production of Donald Margulies' *Dinner with Friends*. (Previously, in 1973, the Outer Critics seemed to be making a point when they named *A Moon for the Misbegotten* Best Play, despite the fact that it had been written thirty years before and had previously played both on and Off Broadway.) In 2000, Drama Desk nominations went to Byrne and Dotrice in their respective acting categories, and to the production for Best Revival. But the Tony Award is the one that marketing plans can be built around, and the production received nominations for Byrne, Jones, and Dotrice, and for the production as Best Revival of a Play. Byrne was also honored with a Theatre World Award for his debut performance on Broadway and with an award from the Drama League. Using illness as his excuse, Byrne asked Jones to attend the Drama League ceremony in his place, and she complied. On the same evening, however, Byrne was photographed out on the town with a female friend, a move that did not endear him to the Broadway community, which expects its honorees to appear.

In the press, Byrne had acknowledged his interest in winning the Tony Award; without it, he would certainly not extend his run in the play. With Byrne in attendance at the Tony Award ceremony, the 2000 revival of Stoppard's *The Real Thing*, directed by David Leveaux, won in several of *Moon*'s categories, including Best Actress, Jennifer Ehle; Best Actor, Stephen Dillane; and Best Revival of a Play. From the *Moon* cast, only Roy Dotrice went home with the Tony, as he had with the Drama Desk Award, but this would not be enough to sustain audience, or Byrne's, interest in the play. One can only speculate as to whether Byrne's dodging the Drama League ceremony, and the subsequent bad publicity, diminished his Tony chances. But apparently, there were no hard feelings, as Byrne would return to Broadway and to O'Neill in 2005, as Con Melody in *A Touch of the Poet*, in a production acclaimed primarily for his performance.

After 120 performances and 15 previews, *A Moon for the Misbegotten* closed, barely breaking even. Unlike the 1973 revival, which exists on video, the production was not filmed by Lincoln Center for its archives or by a cable channel like Showtime, which had saved for posterity the 1999 production of *Death of a Salesman*, with Brian Dennehy, adding to its profitable run. The 2000 revival would exist only in the memories of those who had experienced it firsthand.

The play having been deemed a masterpiece in 1973, there was no going back. Even amidst claims of overwriting or excessive repetition, the play's status was confirmed; all that remained were the players. As Michael Phillips had pointed out, greatness did not seem beyond them. Yet the production as a whole, though rock solid, did not find itself in the company of greatness. When the production tried out in Chicago, Chris Jones saw "a widely disparate trio," each in a different production of the play, with Roy Dotrice's Phil Hogan firmly in the foreground, a placement that "unbalanced" the production (25). In Chicago, Richard Christiansen also saw a play off balance, due to what he identifies as Jones' sweetness in the early scenes, making the anticipated change "as she turns Earth Mother for Jim ... much less effective when she seems to be a fairly soft person to begin with" (D1).

The imbalance had been stabilized by the time the production reached New York. In the place of three plays, now there were two. Dotrice and Jones had bonded as a believable father/daughter duo, with Jones more comfortable in the Irish folk comedy of the play, but still too refined to be found anywhere near a hog wallow. Although Dotrice's Phil displayed a level of hygiene worthy of a character based on a character named Dirty Dolan, Jones' Josie seemed too squeaky clean, from the top of her head to the core of character, to be fully accepted as a woman who works the farm in bare feet and outpaces her brothers. At the same time, Gabriel Byrne was in another play entirely, perhaps closer to the one O'Neill wrote, playing a man more than a little in love with death. The twain met only in the third act, when Josie, who dreams of a life with Jim, gives herself to him not as a lover but as a forgiving mother-figure so that Jim can end his life having achieved a small measure of peace. A production of *Moon* must reconcile the comedy of the first half with the tragedy of the second. When the actors are in two functionally different plays, this makes a reconciliation nearly impossible.

With Cherry Jones the better known theater name, and Gabriel Byrne the unknown quantity, at least as a stage actor, those who came to see the production anticipating that Jones as Josie would dominate the proceedings were surprised by the result. When the two leads settled into their roles and the focus shifted from Dotrice, who had taken center stage in Chicago, Jones's self-effacing performance made *Moon* Jim's play, with Byrne's performance becoming the focal point of the production. Although clearly not intended as revisionist, the production did, in its own way, challenge pre-conceived notions about both the play and the players, adding to the history of the play in completely unexpected ways.

Regional Productions

After 1973, *A Moon for the Misbegotten* was frequently revived on regional stages. Despite the challenge of casting the roles and sustaining the performances, the combination of a single set, a small cast, and Eugene O'Neill continued to appeal to regional producers. If the demands of the play were not daunting enough, there were always the comparisons to productions past. Writing in the *Boston Phoenix* in 1979 about a revival of *Moon* at the Lyric Stage, Carolyn Clay asks the logical question: "Does the fact that Ron Ritchell's Jim Tyrone is not Jason Robards' make it worthless?." Clay provides the logical answer: "Of course not" ("Flip Side of a Masterpiece" 14). Unfortunately, few critics shared her view, instead expecting revivals to compete with a production that had gone from mortal to myth.

Yet, many were willing to risk the comparisons. In 1991, Lloyds Richards chose *A Moon for the Misbegotten* as the final production of his twelve-year tenure as Artistic Director of the Yale Repertory Theatre, with Frances McDormand, a 1996 Oscar recipient for her role in *Fargo*, as Josie Hogan, and David Strathairn, a 2006 Oscar nominee for *Good Night, and Good Luck*, as Jim Tyrone. In his review of this production, Alvin Klein had almost as much to say about the 1973 revival: "The play can be illuminated through transcendence. That was proven in 1973, when Jason Robards, Colleen Dewhurst, and the director Jose Quintero appeared to have established a communion with the ghost of the playwright." As Klein describes the Yale production, "without a superimposed fatalistic view, the director seems simply to be waiting for tragic inevitability, as if presuming that life-sized characters will be enlarged from within by a sudden moment of revelation." Klein continues, "On their fabled 'moonlight date'—the play's crucial lifeline—the elusive connection, the moment of truth, is not reached, [in] performances that fail to fill the theater" (C16). Writing in the *Boston Globe*, Kevin Kelly rejects the possibility that McDormand can play the part: "she is physically all wrong for [Josie Hogan].... In 1984 Kate Nelligan, comely and small, was able to play against the contradiction by using voice and manner, both highly skilled, to suggest Josie's amplitude.... McDormand is utterly awkward and artless where, for example, Nelligan was artlessly awkward." As for David Strathairn as James Tyrone, Jr., Kelly states that the actor plays Tyrone "as though he's about to lurch into 'Yankee Doodle Dandy,'" describing the performance as "a stock embarrassment" ("A Misguided 'Moon'" D14). The production may not have achieved the tragic scope inherent in the O'Neill play, but it was mythic grandeur that was expected, and that is nearly impossible to realize.

In 1992, the play was revived Off Broadway at the Pearl Theater Company. Critic Wilborn Hampton, clearly not a fan of the play, describes the experience as "viewing disagreeable, if not downright despicable, characters through the prism of a rosy memory." Yet, Hampton is able to summon praise for the performances of Jim and Josie by Paul O'Brien and Joanne Camp, who "achieve a credible and touching rapport that expiates much of O'Neill's rather trying romanticism," with "Mr. O'Brien [delivering] a fine reading of Tyrone, bringing some blood to a very talky play." Continuing to praise with faint damns, Hampton calls the production "a revival that the play's admirers will find worthy, but that is not likely to win any converts from its detractors" (C16).

A decade later, the Trinity Repertory Company in Providence, Rhode Island, revived *Moon*. In *Theater Mirror*, Carl A. Rossi begins by offering his personal history with the play, saying, "the Dewhurst/Robards pieta haunted me for years." Rossi praises what he calls the Quintero 'Moon,' which "put the play on the map and remains the yardstick against which other productions are measured." He was less impressed after seeing the production on DVD, describing the Hogan farm as "a stage setting in a television studio through which the winds of Great Theatre solemnly blow." The many close-ups reveal to Rossi both the play's artifice and a "too mature" Dewhurst as the 28-year-old Josie, with Jason Robards, "a

surprising disappointment considering his reputation as an O'Neill interpreter." Rossi claims that the dark portrayal of Jim is "cold, reptilian ...
[and] based more on the saturnine Mr. O'Neill than his supposedly charming, wayward brother."

Although many would disagree with Rossi's assessment of the 1973
production of *Moon* on DVD, the critic does offer a convincing reason to
share his opinion of Trinity Rep's revival. As Rossi writes, "The Trinity
production, under the direction of Amanda Dehnert, triumphs in the long
run by ignoring the Quintero yardstick." For this production, that means
using a naturalistic physical setting, down to the "real, tamped-down soil
covering most of the playing area," and a production tone that is, as per
O'Neill's specifications for the original production, "distinctly Irish." Rossi
defines this quality not as a question of nationality but of comic intent:
"Ms. Dehnert satisfies much of O'Neill's demands by punching up all of
the bravura comedy hiding in plain sight ... and Ms. Dehnert knows when
to stop the blarney and to pluck at the heart strings." Dehnert's approach
corresponds to Ted Mann's in 1968, when he was accused of interpreting
the play far too lightly by *Village Voice* critic A. D. Coleman, and responded
by saying, "[*Moon*] was not meant to be performed as three hours of unrelenting, tragic doom." Rossi favors Dehnert's approach to the play: "those
expecting three hours of Gloom and Doom will be delighted at how their
lusty laughter makes the tragedy go down easier."

With Trinity Rep's resident actors Janice Duclos and Fred Sullivan, Jr.,
in the leading roles, Rossi begins with the inevitable comparisons: "Mr.
Robards' Jim is an iron fist of self-hatred and hard to love; Mr. Sullivan's
Jim ... is not the 'damned soul' that Josie tries to save, but, rather, a tipsy
playboy who has wandered into 'Tobacco Road.'" Janice Duclos fares much
better, in Rossi's estimation: "Ms. Duclos is not the giantess that Mr. O'Neill
calls for; she is of medium build and fat (her bulk becomes her freakish-
ness), but she loses her fatness when she steps into the arena." Described as
"young enough, warm enough and more than pretty enough to make many
a Jim turn to her for comfort," Rossi sees "nothing Epic in Josie as written;
the Epic lies in the heart's journey this ordinary, overlooked woman must
take as she passes from reputed Magdalene to shanty Madonna ... [with] a
purity that no amount of dirt, slops or stagnant water can pollute." According to Rossi, in this production, "Duclos' Josie is the crowning glory."

More recently, the play has been seen on a number of stages across the country. In 2005, *A Moon for the Misbegotten* was produced at the Madison Repertory Theatre in Madison, Wisconsin; the Orlando–UCF Shakespeare Festival in Orlando, Florida; Triad Stage, in Greensboro, North Carolina; The Heritage Theatre Company, in Chevy Chase, Maryland, and the Thalian Hall Center for the Performing Arts in Wilmington, North Carolina. Proud of the fact that O'Neill wrote the play across San Francisco Bay in Danville, California, the American Conservatory Theater produced *Moon* with Robin Weigert, better known as Calamity Jane on HBO's *Deadwood*, as Josie. Endorsing Weigert's Josie as "smartly played," reviewer Phyllis Butler is unconvinced by the premise of the play, finding that Jim's secret, "having sex with a 'blonde pig' at $50 a night on the train while his dead mother lies in the baggage car — is not shocking enough by today's sensibilities," and not sufficient cause for his self-hatred and self-sustaining alcoholism. In 1947, it should be noted, these were considered sufficient cause for shutting down the production. The critic is clearly a fan of Mario Barricelli in his final performance as a company member at the ACT. She writes, "Not to take away from the attractive Weigert's performance, the drama's initially talky and farcical scenes didn't really speak to me until the much spoken of James Tyrone arrives.... As portrayed by Barricelli, a big guy with a big presence and voice to match, Jamie/Jim ... [is] full of false bravado, and increasingly vulnerable as the story progresses." Although Butler manages to avoid comparisons to previous productions, the online review includes a link to information on the Broadway production with Cherry Jones and Gabriel Byrne.

Writing in the *San Francisco Chronicle*, Steven Winn praises Weigert's "buoyant, emotionally mobile performance," stating that "Director Laird Williamson's staging doesn't try to wring the same kind of pathos or operatic angst out of the script that other directors have," adding that "the comedy is generous-hearted. The grief, although underdeveloped in spots, is genuine and never milked." In the famous scene of Act III, Weigert becomes "something of an accompanist" to Barricelli. Winn also notes that "Barricelli resists the impulse to play it as a drunkard's aria. He tells us all we need to know about James' intoxication with the mock-heroic lighting of a cigarette." When the character begins to come apart, "even his speech comes apart, into little spasms and disjointed, toneless phrases"

("Nimble pas de deux" E1). The actors' relationship echoes that of Cherry Jones and Gabriel Byrne in 2000, when Jones seemed to defer to Byrne in the climactic scene, in a performance that some critics found constrained.

In 2005, the Long Wharf Theatre in New Haven, Connecticut, presented *Moon* in a production that moved to its "sister" theater, the Hartford Stage, in 2006, and then to the Alley Theater in Houston in 2007. Directed by Long Wharf's artistic director Gordon Edelstein, its set by Ming Cho Lee was described as "a bleak Andrew Wyeth landscape" (Robertson C11), which was "perched precariously on a hard-packed dirt slope punctuated by boulders" (Bovard). With conditions as harsh as the landscape, humor, in the form of relentless kidding, became an essential form of self-protection.

But who was kidding whom? Again, critics debated the topic of casting the uncastable play. Having previously appeared at Hartford Stage as Maggie the Cat in Williams' *Cat in a Hot Tin Roof*— a far cry from Josie Hogan — Alyssa Bresnahan made no concessions to O'Neill's stage directions, and used no padding. In her review of the production, Anita Gates states that "Josie Hogan just seems to get skinnier and skinnier," suggesting that the actress "looks as if she should be starring in 'The Kate Moss Story' instead" (C8). Similar to Kate Nelligan in 1984, what Bresnahan lacked in the physical, she more than made up for in physicality, striding around the stage with a lumbering gait, and, at times, speaking in a growl. Bill Raymond, as Phil Hogan, is an actor with a light comic touch, usually seen in gentler roles, and known in Hartford as a comic Scrooge in Dickens' *A Christmas Carol*. Yet, according to most of the critics, the casting seemed to work. As Karen Bovard writes in the *Hartford Advocate*, "we get to see talented actors doing something they rarely get to do, the way American theater is structured: step beyond their standard type, exercise their range, [and] live with a role long enough to inhabit it."

One point of contention was the performance of John Procaccino as Jim Tyrone, a character described by O'Neill in the stage directions as reflecting "the ghost of a former youthful irresponsible Irish charm — that of the beguiling ne'er-do-well, sentimental and romantic" (*Moon* 875). Procaccino is described by critic Campbell Robertson as having none of the above. While Robertson finds Bresnahan's performance "compelling

despite its flaws," referring to her undisguised "good looks," he writes that "Long before the Pieta scene at the end, when Tyrone experiences his catharsis against Josie's breast, one wishes he would go back to repressing." Robertson does acknowledge that "a pleasant fife music [plays] over this heavy bass" in the performance of Bill Raymond as the rustic Phil (C11).

When the Long Wharf production moved to Hartford, Procaccino was replaced by James Colby, who had often played opposite Bresnahan, and was also playing against type, unless Stanley Kowalski and Jim Tyrone come from the same play book. For once, here was a Tyrone too physically large for the role, a condition masked, as Joanne Greco Rochman observes, by "his too big suit and slouched and droopy body language [suggesting] the image of an ailing man." Opening with Faure's "Requiem," the production moved to its iconic image in Act III, and, as Rochman writes, "By the time Jamie collapses in the lap of Josie Hogan, played by Allysa Bresnahan who nailed the role at Long Wharf and now melds with Colby, O'Neill's holy, word-sculpted Pieta is complete. It is a stunning and breathtaking theatrical moment."

In January 2006, Princeton's McCarter Theatre Center offered its version of *A Moon for the Misbegotten*, O'Neill's explanation and expiation of his brother's sins. In directing the play, Gary Griffin made a concerted effort to avoid the charge that *Moon* is a static and long-winded play. This was a physically active production, at least for the Hogan family. After dispensing with her youngest brother, Mike, by giving him train fare to Bridgeport, thus freeing him from their father's tyranny, Josie, as played by Kathleen McNenny, mops the floor, peels the potatoes, repairs a rip in her father's shirt while he's still wearing it, then grabs a pitchfork to finish the work left by her departed brother, all in the first twenty minutes of the play. No one who works this hard would ever gain weight. (On the other hand, Jack Willis, as Hogan, is called upon to urinate and to vomit, upstage, luckily, in the course of the action.) Griffin may have made this directing choice to account for the fact that McNenny, a Juilliard-trained actress previously seen on Broadway in *After the Fall* and *The Constant Wife*,

Opposite: Andrew McCarthy as James Tyrone, Jr., and Kathleen McNenny as Josie Hogan in the 2006 production of *A Moon for the Misbegotten*, directed by Gary Griffin, at the Berlind Theatre of the McCarter Theatre Center. Photograph by Rich Tepper/McCarter Theatre Center, Princeton, NJ.

lacked the physical size of Josie as written, although, as the ungainly woman who privately moons over Jim, she had the sound and style of a woman willing to sacrifice anything, even her own dreams, for the man she loves. The frantic activity helped to explain why this Josie had normal-sized arms and legs and a large, albeit padded, frame.

But Josie's emotional size is something that McNenny got just right. O'Neill expected everything of his Earth Mothers: they were both lover and mother. This production placed that burden squarely on the sturdy shoulders of McNenny's Josie, and in the process, what is usually a duet, or possibly a trio, became a solo. As critic Naomi Siegel writes, "In total command of the role, [McNenny] makes it almost impossible to focus on the other two legs of the author's dramatic tripod." Without suggesting any form of imitation, there were Dewhurstian echoes in the force and power of McNenny's performance. Or, as critic Siegel puts it, "Ms. Dewhurst, meet Ms. Kathleen McNenny. One great Josie deserves another" (C9).

As the character based on O'Neill's dearly loved and sometimes hated older brother, Andrew McCarthy faced an even greater challenge than playing James Tyrone, Jr. Although he had appeared on Broadway in Warren Leight's *Side Man*, and played Jamie Tyrone in *Long Day's Journey Into Night* at the Hartford Stage, McCarthy has yet to escape his reputation as a member of the Brat Pack, a group of young actors, including Demi Moore and Rob Lowe, who starred in films such as *St. Elmo's Fire* in the 1980s. Even behind a mustache, the forty-four-year-old McCarthy lacked both the physical and emotional heft to play a middle-aged man on a determined march to an early death. Unlike previous Tyrones, who occasionally sent Josie flying, this Tyrone is the one who took a tumble. Between moments of mothering the wounded calf that is Jim Tyrone, at one point, McNenny's Josie nearly knocked him off the stage. As O'Neill said of his brother in a letter to a friend, "Bad booze got him in the end" (*Selected Letters* 378). McCarthy played Tyrone as if in the throes of a bad headache. The performance was redeemed for some, however, in the long speech in Act III in which Tyrone reveals the cause of his torment. As Simon Saltzman writes, "It's a daring undertaking for Andrew McCarthy to tackle the role of the physically eroding James Tyrone, Jr. McCarthy, however, comes very close to revealing a good many of the darker shadows of this superficially dashing knight-errant and the half-living shell of the deluded dreamer-survivor."

For the Princeton production, Eugene Lee designed a memorable set that takes in two of the major schools of thought regarding the Hogans' ramshackle farm. In 1973, the house was expressionistically rendered, with no front or side walls, and widely-spaced wooden slats to indicate the roof and back wall. In his own design for the Broadway revival of 2000, not a rock seemed to be missing from Lee's rendition of the home, in keeping with O'Neill's naturalistic stage directions. Lee's design in Princeton followed both directions: the house was open-faced, lacking a front wall. Josie's bedroom had solid walls at the side and back, with the back of the living room and the roof over their heads suggested by wooden boards. As C. W. Walker describes the home, "the fully furnished rooms in the front fade away into a half-constructed silhouette of bare beams — a tangible symbol of unfinished dreams." At Princeton, Lee expanded on his previous design, bringing the set, and therefore, the action, further downstage. He reconfigured the first three rows of the 360-seat Roger Berlind Theatre to accommodate a thrust stage, the additional playing area bringing the audience even closer to the action in a production that "draws us in and cradles us as well," according to David Anthony Fox in Philadelphia's *City Paper*.

While Connecticut farms can be rocky, unless the Hogans live in a quarry, there was no adequate explanation for the wrinkled brown paper on the upstage wall and the sides of Lee's set, although lighting designer Jane Cox does refer to it in an interview as a "burlap sky ... malleable with light." Through the trees, a lovely full moon could be seen that rises and falls for the would-be lovers, courtesy of designer Cox. Josie's best dress was a tragedy all its own. Designed by Jess Goldstein, the navy sack was more suited to a school marm than a special date, making Josie's desire for Jim all the more pathetic in this sad uniform for seduction.

Director Gary Griffin, whose next stop was the musical *The Color Purple* on Broadway, cast a younger pair in the two main roles, closer in age to the characters as originally envisioned by O'Neill. The results of this decision were mixed. While McCarthy was not entirely up to the task, McNenny's performance was generally well received, though she was still regarded by some as too pretty, not physically big enough, or, simply put, not Colleen Dewhurst.

Yet, Griffin also saw the humor in the play. He is quoted as saying, "I would love for this to be the funniest production of *Moon for the Misbegotten* that people have ever seen. I think O'Neill believes in the survival power of humor." Acknowledging the previous associations with particular actors in the leading roles, Griffin added, "There was the Colleen Dewhurst/Jason Robards version, the Cherry Jones version. I hope people will think of this as the O'Neill version." Especially for those new to the play, the intimate and naturalistic production provided access to a difficult play, even if it did not fully explore that difficulty. More comfortable with the comic banter than the emotional bleeding, the production was finally more likeable than fully tragic. The frequent and varied revivals continue to attest to the enduring appeal of the play as well as to the difficulty of achieving its full potential.

5

Broadway Revival, 2007

As in 1984, the next major revival of *A Moon for the Misbegotten* originated in London, this time at the Old Vic Theatre. The Old Vic had a
storied past, with actors such as Sybil Thorndike, Edith Evans, John Giel-
gud, Ralph Richardson, Peggy Ashcroft, Michael Redgrave, Alec Guin-
ness, Laurence Olivier, Helen Mirren, and Richard Burton having trod
the boards. By the year 2000, unlike the National, the Almedia, or the
Donmar, the Old Vic was no longer an essential destination for the theater community. In fact, Frommer's *Guide to London* advised tourists to
call first if they planned to visit the Old Vic, described as up for sale, "and
what will happen is anybody's guess" (285). With a roof that had been
leaking since bomb damage suffered in World War II, and walls that continued to ooze water, the theater was in serious need of institutional repair.
With no public subsidy, the Old Vic had been saved from demolition in
1998 by the impresario Sally Greene, who purchased it for 3.5 million
pounds and now serves as the chief executive of the Old Vic Trust. She
assembled a board of directors for the theater that included the actors
Dame Judi Dench, Jeremy Irons, and David Suchet.

By 2003, the theater's fortunes seemed to improve. In February, the
actor Kevin Spacey was named Artistic Director. It was Green who first
met with Spacey in 2001 and convinced him to take the job, a secret she
and Spacey managed to keep for two years before the official announcement. Trained at Juilliard, with a Tony and Oscar awards to his credit, the
new artistic director was introduced by Elton John, the chairman of the
Old Vic's board of directors, who praised Spacey's ability to bring "a totally

new dynamic so that the Old Vic remains one of the most important theatres in the world" (qtd. in Jeffries). As Spacey later told interviewer Harry Haun, "For a long time, I was focused on my own personal career, but I got to a point where I no longer cared about that. I wanted to do something outside of myself, bigger than myself, that would—as I see every day at the Old Vic—affect people's lives."

With Dame Dench by his side, Spacey announced plans to form a permanent company, with performances beginning in Fall 2004 for an eight-month season. Using himself "as a magnet to attract great writers, actors, and directors to this theatre that has been kind of lost" (qtd. in Gibbons), Spacey would entice others to take the inevitable pay cut for the honor of performing at the Old Vic. The actor would continue his film work and be available for two stage productions per season. The then 180-year-old theater would also be available for use during the summer by producing organizations such as the Royal Shakespeare Company. David Liddiment, former director of channels at ITV, was named producer in charge of locating financing from commercial backers. The theater had been supported by a variety of private sources, and more investors, like the investment bank Morgan Stanley, would be drawn to the cause.

Spacey made a ten-year commitment to the Old Vic, with "five years to establish myself and build the audience who come and see the work," as he told interviewer Michael Coveney. A board member at the Old Vic since 1998, Spacey previously had invested over 100,000 pounds in the theater. Having first visited the Old Vic as a child, Spacey eagerly relocated to London to assume his post, explaining, "I'm an anglophile, let's face it" (qtd. in Chrisafis). In 2003, his first order of business was to host a gala that netted half-a-million pounds for the theater, thanks to a celebrity line-up that included the musicians Sting, Sinead O'Connor, and Elvis Costello. Planning an aggressive community-outreach program, Spacey was eager to develop younger audiences, offering over 100 seats per performance available at twelve pounds (approximately twenty-five dollars) for those under the age of twenty-five. He also hoped to transfer Old Vic productions to the United States, and bring American theater to the Old Vic.

Spacey's choice for his first production, the play *Cloaca*, gave some pause. Written by the Dutch playwright Maria Goos, *Cloaca* is a word that means *sewer*. "The play is like a gutter," according to its author (qtd. in Jeffries); others described it as a bleak contemporary comedy that follows four men through their respective mid-life crises. A hit in Holland, followed by a successful film adaptation, *Cloaca*, directed by Spacey himself, would make its London debut. This would be followed by more family-friendly fare, with Ian McKellen playing the Widow Twankey in a new version of the pantomime *Aladdin*, a role sought out by the noted British actor, and which he happily repeated the following year. The Christmas pantomime revived the Old Vic tradition of the nineteenth century but with a twist. In his first attempt at a pantomime, Sean Mathias, best known for directing *The Elephant Man* on Broadway and Martin Sherman's *Bent* on screen, would lead the production. The season continued in 2005 with the British premiere of Dennis McIntyre's *National Anthems*, a dark comedy about American materialism. The cast included Mary Stuart Masterson, Steven Weber, and Spacey in a role he had first played at the Long Wharf Theatre in 1988, that of a fireman who infiltrates the household of a yuppie couple in Detroit and exposes the fraudulence of American materialism. This production was followed by Philip Barry's *The Philadelphia Story*, with Jennifer Ehle as Tracy Lord and Spacey as C. K. Dexter Haven, a role played on film by Cary Grant.

Given the mixed response to his first season as artistic director, Spacey would need a generous time frame to gain the trust of the theatergoing audience. *Cloaca* was a bold beginning, but the critics were not impressed. Natasha Tripney's assessment of the play echoes the views of a number of critics when she describes it as "a rather flat tale of men in middle age that too closely resembles Yasmin Reza's *Art*." They applauded Spacey's performance in *National Anthems*, but the production itself received mediocre reviews. Two dark comedies in a row were more than the audience could take. McKellen's Widow Twankey in the Christmas pantomime *Aladdin* was a critical favorite, although many of the audience members came to see Gandalf of *Lord of the Rings* fame and not the distinguished classical actor taking a busman's holiday. Both audience and critics warmed to *The Philadelphia Story*, but box office receipts dipped and audiences were disappointed during the six weeks Spacey left the production to play the villain Lex Luthor in *Superman Returns*, directed by Bryan Singer, who had previously directed him in *The Usual Suspects*.

Spacey had to strike a delicate balance: he needed to continue in films to sustain his celebrity; at the same time, he needed to make artistic choices that would establish him as more than a famous face, as a viable theatrical force. With the London press asking questions like "Will a great American actor embarrass the London theatre world by beating it at its own game?" (Jeffries), Spacey was well aware that he was "a big target" (qtd. in Coveney). This made for a contentious relationship with the press. As he himself said after the first season, "If you look at how most artistic beginnings have been greeted in this country, I'm in very good company. I know I'm a bigger target as long as I'm seen as a Hollywood movie star instead of as an actor of the theatre, even an artistic director. They don't accept that I come in to work here every day, and have done so for the last two-and-a-half years, and will continue to do so" (qtd. in Coveney). Not only had Spacey been onstage for thirty-six weeks in three different plays during the first season, but the theater had played to houses at approximately seventy-percent capacity, a more-than-respectable average. Both were significant indicators of his commitment to the theater and of its emergent success.

Spacey's first season offered no new commissions by the theater nor any Shakespeare play, a situation rectified in the second season. First, Spacey took on the role of Richard II, and his modern-dress Richard won critical acclaim. Eighteen months into his tenure at the Old Vic, Spacey received the award for Best Actor at the Critics' Circle Awards, the first outward sign of approval for his efforts at the Old Vic. As critic Mark Lawson wrote in *The Guardian*, "Surely, this tells us something: that great stages require great plays. Spacey should dive in at the deep end and give us a series of knockdown masterpieces; preferably with himself in the lead." The second season also included an event that was intended to be the theatrical highpoint. Legendary film director Robert Altman, who had just turned 80, would make his London theater debut directing *Resurrection Blues*, one of the last plays written by legendary playwright Arthur Miller. Miller had stated his desire to bring the play, which he continued to rework up until his death in February 2005, to London, specifically to the Old Vic, one of his favorite theaters. The play is a departure for Miller in that it does not invoke the social or political commentary usually associated with works like *Death of a Salesman* or *The Crucible*. It is instead a black comedy set in an unnamed banana republic. A young revolutionary has been captured, and the television rights to his execution by crucifixion have been sold to an American company by a military dictator who wants it to be televised as a live spectacle, with merchandise and a theme park to follow. The cast included several notable American actors, among them, Matthew Modine, Maximillian Schell, and Jane Adams.

Unfortunately, the many promising elements of the production never coalesced. Altman had limited experience with dramatic texts, and according to *The Guardian*, the director admitted, "I don't really know this script" (qtd. in Billington, "Without the classics, Old Vic is a farce"). The production's reviews were dismal. Jeremy Austin, in *The Stage*, wrote, "for the most part, *Resurrection Blues* is a mess, never really settling upon one theme or another. Did God create man or did man create God? It begins to ask at one point before failing to explore this satisfactorily." According to Lizzie Loveridge of *Curtain Up*, "Altman's film directing style — letting the actors develop their role — is fundamentally unsuited to Arthur Miller's precise and carefully thought out writing." Paul Taylor, in *The Independent*, lands the final blow: "It takes an almost ingenious ineptitude on the part of a producer to bring together two American giants — dramatist Arthur Miller and director Robert Altman — and contrive to expose them both to ridicule through the exercise."

Altman's words to Jane Adams, reprinted in the program, suggest part of the problem. As he told her, "We don't have to hear every word — it's ok if it's a bit of a mish-mash. I don't care what you're saying to your mother on the phone, Jane. People don't have to hear every line." But, in the theater, they do. Jane Adams received positive reviews for her performance as Emily Shapiro, the commercial director with a conscience, but during one matinee performance, when Adams exited the stage, she kept on going, never to return. The show did go on, but not for long; opening in March, it closed prematurely in April. This left the theater empty until September 2006, a situation that had critics calling for Spacey to step down. Spacey shrugged off the criticism, saying, "I will never, ever stop believing that this is a good idea. If you believe in something enough, then nothing can dissuade you from doing it" (qtd. in Brown).

Apparently, the third season was the charm. Spacey announced that beginning in September 2006, he would be playing Jim Tyrone in O'Neill's

A Moon for the Misbegotten, directed by Howard Davies, who had previously directed Spacey in O'Neill's *The Iceman Cometh*, which transferred from the Almeida to the Old Vic in 1998, which was followed by a successful critical and commercial run on Broadway. Spacey had previously played Jamie Tyrone in the 1986 Broadway revival of *Long Day's Journey into Night*, directed by Jonathan Miller, with Jack Lemmon as the elder Tyrone.

As a director, Davies was known for his work on both sides of the Atlantic. Currently the Associate Director of the National Theatre, Davies also directed the Broadway productions of *Piaf* (1981), *Good* (1982), *Les Liaisons Dangereuses* (1987), *Cat on a Hot Tin Roof* (1990), *My Fair Lady* (1994), *Translations* (1995), and *Private Lives* (2002), in addition to *The Iceman Cometh* (1999). In casting the production, as far as director Davies and artistic director Spacey were concerned, Eve Best was the only choice to play Josie. Best, who first name is Emily, and this is how she is known to her friends, took her grandmother's first name, Eve, when British Equity already had an Emily Best among its members. Little known outside of the London theater world, Best had become a decorated veteran after only a short career. After graduating with a degree in English from Oxford University, Best studied acting at the Royal Academy of Dramatic Art, which had rejected her the first time she applied, before she enrolled at Oxford. In 1999, she received the London Evening Standard Theatre Award for Best Newcomer for her performance in John Ford's *'Tis Pity She's a Whore*, which she performed at the Young Vic Theatre opposite Jude Law, as well as the Critics Circle Theatre Award (Drama) for Most Promising Newcomer. In 2003, she was awarded the London Critics Circle Theatre Award for Best Actress for her performance as Lavinia in *Mourning Becomes Electra*, directed by Howard Davies at the Royal National Theatre. For her performance as Hedda Gabler, Best accepted both critical acclaim and an Olivier award. At the age of thirty five, Best would approach the part like most of the actresses who played Josie, not fulfilling the physical requirements stated in O'Neill's stage directions.

Interviewed with Eve Best and Kevin Spacey before rehearsals began, Davies was steadfast in his defense of O'Neill's play, objecting to the charge that the plays, in general, are repetitious, and that, according to some academics, O'Neill has a "tin ear." Davies stated that "it's not the language of analysis; it's not about people describing their lives. It's about language as an expressive force. It is about language as a part of life." With this, Best concurred, adding, "that's how people talk in life, those repetitions happen when emotions are charging through you, and you pick up on the same words that somebody has used." Spacey finished her thought: "And as a way of avoiding saying something. There's a lot of that in this play, when you're not saying what's there," which Spacey described as "a chess game of emotion" (qtd. in Cavendish). Clearly, the actors and director were already in agreement on at least one point.

The role of Phil Hogan would be played by Colm Meaney, an actor who had played a number of Irish fathers in his career. Although he began his acting career with the Focus Company in the late 1970s in Dublin, alongside Gabriel Byrne and Stephen Rea, Meaney is probably best known for film and television roles, including *The Commitments* (1991) and *The Snapper* (1993). In addition, Meaney played Chief Miles Edward O'Brien for twelve consecutive years, from 1987 to 1999, on *Star Trek: The Next Generation* to *Star Trek: Deep Space Nine*; along with Michael Dorn, Meaney is one of only two actors with this kind of longevity on the series. The cast of *Moon* was completed by Eugene O'Hare as Mike Hogan and Billy Carter as T. Stedman Harder. In addition to the Old Vic Theatre Company, producers included Nica Burns, who owned the UK rights to the play, and Americans Elliot Martin, who had also produced the American revival of the play in 2000, and Max Weitzenhoffer.

Once the production opened, it was apparent that all was forgiven, if not forgotten. Identifying himself as "one of the harshest critics of the Spacey regime," Paul Taylor wrote in *The Independent*: "Kevin Spacey's last season at The Old Vic petered out wretchedly with the critical disaster of *Resurrection Blues*." But Taylor quickly changed his tune, adding, "So it's a joy to report a glorious bounce-back." Describing director Howard Davies as "the greatest British interpreter of O'Neill," and the production as "beautiful, funny, and cathartic," Taylor praises the actors who "appear to have achieved the deep rapport experienced by the characters — two people who can kid the world but can't fool themselves" in a production that is "exquisitely judged in terms of lighting, shifts of mood and undulating pattern of raised and dashed hopes."

Another of Spacey's critics, Michael Billington, finally found something to praise. In his review, he calls the Old Vic production "the highlight of the Spacey regime to date." In discussing the actors, he notes that "Eve Best makes no pretence at being the ungainly, 180-lb figure O'Neill describes in his stage directions. Instead, her Josie is a hard-working rustic slave who has grown used to hiding her feelings and who deflects every compliment with a shy, nervous laugh. It is a beautiful performance, about the pain of living a constant lie, perfectly matched by Spacey's Jim.... Watching Best and Spacey together is like seeing two desperate people stripping their souls naked." Billington adds, "Bob Crowley's ramshackle rural set and Colm Meaney's self-deceptive Hogan lend weight to a production that offers the rarest of theatrical treats: an evening of raw, powerful emotion."

In the London *Times*, Benedict Nightingale found much to praise in the production, though less to praise in the play, writing in his review that "Howard Davies' revival, with Kevin Spacey and Eve Best ablaze at its epicenter, is both a major triumph and, inevitably, a bit of a failure. It proves impossible to disguise that the play is an awkward mix of rustic laugh-in and searing confessional, but it's equally impossible to miss the force of the long denouement that only O'Neill had the passion and the power to create.... In the half-dark the two protagonists do what O'Neill characters find so difficult. They shed their protective masks and ditch their life-lies." Describing the acting by Best and Spacey as "superb," Nightingale asks, "Is there better acting to be found anywhere?" to which he answers, "I'd be surprised."

Critic Kate Bassett, writing in *The Independent*, also praises the rapport between the actors: "Best's towering, barefoot Josie combines swagger with lovely, funny flurries of shy yearning. And when Spacey looks at her and smiles, a wonderful seductive chemistry sparks between them." In a similar vein, Charles Spencer notes in the *Daily Telegraph*, "Spacey seizes all his chances. When we first meet him, his thirst for the booze seems comic, but this extraordinarily comic actor gradually lays bare a man enduring a living death.... More movingly still, Eve Best gives one of the most beautiful accounts of aching, unconditional love I have ever seen as she listens to his confessions, cradles his head against her breast, admits to her own long denied virginity and finally, devastatingly, understands that love is sometimes ineffective against the worst horrors of this world."

Several American critics crossed the pond for this theatrical event, among them Ray Bennett of the *Hollywood Reporter*, who describes the revival as "a powerful demonstration of how superlative acting — in this case by Kevin Spacey, Eve Best, and Colm Meaney — can elevate a flawed play so the whole thing resembles a masterpiece." As Bennett continues, "The clunky plot and motivation in all of this does not bear close inspection, but they are merely pegs on which O'Neill hangs his story of self-deception and compassion with some gorgeous words and phrases to light the way. Spacey wears Tyrone's defeat like a whiskey-soaked suit, spurning the obvious temptation to be lyrically Irish and showing instead the ruin of a man too far gone to save himself." Speaking of Best's performance, Bennett writes, "With breathtaking simplicity she inhabits a character whose inner strength emerges only when she sets aside the carapace of denial." Praising Howard Davies' direction as well as "Bob Crowley's atmospheric design, Paule Constable's subtle lighting and Dominic Muldowney's bluesy music," Bennett concludes by saying, "What begins as a folksy tale threatening a cup of blarney ends up as a deeply moving drama brimming with emotion and fortitude and made unforgettable by actors at the peak of their powers."

In *Variety*, David Benedict focuses more on the elements of the production, stating that "If there's one idea coursing through Howard Davies' incandescent Old Vic revival of "A Moon for the Misbegotten," it's that naturalism is not the answer. The clue is the language. Eugene O'Neill's dialogue is unyielding, poetic, even hectoring in its potentially numbing repetitions. Aiming instead for the elemental, Davies abandons most of the playwright's stage directions. Armed with Eve Best and Kevin Spacey, two of his favorite O'Neill actors, the director turns intransigence into magnificence. Like a conductor taking on an unwieldy late symphony, he keeps a tight rein on the seismic ebbs and flows of O'Neill's great soul-searcher, ensuring it never peaks too soon."

On Bob Crowley's set, the wide open spaces expected of a rural setting were replaced by a narrowed stage. As described by Benedict, "the Hogans' ramshackle homestead perches on a set that's a long corridor, its perspective staked out with telegraph poles pulling the eye almost endlessly back to a tiny horizon. We're told that it's Connecticut, but with bare, steep walls glowing in super-saturated blue light, the space looks mythic." With the inclusion of a working water pump that limits the acting space on a severely raked stage covered with red earth, a certain claustrophobia results, but one which Benedict finds "dramatically useful — the characters cannot escape one another — it allows for unusually engrossing 'business' as Josie crabbily sets about washing clothes or releasing a glorious cascade of water over estate owner Harder."

Benedict has high praise for the actors. In discussing Spacey's performance, the critic admits that "Part of Spacey's incontestable stage charisma stems from his self-evident pleasure in performing. What better role could he order up, therefore, than that of an actor who is a self-dramatizing drunk?" Benedict also acknowledges that "there are moments when Spacey cannot resist playing the audience rather than the character. When Josie mentions his crucial train journey, he rounds on her, but his eyes dart out front to ensure that we have appreciated his lightning change of mood." Benedict finally comes to the conclusion that "ironically, Spacey's Tyrone comes fully, scarily alive when consumed by self-disgust. His tormented self-loathing as he tells of his whoring in the wake of his mother's death is lacerating." At the same time, Benedict admits that "The less 'acting' Spacey does, the more powerful his performance grows," for example, when "seemingly without effort, he sweetly conveys innocence as he wakes up in the final act. When he's suddenly stopped short as the memory of the night before floods back, the startling glimpse of his ravaged hope is devastating."

As for Best's Josie, the critic acknowledges the obvious: "Physically, Best is far from the giant of O'Neill's directions. Tall and almost gaunt, she makes up for in tensile strength what she lacks in brawn.... She may look weatherbeaten and plain, but stomping around, awkwardly swatting the air and terrified of holding anyone close to her, she is utterly convincing in her belief that she is 'a great fat cow.'"

Best and Spacey's rapport was unmistakable. Benedict called their handling of the seduction scene "riveting," adding, "The longer this operatic duet goes on, the more the actors focus on the moment-by-moment detail rather than losing themselves to O'Neill's bruising poetry. Their commitment is so complete, they even manage to make Jim's (and O'Neill's) whore/Madonna complex genuinely moving." Benedict ends his review by saying, "If Spacey can continue to mount productions of this caliber, his tenure as Old Vic artistic director could be longer than the naysayers predicted."

David Finkle, writing for *TheaterMania*, attributes another motive to Spacey: "after the death of preeminent O'Neill interpreter Jason Robards, Spacey likely wants to make it clear that he's assumed the late actor's mantle." (Actors Liam Neeson and Gabriel Byrne might have something to say about that.) Although Finkle describes the first half of the production as "no more than acceptably workmanlike," he praises the second half, "which blossoms like an exotic flower growing unexpectedly on Bob Crowley's nearly barren set. Crowley has covered the severely raked stage with red earth for O'Neill's down-to-earth characters to tread, squat, and collapse upon." According to Finkle, the second half of the production is a "stunner" as Spacey's Jim Tyrone and Best's Josie Hogan "strip the illusions they have about themselves in order to face the truths of their lives, no matter how devastating those truths are to bare and bear." As Finkle describes Spacey's performance, "his graphic depiction of Tyrone's torment is like watching a man being eaten alive from the inside out."

While acknowledging that Best is not an obvious casting choice for an earth mother type, her slim build undisguised by Lynette Mauro's deliberately "shapeless" costumes, Finkle finds Best a convincing earth daughter, "engaging Spacey with her concomitant emotional honesty." After her performance in *Mourning Becomes Electra* in 2003 at the National Theatre, Best, according to Finkle, "continues to stake her claim as an O'Neill player of note." Finally, Finkle finds the charge that O'Neill is "relentlessly prosaic" to be "nonsense," although the critic does object to the "extended blarney about Josie's relationship to her bibulous father." As Finkle continues, "when O'Neill gets to the Jim-Josie encounter, he produces a tone poem full of myriad resonant tones. It's indisputably one of the most masterful scenes in American theater literature." Finkle finishes his review with the statement that "This O'Neill work is not misbegotten."

From the time the production began previews on 15 September 2006 through the end of its run at the Old Vic on 23 December 2006, there had been talk of a Broadway transfer. The rave reviews from the London critics cemented this prospect, although an immediate transfer was not possible due to Best's commitment to play Rosalind in a production of *Twelfth*

Night beginning in January 2007. But move it would, after extensive negotiations with Spacey.

Added to the list of producers and the Old Vic Company was Ben Sprecher, who acted as a spokesman for the production. It had been reported that Spacey demanded a weekly salary in the neighborhood of $50,000, comparable to that of Julia Roberts in her Broadway debut in 2006, playing a daughter and then her mother in Richard Greenberg's *Three Days of Rain*. The production was assailed by the critics during its limited run, from 28 March to 18 June 2006, primarily for Robert's lack of theater experience. It still sold out as fans flocked to see the movie star, live and in person. Despite the rumors, Spacey, in fact, received $10,000 for the first half of his limited run. As reported in the *New York Post*, his salary jumped to $30,000 after the show recouped. The producers had convinced all those who would receive a percentage of the box office, including Spacey, to forego it until the production repaid its investment (Riedel, "Spacey 'Moon' Landing").

To achieve that end, the "premium seats," those seats in the center of the orchestra from Row AA to L, would be sold at $200, instead of the standard orchestra price of $101. On weekends, these seats would be $250. This was a significant jump from the top ticket price of eighty-five pounds, or $101.25, when the production played the Old Vic. Even if the show received another set of rave reviews in New York, a three-hour O'Neill drama would still be a hard sell, and some predicted that the prices would have to be lowered. Producer Sprecher insisted that the move was "in line with what other limited-engagement productions — like 'The Odd Couple' [starring Nathan Lane and Matthew Broderick, reunited after *The Producers*] have done in terms of premium seats. If we do well, the show will make money" (qtd. in Riedel, "Extreme $pacey").

Sprecher's great hope was that the production would be extended beyond its 84-performance limited run. Those expecting a direct mail offering for discounted tickets would be disappointed: with the exception of a few email announcements offering discounts for tickets purchased before previews began on March 29, or for Easter Sunday (April 9), there were no discounts available until the production opened, when they became available through TDF (Theater Development Fund) and other ticketing services. In keeping with the Old Vic's policy of developing new audiences, at each performance sixty tickets would be made available to students with valid ID for the reasonable sum of $26.50. According to Spacey, "If you can get the kids in early enough, you might just be part of planting the seed for the next generation of theatergoers. And the truth is, producers have the money to afford it" (qtd. in Cox). Although the producers might disagree, feeling the pinch of a 10-week run, by the time previews began, *Variety* reported on 30 March 2007 that the production had a very respectable advance of 3.5 million. During the first week of previews, 87% of the 1,050-seat theater was filled, followed by 96% capacity, in the weeks before and after the opening. Through the remainder of the run, the percentage of audience capacity ranged from the high eighties to the low-to-mid nineties, with the audience dipping to 83% capacity in the second-to-last week, followed by the highest audience attendance figures, 97% capacity, during the last week of the run. When, on 15 May 2007, a mere five weeks into the run, the producers announced that the production had recouped its initial 2.4 million investment, the news was greeted with some skepticism and seen as a marketing ploy rather than a statement of fiscal fact. When the production ended its run on 10 June 2007, investors did, in fact, receive a 30% return on their outlay, making *Moon* one of the few shows during the 2006–2007 Broadway season to turn a profit (Riedel, "Spacey 'Moon' Landing"). The initial skepticism did not dissuade the producers, however. In the theater listings in the *New York Times*, for example, the production touted itself as "The Most Successful Production of 'Moon' in Theater History." Previously, the advertising campaign has used a numerical countdown to inform potential viewers how many of the 84 performances remained.

While *Moon* was in previews, it was clear that Spacey would continue to play his offstage role as Artistic Director of the Old Vic. During this time, an exchange program was announced between the Old Vic and BAM (the Brooklyn Academy of Music), initially a three-year venture, with Sam Mendes directing Stephen Dillane in *Hamlet* and *The Tempest* on the stage of the Old Vic, opening in May and running through June 2008. The production would then move to New York in January 2009. This would be followed by Mendes directing *The Winter's Tale* and *The Cherry Orchard*, featuring Simon Russell Davies in 2009, with the pairing for 2010, possibly to star Spacey, still under consideration. According to Mendes, Joseph V. Melillo, BAM's Executive Director, and Spacey, the goal was to produce "large-scale, classical theatre for international audiences" (qtd. in Paddock). The company would be truly transatlantic, with fifty percent of the actors coming from the United States and fifty percent from the United Kingdom. Mendes had previously served as the Artistic Director of the Donmar Warehouse in London, and a double bill of *Twelfth Night* and *Uncle Vanya* had transferred to BAM for a successful nine-week run in 2003. Spacey and Mendes had previously worked together on the film *American Beauty*, for which both had received Academy Awards. The Bridge Project, as it would be known, was the culmination of almost a decade of discussions between the director and actor. Two-million dollars would need to be raised to bring the project to fruition, but all of the participants were confident that this could be accomplished. In addition to planning this project, Spacey would appear in David Mamet's *Speed-the-Plow* during the Old Vic's 2007–2008 season. In addition, between April 24 and June 5, Spacey planned to lead six workshops for 180 New York City high school students after they had seen a matinee performance of *Moon*. On 19 April 2007, the Old Vic Theatre Company planned a benefit to follow the evening performance of *Moon*, with a keynote speech by Bill Clinton, an event that netted the theater close to half-a-million dollars.

What Spacey also managed to do was to bring the entire Old Vic cast with him to New York. Spacey himself and Colm Meaney, for that matter, have the star status that would enable them to make the transfer. Eve Best, though relatively unknown outside of London, might be deemed indispensable to the production, and therefore be allowed to perform in New York with the permission of Actors' Equity. What was unusual was that the actors playing the minor roles of T. Stedman Harder and Mike Hogan, Billy Carter and Eugene O'Hare, would also be making their New York debut. Usually, these roles would be played by American actors, given the paucity of parts available to members of Actors Equity. Other than the American understudies, and Spacey himself had no understudy, this production of *Moon* would move intact to the Brooks Atkinson Theatre, with performances to begin on 29 March 2007.

When the ads began to appear in newspapers, it was not surprising to see the two lead actors' names listed above the title of the play, but unusual to see Eve Best's name listed first, before Kevin Spacey, the movie star and known quantity, and a major reason why an audience might be drawn to see a production of *Moon* only seven years after the last Broadway revival. Perhaps this was a gesture on the part of an artistic director who runs a repertory company that does not participate in the star system; instead, actors are usually listed alphabetically to designate a company of equals. But Broadway is run strictly on the star system, with the biggest box office draw most prominently displayed. When the play opened, what might have seemed an act of generosity on the part of Artistic Director Spacey was, in fact, an accurate indication of the show *Moon* had become.

A month before previews began, Eve Best was already being touted as one to watch in the upcoming theater season. At first glance, Best's "willowy and patrician" demeanor might seem an impediment in playing the "ugly overgrown hulk of a woman" described by O'Neill. In an interview with Kathryn Shattuck for the *New York Times*, Best described wearing a pair of boots in rehearsal, the same kind doled out to male cast members, "to find Josie's physical heft, not just her psychological and emotional weight," adding that "I think Josie is more about how you carry yourself." Taking a cue from her director Howard Davies and discounting the physical requirements O'Neill writes into the stage directions, Best continued, "Howard said it's not about that, but rather how she feels in herself and her self-esteem" (10). In fact, as Best told interviewer Patrick Pacheco of NY1's *Onstage*, Davies had soundly rejected any suggestion from the actress that she pad herself for the role, insisting that she would look "ridiculous." Though not ideally suited, at least physically, for her performance, in the minds of almost all, Best's performance was an unqualified success and, according to some, the saving grace of the production.

Ben Brantley, chief theater critic of the *New York Times*, states that "the night belongs to Ms. Best, who clearly and winningly maps the contradictory levels of Josie Hogan, both the blustery façade and the sensitive core. Her not matching O'Neill's description of a big bruiser only feeds our sense that Josie has a created a persona to hide behind, as Ms. Best clomps about the stage like a wrestler in search of a match." Brantley saw in Best's performance a metaphor for the evening as a whole: "The toll of sustaining this façade registers with touching specificity in the play's penultimate scene, when a weary Josie collapses like a marionette with its strings cut. It has been hard shouldering all that pretense for so long. Of course the realism of the moment is probably enhanced by Ms. Best's also having to shoulder the entire emotional weight of a heavy play" ("A Moonlit Night on the Farm" E8).

Several critics shared this opinion. Michael Kuchwara, of the *Associated Press*, describes Best's performance as "one of the glories of the current Broadway season," adding, "It would be a serious mistake to miss her extraordinary performance, a remarkable balancing act of power and vulnerability, sexuality and innocence." Although David Sheward of *Backstage* admits that Best "doesn't fit Tyrone's description of her as 'voluptuous,'" he acknowledges that the actress "powerfully conveys the character's humor, vitality, and bone-deep longing for intimacy with the right man," features more essential to the character. David Rooney, in *Variety*, identifies "the beauty of Best's performance [in] its emotional transparency. Her Josie is all bluff and bravado, stomping about in an ungainly fashion as if to dispel the idea she's a woman." But whenever Best's Josie gets close to Spacey's Tyrone, she "softens visibly, her face dissolving into a gentle, incandescent smile that erases her grubby plainness so we know Jim isn't lying when he says she is beautiful." As Rooney continues, "while maintaining the façade of imperviousness, her vulnerability becomes so acute that every tiny spark of happiness or hurt plays across her face like music."

While Linda Winer, in *Newsday*, could not avoid a reference to a previous Josie — "No actress we've seen can inhabit Josie with the earth-mother comfort of Colleen Dewhurst" — she does admit that Best "finds a shimmering balance between the sturdy, bat-wielding, brazen giant of a slut she wants to be and the virgin she keeps hidden inside." Simply put by Matt Windman of *am New York*, Best's performance is "simply mesmerizing." "A star-making turn," according to Chris Jones of the *Chicago Tribune*.

Jones also approaches the question of whose play this is, an area in which the critics disagree. From the time the play was written, Josie has always had more stage time but was often seen as secondary to Jim Tyrone. According to Jones, "Best's raw beauty has the effect of empowering Josie, raising the character up from its usual post as a self-ameliorating enabler and intensifying the profundity of her capacity for love." Far from serving as a means to an end, many critics see Josie as Jim's equal in terms of importance to the play. According to David Rooney, "Many argue whether the drama's emotional center is citified Jim (based on the playwright's alcoholic older brother, James) or Josie Hogan, the earth-mother farmer's daughter whose unrequited love warms their moon-bathed, bourbon-soaked night of bared souls. For this lyrical, character-driven play to be fully effective, Jim's inescapable sorrow and Josie's wounded strength need to be invested with equal truth." Or, according to Jacques Le Sourd in *The Journal News*, "Ever since the landmark revival in 1973, with the late Colleen Dewhurst as the two-fisted moll Josie Hogan, *A Moon for the Misbegotten* has been Josie's play." Le Sourd concludes that with Spacey in the role, "The play now belong to James, a Broadway smoothie with dark secrets to tell."

This was, in fact, a minority opinion. While Le Sourd describes Spacey's performance as "luminescent" and "something to see," other critics begged to differ. As Ben Brantley describes Spacey's "beat-the-clock" performance that brings the curtain down in under three hours, "Mr. Spacey is as lively as a frog on a hot plate. When this Tyrone rails against the universe, it is with the frenzy of a 2-year-old who has been told to eat his spinach. And he rattles off the play's confessional soliloquies as if they were the final verses of Gilbert and Sullivan patter songs." David Rooney finds that "From the moment Jim enters, Spacey gives a performance of such swaggering self-regard that it's impossible to believe him as a man made hollow by grief and guilt." According to Rooney, "When [Spacey] sinks into Jim's cancerous self-disgust, there are flashes of the role's affecting torment. But he continually undercuts the pathos by shamelessly courting the audience, too often punctuating the bleak revelations with smug line-readings colored by sardonic humor." Andy Propst, writing for *American Theater Web*, describes "a curiously idiosyncratic performance of Jim by Kevin Spacey.... Spacey's choice for emphasizing Jim's humor as a means of self-defense is valid, but as he rarely wavers from this approach, theatergoers rarely have the chance to glimpse much of what makes the character pitiable."

Chris Jones sees the performance a little differently: "Eschewing the usual booze-deadened softness of this wounded character, Spacey here unleashes a dazzling, energized study in sharp-edged contrasts, wherein

153

hyper-articulate irony undercuts raging agony, oh, about as often as raging agony undercuts hyper-articulate irony." As Jones continues, "Were it
not for his last half-hour, when Spacey's Tyrone seems to come apart at
the nocturnal seams before your eyes, you'd be tempted to dismiss all this
as clever trickery. And indeed, you form an initial case that the addition
of some of Spacey's contemporary colloquialisms has a jarringly post-mod-
ern effect." (At one point, Spacey caps a speech with "Hello?": spoken as
a question it creates a comic effect, a technique used throughout his performance to undercut the tragedy by emphasizing or interjecting the
comic.) Jones finds Spacey's connection with Best "palpably real and
intense," saving both the performance and the play: "when Tyrone finally
loses control of his shtick, the vacuity of what's left boggles the eye" ("Two
Stellar Leads Make 'Moon' Shine").

Several critics account for Spacey's choices by noting that the actor
is playing an actor. According to Robert Feldberg, writing for *The Record*,
"In dramatic encounters, [Spacey] will suddenly make a face or toss in a
gesture that gets a laugh. It seems odd, but then you realize that, as an
actor, he just might do that." David Sheward notes that "[Spacey gives]
Tyrone's self-deprecating jibes plenty of vaudeville spin. It's a risky choice,
because if such antics are carried too far, the characterization becomes a
parody. Spacey knows just when to pull back so that the laughter at
Tyrone's clowning catches in the audience's throats." While Brantley "was
always more conscious of the actor Kevin Spacey than of the actor James
Tyrone," Brendon Lemon, writing for *The Financial Times*, describes
Spacey's performance as "gloriously entertaining, technically suberb," while
Michael Kuchwara is impressed by Spacey's ability to transform the words
of the play: "O'Neill's dated language can be melodramatic, even florid,
but Spacey has the gift of making these outbursts sound genuine." Revis-
iting the production in New York, David Finkle of *TheaterMania* again has
vivid praise for Spacey's performance: "His graphic depiction of Tyrone's
torment is like watching a man being eaten alive from the inside out." And
in concert with Eve Best, Spacey receives high praise indeed from Finkle,
who writes, "Their colliding and clinging during one long night's journey
into day is the new standard by which the O'Neill opus will be judged for
the foreseeable future.... It's safe to say that Spacey is the new Robards;
and keeping right up with him, Best is the new Dewhurst." According to

Finkle, following his success as Hickey in *Iceman Cometh* and Jamie in *Long Day's Journey*, Spacey "confidently [assumes] the mantle of being the foremost O'Neill interpreter—a title that has been up for grabs since Robards' death."

As Phil Hogan, Colm Meaney did not turn the role into a scene-stealing turn, unlike his predecessors Roy Dotrice and Ed Flanders, both of whom received Tony Awards for their efforts. Although Finkle attributes to Meaney's Phil "his fair share of scene-grabbing," Propst finds Meaney's rendering of Phil "truly complex." In an interview on NY1's *Onstage*, Meaney himself suggests that the play is about "people who are not saying what they mean." This extends to Phil's relationship with his daughter. As Meaney notes, every time Josie criticizes herself in the play, her father counters with a compliment. This paternal concern contradicts Phil's pose as a father eager to use his daughter to gain a more lucrative future for himself.

Like Eve Best, Colm Meaney was physically incompatible with the character he played; as described by his daughter, Phil Hogan is "an ugly little billy goat (*Moon* 861) and "as spry on his stumpy legs as a yearling" (*Moon* 862). Matthew Murray, in *Talkin' Broadway*, feels that "Meaney looks far too young to play [Best's] father, but finds all the right devious joviality and canny business sense to convince as a new breed of 20th century frontiersman." While Feldberg sees the actor as "too young and too clean for the old reprobate" (Sheward also finds him "too tall"), Brantley attributes to Meaney "a solid, likeable performance as Hogan that resists Pappy Yokum cuteness," grateful, as were many critics, that the actor didn't overdo the part.

It is not unusual for the actors playing the small and smaller roles of T. Stedman Harder and Mike Hogan to receive little critical attention, although Sheward notes that "Billy Carter and Eugene O'Hare ably fill the walk-on roles of Josie's runaway brother and a snobbish neighbor," and Finkle describes them as "strong in their brief performances." It is curious, however, that the direction of Howard Davies received somewhat limited attention from critics. As Kevin Spacey told interviewer Charlie Rose, "[Howard Davies is] a great, great director, and I think he very often doesn't get the credit he deserves because you don't notice his direction, that's how good it is." In discussing Davies' contribution, most critics referred to his previous success with the production of *Iceman Cometh* eight years before; of those, many were disappointed that the production of *Moon* did not repeat it. Among other critics, Brantley notes that "the I'm-talking-as fast-as-I-can delivery, which Mr. Spacey used to more persuasive effect in Mr. Davies' fine 1999 production of *The Iceman Cometh*, mostly registers as shtick." Matthew Murray acknowledges Davies' attempt at "[stripping] this *Moon* of all its ties to the poetic realism that was always O'Neill's trademark; David Rooney states that "Davies makes clear from the start that he has little interest in naturalism." While Finkle describes the production as "directed with gritty intelligence by Davies," Rooney notes that "the director's heavy hand plays up the gabby first act's farcical tone.... while this approach feeds into O'Neill's scheme of shifting by degrees into sadness, the production's destabilization begins here." What results is a speedy and comic rendering of the play. Again, considering the contribution of the direction, and without underestimating the actress' ability, the praise for Best's performance might, at least in part, be attributed to Davies, a director with whom she had worked previously in O'Neill's *Mourning Becomes Electra*.

One aspect of the production that did receive much attention was the set by Bob Crowley. During the 2006–2007 Broadway season, the Irish-born Crowley was represented by five productions running concurrently: along with the set he created for *Moon*, he had designed and directed the musical *Tarzan*, complete with bungee-jumping gorillas, and he created the scenic design for Tom Stoppard's trilogy *The Coast of Utopia* at Lincoln Center and Joan Didion's *The Year of Magical Thinking*, as well as the sets and costumes for *Mary Poppins*. The previous season, Crowley had received a Tony Award for his scenic design of *The History Boys*, which made effective use of projected images to enhance the play. The set for *Moon* was another matter entirely, with Crowley's choices seen as highly controversial.

Simply described by David Rooney in *Variety*, "Bob Crowley's design sets the Hogans' crooked, weather-beaten shack on a barren patch of dirt and rocks with telegraph poles stretching back to an empty horizon, overhung by an azure sky made unnaturally brilliant by lighting wizard Mark Henderson." The bright cerulean blue of Henderson's lighting design made the drab browns and dirty beiges of the costumes stand out in sharp relief, although, when the time came, there was a striking lack of a moon, as the actors looked out in the direction of the audience to see the moon, the changes in lighting evoking the passing of the night into day. For *Talkin' Broadway*, Matthew Murray extends the description of the set: "Staring out over the desolate expanse before you might lend the impression you're overseeing the aftermath of a nuclear holocaust, or in the best case scenario, an abandoned war zone. So decimated is the landscape that even the telephone poles and the lone farmhouse in view appear to be at odds with traditional vertical space. Angles, gravity, you name it — nothing works normally here." "Weirdly surreal" is how Michael Kuchwara describes the farmhouse, "pitched to one side of the stage.... The structure looks as if it could collapse at any moment, much like the relationships in the play." Yet the farmhouse, surprisingly, never does. Although it looked as if it had been banged together with whatever piece of wood or metal was handy, the house, despite appearances, stood solid as a rock, even with a front door that frequently slammed.

In the setting, many critics saw Oklahoma at the height of the Great Depression rather than Connecticut in the early 1920s. "Do all British designers visualize America as one big Walker Evans desert?" asked David Cote in *Time Out New York*. It was "*Tobacco Road* on a bad day," according to Jacques Le Sourd. In fact, the rocky terrain described by O'Neill had been replaced by a red, sandy expanse more typical of Santa Fe than the red clay of Connecticut. Eve Best's only reservation about her experience in *Moon* centered on the sand: "I've had it with the dirt," she admitted, with a laugh, to interviewer Kathy Henderson. "We're Irish pig farmers, so we have to look really filthy. Every night, we put on *so* much dirt, and it takes hours to get it off. I take two showers after the show, but in the morning, my sheets are covered with little bits of red gravel that get in my hair."

Critic Jeremy Gerard did not share Best's sanguine response to the scenic design, complaining that the production "is first undone by Bob Crowley's stylized mini-shack, which could not house a single person, let alone a family of six.... The shack is backed by a refulgent sapphire-blue cyclorama with cotton-candy clouds that change hue as day fades into night and then morning. The effect is not so much an O'Neill melodrama as low comedy: *Li'l Abner*, perhaps." Yet, as Linda Winer points out in

Newsday, "Oddly enough, despite the mythic expanse of an almost abstracted landscape, Crowley bothers to go realistic with a pump that spits real water." The working water pump, downstage right, was a highlight of the set and the action, especially in the first half. For a woman who lives without indoor plumbing, Eve Best's Josie worked hard to be clean, frequently washing herself or whatever clothing came her way, as well as the visiting T. Stedman Harder, when he was in need of a comeuppance. With the pump a frequent destination for the other actors, the ablutions continued: at one point, Spacey as Tyrone treated the base of the water pump as a divan, reclining and blowing smoke rings, more typical of a movie diva than the self-described third-rate ham.

The critical response to the production ranged from the sublime to the ridiculous: like the set, it was seen as either brilliant or off-kilter. O'Neill told the actors in the original production not to sacrifice the comedy of the first two acts for the tragedy that followed. In his interpretation of the role, Spacey admitted to Charlie Rose that the key to Jim Tyrone was in the character's belief that "[he doesn't] deserve to be loved." Spacey had clearly worked hard, perhaps too hard, to make his Jim Tyrone as dissimilar as possible from the performance of Jason Robards, a friend with whom he shared a birthday, and a hero whose work Spacey greatly admired. Unlike the more melancholic portrayal by Robards, Spacey invested his lines with more comedy than they held or possibly could hold. Eve Best's performance, on the other hand, was almost universally admired, and when award season began in April 2007, her name was among the nominees for every major award. Like Spacey, Best was nominated for a Drama Desk Award. The Drama Desk places performers from productions on and Off Broadway in the same category; included in Best's category was Meryl Streep's highly respected performance as Mother Courage during the previous summer at the Delacorte Theater in Central Park. In this august company, Best's win became all the more impressive. In addition to a Drama League nomination, Best also received the Outer Critics Circle Award for Best Lead Actress in a Play and a Theatre World Award for her Broadway debut. When the nominations for the Tony Awards were announced, Best's nomination was the only one received by the production. Although Best had been considered a frontrunner for the award, on 10 June 2007, a few hours after the production of *Moon* had closed, when the winner's name was read, the award went to Julie White for her comic performance as an unscrupulous agent in Douglas Carter Beane's *The Little Dog Laughed.*

Yet, the overwhelmingly positive response to the actress' performance serves to emphasize the greatest strength of this production. Before Colleen Dewhurst, the actresses playing Josie had been criticized for not inhabiting the role as the quintessential earth mother described by O'Neill. After Colleen Dewhurst, actresses were criticized for not being Colleen Dewhurst. What Eve Best's performance made clear was that that a lack of weight did not result in a performance that lacked substance, and that an earth daughter could succeed admirably in the role.

Conclusion:
"What's past is prologue."

Of the iconic figure Willy Loman, Arthur Miller said, "There'll never be a standard Willy. There'll always be a new one, depending on the actor playing him. There's no comparison, really, except to music. It's like hearing the same composition played by one conductor and then another. It's the same notes, it may even take the same length of time to perform — but they're different" (qtd. in Kakutani 1). The same is true of the protagonists in O'Neill's *A Moon for the Misbegotten*. O'Neill had specific ideas of how the characters should be presented, but even with a slavish devotion to the stage directions on the part of an actor or director, it would be impossible to achieve a performance exactly as written. At the same time, no one aspires to be a standard Josie or Jim Tyrone, and the recent Broadway revivals suggest that a standard production is virtually impossible to achieve. In 1984, director David Leveaux was criticized for his revisionist reading of the text, while, in 2000, Daniel Sullivan was criticized for a more naturalistic approach to the play. In 2007 Howard Davies emphasized the comic potential of the play, but after experiencing the antic disposition of Kevin Spacey's Jim Tyrone, some critics, like *USA TODAY*'s Simon Annand, waxed nostalgic about the 2000 revival, which had received mixed reviews. In retrospect, Annand praised Gabriel Byrne and Cherry Jones' "witty but heartbreaking performances that elicited more tears than chuckles." Clearly, the 1973 revival of *Moon* served as the seminal moment in the play's history, with its confluence of a director and a cast of actors at the ideal moment in their careers to play these roles: even the critics who had previously rebuffed the play acknowledged its greatness. But with this well-deserved success came the assumption that these performances and this production were definitive.

But if we are to bow to the idea of a definitive performance, then theater should simply pack up and go home whenever a performance, or a production, has been deemed a landmark. The great plays of O'Neill and of Shakespeare, for that matter, would be off limits; once the performance has been committed to tape or to memory, there would appear to be no point in attempting to equal or surmount this success. Yet a great play can sustain a variety of productions and interpretations, a reality that serves as proof of its greatness.

Certain roles are seen as a testing ground — for example, a young actor must have a Hamlet in his repertoire for his career to be taken seriously. If given the choice, however, most actors would prefer to originate a role rather than compete with the ghosts of performances past. While the risk exists of being forever associated with the role, as in the case of James O'Neill in *The Count of Monte Cristo*, the rare opportunity to create something new usually overcomes the fear of being trapped in a single part. In the end, however, the actor uses the same preparation for a new role as for a classic role, by approaching the part through the words of the play, and through the words, finding a point of intersection between the actor and the character. Whether the individual is originating a role or playing a classic one, the desired outcome is to create a performance that is original. Both prospects test the actor, but the greater challenge may be to succeed in a part that has been well worn by others.

In productions of *A Moon for the Misbegotten* over the past sixty years, there has been a wide range of opinion as to what a Connecticut pig farmer's home looks like, for example, with settings that appear to span the American landscape from New Mexico to Oklahoma and back to New England. The widest range of opinion, however, seems to focus on the role of Josie Hogan. Admittedly, Colleen Dewhurst most successfully executed the role of Josie as Earth Mother, at a time in her career when she was twenty years older than the character as written. Yet, the earth daughters who followed and preceded her, regardless of the success of their respective productions, each brought something of herself and of her time to the part, reflecting not only what O'Neill had written but also the decade in which the play was performed. Described by Jim with both affection and sarcasm as "[his] Virgin Queen of Ireland," Josie Hogan, although not as infinite in her variety as Shakespeare's Cleopatra, does share one feature with the Queen of the Nile. From the vamp of Theda Bara in 1917 to the bee-stung lips of Claudette Colbert in 1934 to the sloe-eyed Elizabeth Taylor in 1963, the actresses playing the character on screen often reflected the fashions of their times. Clearly, their performances were more than the sum of their style. In a similar fashion, most of the performers playing Josie Hogan have brought visible reminders of the world in which they lived to the stage on which they performed. In their enactment of the character was a subtle indication of the social attitudes of their own time and place.

Unless the director cut the script during the rehearsal process, the words of the play remained the same, the published version in 1952 having replaced the language that was hastily cut by the censors during the play's original production in 1947. But the effect of those words has been remarkably different, depending upon when they were spoken. Beginning with Mary Welch, the original Josie, the part, like the play, has been controversial. The Theatre Guild hedged its bets in casting James Dunn, a charming but alcoholic movie star, best known for playing the charming but alcoholic father in *A Tree Grows in Brooklyn,* as the charming but alcoholic James Tyrone, Jr. Through the course of his life and career, Dunn had already drunk his way into the part, but Welch was forced to eat her way into hers. O'Neill himself describes the five-foot-eleven-inch, one-hundred-and-eighty-pound Josie as "almost a freak." In the 1940s, when the play was written, and in the 1920s, when the play was set, a woman this size would be considered freakishly large, making it difficult not only to locate an actress to play her, but also to imagine a woman this size as a member of the acting profession, and not simply for the problems anticipated by producer Lawrence Langner: "Well, I'm afraid you're a rather big girl — how are we to find a man tall enough to play against you?" The character Josie Hogan also has a hard time with her size, distanced from, yet painfully aware of, the flapper society of the 1920s, which admired petite, boyish bodies capped by short, bobbed hair. As previously noted, the size of the character was more essential to O'Neill's emotional reality than to Josie's physical one. As Kate Nelligan insisted, "it's not a play about a fat girl, it's a play about Eugene O'Neill's — and Jim Tyrone's — emotional needs" (qtd. in Freedman "Ghosts Haunt the Stage"). Performing in the 1940s, however, Welch had no choice but to eat up, as if the key to the character was her size. According to Welch, the playwright himself told her that it was essential that she understand "how Josie feels" (qtd. in Welch 84), a point lost on the management of the Theatre Guild.

Wendy Hiller, the first Josie on Broadway, came to the part after having acted the role of plain Catherine Sloper in *The Heiress*. To her resume, Hiller also added the scruffy Eliza Doolittle of Shaw's *Pygmalion*, which she played both on stage and in film. This combination of dirt and determination would seem to be useful training to play the daughter of a pig farmer in O'Neill's play. Using minimal padding, and wearing a simple dress and a straw hat, Hiller successfully demonstrated that the part was playable without a significant weight gain. Although critic Tom Donnelly admired Hiller's ability to put out a cigarette with her bare foot, and critic John McClain insisted that Hiller carried the part "by sheer force of animal vigor" (18), the 1957 production seemed to emphasize the lady rather than the tiger. Even living in a shanty complete with broken windows, Hiller's Josie was able to unearth a clean and proper, even be-ribboned, navy dress for her date with Jim, a choice more in keeping with the style and social mores of the 1950s than the rough-hewn and dirt-infested life of Josie Hogan.

In the two productions that followed, Off Broadway in 1968 and on Broadway in 1973, it was clear that the Age of Aquarius had dawned, in part, reflected by the costumes worn by the respective Josies, Salome Jens and Colleen Dewhurst. This is not to suggest that the groundbreaking production of *Hair*, which had originated downtown at the Public Theater, and played on Broadway from 1968 to 1972, had any direct influence on these two revivals of *Moon*. But the profound societal disruption that resulted from opposition to the war in Vietnam led to a way of looking at the world that permeated these entirely separate theatrical universes, both the countercultural *Hair*, the first time hippies found their way to Broadway, and the cultural arena of *A Moon for the Misbegotten*, the last word of a great American playwright. While O'Neill might have approved of *Hair*'s experimentation, that would seem to be the only point of intersection. Yet, neither production was immune from the influences of the world outside the theater.

Tall and smoky voiced, with long, straight hair, and casually dressed in a simple dress, even barefoot, Salome Jens would not have appeared out of place in 1968. Her Josie was not a hippie, but her fashion influences were, her style effected also by the limited finances of an Off Broadway production. Again, in 1973, as the Resurrection Company restored life to the play and to the careers of the players, the production had to work on a tight budget. Colleen Dewhurst's dress came from a Los Angeles thrift shop, unavoidably echoing the fashion, if discarded, of the time. Dewhurst, too, in her simple dress and bare feet, served as a reflection not only of a pig farmer's daughter in 1923, but also of her own cultural context. Dewhurst was a part of the theatrical equivalent of the counterculture, beginning her career working with Joseph Papp, whose mission was to make theater, particularly Shakespeare, accessible to all people. This movement began when a flatbed truck broke down in Central Park, and Papp refused to move it, creating performances on that site. With her husky voice and hearty laugh, Dewhurst was often cast by Papp and other producers as an earth-mother type, a role she played only on the stage. According to T.E. Kalem in *Time* magazine, "No woman has been big enough for the part before, not only physically but in that generosity of heart, mind, and spirit which Josie must convey" (42). Dewhurst may have been giving the performance of her life, but, as recent incarnations have demonstrated, there are many ways to play the part.

The outspoken Kate Nelligan was the next Josie on Broadway. By her own admission, Nelligan was often hired "to play from the eyebrows up" (qtd. in Freedman "Ghosts Haunt the Stage"), cast as an intellectual, confident, and sophisticated woman. Josie is none of these. Following Dewhurst in the next major revival of *Moon*, Nelligan felt less of a burden in facing the inevitable comparisons, given how vastly different she was in appearance and type from the persona established by Dewhurst. Nelligan's Josie was more of a wild child, aggressively unkempt, making it harder to see the beauty, either of Josie or of Nelligan, under the dirt and matted hair. The Leveaux production made no attempt to create real people; rather, it populated the play with mythic types. No whiff of the Reagan era wafted through the production, which was not anchored to a naturalistic foundation nor influenced by a specific time and place. Yet Josie's longing for Jim's love, and her utter devastation when it was not forthcoming in any lasting way, cut through the Irish mists that suffused the production to achieve the same heartrending conclusion.

In the year 2000, sixteen years after *Moon*'s last visit to Broadway, the arrival of Cherry Jones, coupled with that of Gabriel Byrne, was highly anticipated. Like Hiller before her, Jones had made her name as Catherine Sloper in *The Heiress*, and rarely had heard a discouraging word since her arrival on the New York stage. In Josie, Jones may have met her match, though not in the way she intended. Jones was deeply influenced by Colleen Dewhurst; seeing her perform the role of Josie inspired not only Jones' career choice but also the type of career she would emulate. As an American actress, Jones felt deeply the inevitable comparisons, which Nelligan, a Canadian trained in the British system, could choose to ignore, less influenced by the recent history of the play, which was so well known to American theatergoers.

For the first time in Jones' career, in the place of unanimous praise, there were critical rumblings that she had been miscast, not rough and tough enough to convey all the facets of Josie, a criticism also laid at the feet of Mary Welch in the original production. Compared to her predecessors in the role, Jones' were the feet most used to shoes, her character, the most comfortable in her nice clothes when she dressed up for the date with Jim Tyrone. Even her haircut, a stylish bob, came in for its share of criticism, seen as too chic for the pig farmer's daughter, and having more to do with the world outside the theater than the world of the play. Ironically, this haircut would have been seen on fashionable women in 1923 as well as in 2000; unfortunately, Josie was not one of those women. Jones' performance was equidistant from the all-forgiving Earth Mother of Colleen Dewhurst and the untamed emotion of Nelligan's Josie; hers was a more moderate approach to the role in a highly naturalistic treatment of the play. Unlike the mythic atmosphere of the previous production, the world presented was a recognizable reality, perhaps too much so to convey the world of O'Neill's play.

Praised throughout her career for her ability to be both theatrical and completely real, Dewhurst enjoyed rapturous critical approval for her performance. She may have been ideally cast in the role, but hers was not the only rendition to be so admired. On regional stages, frequently populated by Josie Hogans, others were also able to make their mark. Even with the

1973 production a not-so-distant memory, and with critics prefacing their remarks with comparisons to previous productions, the critical community was still able to applaud a variety of interpretations. In 2003, reviewing the Trinity Rep production, critic Carl A. Rossi, after acknowledging Janice Duclos' physical size and emotional expansiveness in the role, describes her performance as the "crowning glory" in a production that he praises for "ignoring the Quintero yardstick" by "punching up all of the bravura comedy hiding in plain sight," and at the same time, "[knowing] when to stop the blarney and to pluck at the heart strings." In 2006, at the McCarter Theatre in Princeton, Kathleen McNenny had to work overtime as Josie, not only because director Gary Griffin had given an endless number of tasks to fulfill, from peeling potatoes to repairing her father's shirt while he still wore it, but also because she had to carry the play. Her co-star, the more recognizable Andrew McCarthy, was over-matched by the role of Jim Tyrone, which he was courageous to attempt in the first place. McNenny's lack of physical size could be forgiven or ignored, her physicality in the role serving to mask her limitations. McCarthy's limited stage presence, however, was inadequate to the task of playing a third-rate "ham" actor, and his offstage presence as a former Brat Packer, a persona he has yet to shed, compounded his difficulty in playing the role as well as McNenny's challenge in playing opposite him. Further saddled with one of the saddest costumes seen on any Josie, a navy sack dress more appropriate for teaching Sunday school than attempting seduction, McNeeny still managed to prevail. Naomi Siegel, writing in the *New York Times*, faced the Dewhurst question directly when she praised McNenny's performance, stating, "Ms. Dewhurst, meet Ms. Kathleen McNenny. One great Josie deserves another" (C9). In the history of this play, there has been more than one great Josie.

Beginning in 2006 at the Old Vic Theatre in London, and arriving on Broadway in 2007, Eve Best was the next to play the role. She too brought a contemporary gloss to the role, with her long, dark hair wrapped in a sloppy uptwist, a more functional than fashionable rendition of a popular contemporary hair style, and an unexplained rope bracelet on her right wrist. But what Best brought to the role far outstripped her choice of hairdo. Thirty-four years after Dewhurst seemingly set the standard, Best created a new paradigm. Described as "a remarkable balancing act of power and vulnerability, sexuality and innocence," by the Associated Press' Michael Kuchwara, Best's performance made clear, in a meaningful and, hopefully, lasting way, that a convincing portrayal was possible by someone other than Colleen Dewhurst. Simply put by David Finkle in *TheaterMania*, "Eve Best is the new Dewhurst." Dewhurst's performance was a momentous contribution to the play's distinguished past, and any attempt to erase this indelible impression would be both unwarranted and impossible. Best's performance, however, epitomizes the play's future, with an earth daughter finally coming into her own in the earth mother's sphere of influence, her accomplished performance, both innovative and accessible, encouraging a wider range of possibilities in the casting of future Josies and the choices they make in their performance of the role.

Producer Lawrence Langner complained of the difficulty of finding an actress to play Josie, a virtual impossibility if the Theatre Guild wanted to follow the instructions stated by O'Neill. A compromise was reached in the casting of Mary Welch, although it was not an entirely happy one, either for the Guild or for the author. The commercial producers who followed Langner enjoyed one advantage in not having the author available to second-guess their choices, but they faced similar challenges. In casting the role, they probably would not be able find an actress who fit O'Neill's specifications, but, particularly in the case of the Broadway productions, that was not their intention.

The actress playing Josie on Broadway would need to be able to act the role, but, plainly, looking the part was not a requirement. The practical reality was that producers needed a star, or at least a well-known performer, to draw in viewers. She would attract an audience while playing down her own attractiveness in the role. Thus, we have the casting of Wendy Hiller, Kate Nelligan, and Cherry Jones. All were recognized names in theater, film, or television, yet they were willing, even eager, to disguise their more recognizable selves in order to play Josie. On the other hand, Colleen Dewhurst was well known as an O'Neill interpreter, and masked only her age, if that, in presenting a physical self that seemed to define the role. Little know outside of London, Eve Best was the first choice of director Howard Davies and the Old Vic's artistic director Kevin Spacey to play Josie; she may have arrived in New York a relative unknown, but, as sometimes happens, she went home to London a Broadway star.

The actresses playing Josie may have had to mask their attractiveness in order to be convincing in the part, but the character is not without her physical charms. The character's size has been well documented, but O'Neill, in his opening stage directions, while admitting that "[hers] is not a pretty face," acknowledges that "her dark-blue eyes give it a note of beauty, and her smile, revealing even white teeth, gives it charm" (*Moon* 857). Jim Tyrone, insisting on her attractions to the point of embarrassing her, extols her "beautiful strong body ... beautiful eyes and hair, and a beautiful smile and beautiful warm breasts" (*Moon* 916). More than that, he admires her for being "real and healthy and clean and fine and warm and strong and kind" (*Moon* 915), ideally suited to the role of mother confessor. Even Josie's father, rare in his compliments, praises her for being "a fine strong figure of a woman ... with beautiful eyes and hair and teeth and a smile," in an immediate counterpoint to Josie's statement that she is nothing more than "an overgrown lump" (*Moon* 870). And yet, to contradict Kate Nelligan's statement, finally, the play is about a fat girl. There must be some physical defect, real or imagined, that thwarts Josie's ability to see herself as a person worthy of another's affection. Her abnormality may not be external, but whatever her appearance, Josie is misbegotten in her belief that she is unattractive and therefore unlovable, especially when the physical evidence contradicts her claim, as does the emotional evidence of Jim's genuine, if impossible, love for her. The actresses playing Josie seemed to have come to this conclusion out of necessity, as a result of their literal inability to fill Josie's shoes. Whether or not they were aware of O'Neill's advice to Mary Welch of the need to "understand how Josie feels," they seemed to follow this suggestion, relying on an emotional point of intersection between performer and role, rather than approaching the role primarily from a physical standpoint.

Theatergoers have long memories. While this can be helpful to theater historians, it can also serve as a hindrance to the re-creation of classic works. Audience members who have a long history with a single play more than likely will have a preference among the previous productions. Fifty years after *A Moon for the Misbegotten* debuted on Broadway, a few critics are still able to preface their remarks on the 2007 revival with first-hand experience of the 1957 production. Even as their numbers dwindle, the percentage of theatergoers who saw, or thought they saw, the 1973 production continues to grow, in part due to its mythic status, in part due to its existence and availability on DVD. With the assistance of technology, no one will soon forget the production by which all others are measured.

This is not to suggest that audience members should attempt to erase this production from their memories. In fact, rather than serving as a hindrance, a knowledge of the previous productions, 1973 included, should benefit subsequent revivals of the play, by providing a more complete picture of what the play can be. Thus far, the play has been treated as naturalistic, expressionistic, or mythic, populated by actors who are, and are nothing like, the characters described by O'Neill. The diverse readings of the play, with more unquestionably to come, are a testament to its greatness rather than an indication of uncertainty on the part of its interpreters. Future revivals should be praised for their ability to revise the work and not to rehash it.

Beyond success in individual performances, the question remains as to what a successful revival should accomplish. Twenty years ago, what is now identified as the Tony Award for Best Revival was designated as the Best Reproduction of a Play. Unless the goal was to create a museum piece and to present an exact replica of what had gone before, it would be counterproductive and contradictory to honor a reproduction. The first-time audience member discovers a work, but ideally, the successful revival enables the repeat visitor to rediscover the play. Rather than diminishing the work, the revival should create a deeper and more profound impression upon the viewer through subsequent presentations.

The history of *A Moon for the Misbegotten* has been seen by some to follow the pattern of drama itself, with the original production in 1947 serving as exposition, the Broadway debut in 1957 and the Off Broadway debut in 1968 viewed as the rising action, with the 1973 revival seen as the climax. This would make all the productions that followed, including the Broadway revivals of 1984, 2000, and 2007, and the many performances on regional stages, a long and attenuated denouement. Some productions may cast a longer shadow than others, with greater popular or critical appeal, and more, or less, commercial success. Given O'Neill's contempt for the "show shop" of Broadway, it is ironic that his plays are such frequent, if not lengthy, visitors to this venue. The original production never made it to Broadway, closing out of town, while the 1973 revival enjoyed the longest stay with 313 performances. In 1957 and 1984, the play lasted little more than a month. In 2000 and 2007, the embarrassment of a potentially short run was avoided by strictly limited runs of 120 and 84 performances, respectively. Their producers lived in hope that each run would be extended, but in each instance, their hopes were not realized.

Yet, even with a range of possibilities from which to choose, there will never be a single production that is truly definitive. Perhaps no production will escape the shadow of the 1973 revival, but in light of the history of the play, that seems to be beside the point. The play is not limited by, or to, any of the productions that have served it; in fact, it is defined by all of these productions. To identify a single production as definitive serves only to defy the purpose of the enterprise and to demean the efforts of those involved. Plays are written to be produced, but they are not produced in order to create faithful restorations. In fact, judging by the caliber of their work, most directors feel an obligation to make their interpretation of the work as different as possible. It would be impossible to recreate the 1973 revival, at least in part because it long ago exchanged mortal for mythic status. To dismiss the productions that followed, in the same way that the 1947 production was dismissed as an outright failure, may serve the myth but ignores the reality. For far too long, the myth has outpaced reality in discussions of the play. As its history has demonstrated, each production has renewed the play in its creation, not its re-creation, of a world these characters could inhabit, with each interpretation faithful, in its fashion, to the play O'Neill wrote. With countless productions of the play undoubtedly waiting in the wings, the fortunes of *A Moon for the Misbegotten* can only continue to rise.

Production Chronology

Hartman Theater, Columbus, Ohio; Opened: 20 February 1947.
Cast: Josie Hogan: Mary Welch; Mike Hogan: J. Joseph Donnelly; Phil Hogan: James M. (J.M.) Kerrigan; James Tyrone, Jr.: James Dunn; T. Stedman Harder: Lex Lindsay. *Directed by:* Arthur Shields. *Production Designed and Lighted by:* Robert Edmond Jones. *Produced by:* the Theatre Guild. Production under the supervision of Theresa Helburn and Lawrence Langner. *Associate Producer:* Armina Marshall. Pre-Broadway production, closed out of town.

Bijou Theater; Opened: 2 May 1957.
Cast: Josie Hogan: Wendy Hiller; Mike Hogan: Glenn Cannon; Phil Hogan: Cyril Cusack; James Tyrone, Jr.: Franchot Tone; T. Stedman Harder: William Woodson; *Directed by:* Carmen Capalbo; *Scenic Design by:* William Pitkin; *Costume Design by:* Ruth Morley; *Lighting Design by:* Lee Watson; *Produced by:* Carmen Capalbo and Stanley Chase. New York Premiere, Broadway Debut.

Circle in the Square; Opened: 12 June 1968.
Cast: Josie Hogan: Salome Jens; Mike Hogan: Jack Kehoe; Phil Hogan: W.B. Brydon; James Tyrone, Jr.: Mitchell Ryan; T. Stedman Harder: Garry Mitchell; *Directed by:* Theodore Mann; *Setting by:* Marsha Eck; *Costumes by:* Domingo A. Rodriguez; *Lighting by:* Jules Fisher; *Presented by:* Circle in the Square (Theodore Mann, Artistic Director; Paul Libin, Managing Director). Off Broadway Debut.

Morosco Theater; Opened: 29 December 1973.
Cast: Josie Hogan: Colleen Dewhurst; Mike Hogan: Edwin J. McDonough; Phil Hogan: Ed Flanders; James Tyrone, Jr.: Jason Robards; T. Stedman Harder: John O'Leary; *Directed by:* Jose Quintero; *Scenic Design by:* Ben Edwards; *Costume Design by:* Jane Greenwood; *Lighting Design by:* Ben

Edwards; *Produced by*: Elliot Martin and Lester Osterman Productions (Lester Osterman, Richard Horner). Broadway Revival.

Cort Theatre; Opened: 1 May 1984.

Cast: Josie Hogan: Kate Nelligan; Mike Hogan: John Bellucci; Phil Hogan: Jerome Kilty; James Tyrone, Jr.: Ian Bannen; T. Stedman Harder: Michael Tolaydo; *Directed by*: David Leveaux. *Scenic Design by*: Brien Vahey; *Costume Design by*: Brien Vahey; *Lighting Design by*: Marc B. Weiss. *Original Music by:* Stephen Endelman; *Produced by*: The Shubert Organization (Gerald Schoenfeld, Chairman; Bernard B. Jacobs, President) and Emanuel Azenberg; This production originated at the American Repertory Theatre, Cambridge, Massachusetts (Robert Brustein, Artistic Director; Robert J. Orchard, Managing Director), following an earlier production at Riverside Studios, London. Broadway Revival.

Yale Repertory Theatre; Opened: 30 April 1991.

Cast: Josie Hogan: Frances McDormand; Mike Hogan: Jay Goede; Phil Hogan: Roy Cooper; James Tyrone, Jr.: David Strathairn; T. Stedman Harder: John Jellison. *Directed by*: Lloyd Richards; *Set Design by*: Debra Booth; *Costume Design by:* Helen C. Ju; *Lighting Design by*: Jennifer Tipton; *Sound Design by*: Rob Gorton; *Produced by*: the Yale Repertory Theatre, New Haven, Connecticut (Lloyd Richards, Artistic Director) in association with New York Stage and Film (Vassar Powerhouse Theatre). Regional Theater Revival.

Pearl Theater Company; Opened: 22 September 1992.

Cast: Josie Hogan: Joanne Camp; Mike Hogan: Hank Wagner; Phil Hogan: Frank Lowe; James Tyrone, Jr.: Paul O'Brien; T. Stedman Harder: Arnie Burton; *Directed by*: Allan Carlsen; *Set Design by*: Robert Joel Schwartz; *Costume Design by*: Lyn Carroll; *Lighting Design by*: A.C. Hickox; *Sound Design by*: Donna Riley; *Fight Direction by*: Rick Sordelet; *Produced by*: the Pearl Theater Company (Shepard Sobel, Artistic Director; Parris Relkin, General Manager). Off Broadway Revival.

Walter Kerr Theatre; Opened: 19 March 2000.

Cast: Josie Hogan: Cherry Jones; Mike Hogan: Paul Hewitt; Phil Hogan: Roy Dotrice; James Tyrone, Jr.: Gabriel Byrne; T. Stedman Harder: Tuck Milligan; *Directed by*: Daniel Sullivan; *Scenic Design by*: Eugene Lee; *Costume Design by*: Jane Greenwood; *Lighting Design by*: Pat Collins; *Sound Design by*: Richard Woodbury; *Produced by*: Elliot Martin, Chase Mishkin, Max Cooper, and Jujamcyn Theaters (James H. Binger, Chairman; Rocco Landesman, President; Paul Libin, Producing Director; Jack Viertel, Creative Director); Produced in association with Anita Waxman, Elizabeth Williams, and The Goodman Theatre (Robert Falls, Artistic Director; Roche Schulfer, Executive Director). Broadway Revival.

Trinity Repertory Company; Opened 23 September 2003.
Cast: Josie Hogan: Janice Duclos; Mike Hogan: Andy Grotelueschen; Phil Hogan: William Damkoehler; James Tyrone, Jr.: Fred Sullivan Jr.; T. Stedman Harder: Stephen Thorne; *Directed by*: Amanda Dehnert; *Set Design by*: David Jenkins; *Costume Design by:* William Lane; *Lighting Design by*: Deb Sullivan; *Sound Design by*: Peter Sasha Hurowitz; *Produced by:* the Trinity Repertory Company, Providence, Rhode Island (Amanda Dehnert, Artistic Director). Regional Theater Revival.

Long Wharf Theatre; Opened 23 February 2005.
Cast: Josie Hogan: Alyssa Bresnahan; Mike Hogan: Steve French; Phil Hogan: Bill Raymond; James Tyrone, Jr.: John Procaccino; T. Stedman Harder: Wynn Harmon; *Directed by*: Gordon Edelstein; *Set Design by*: Ming Cho Lee; *Costume Design by*: Jennifer von Mayrhauser; *Lighting Design by*: Jennifer Tipton; *Sound Design by*: Nick Borisjuk; *Fight Direction by*: Thomas Schall; *Produced by*: the Long Wharf Theatre, New Haven, Connecticut (Gordon Edelstein, Artistic Director). The production moved in January 2006 to Hartford Stage, Hartford, Connecticut; and in January 2007 to the Alley Theater, Houston, Texas. Regional Theater Revival.

American Conservatory Theater; Opened: 4 May 2005.
Cast: Josie Hogan: Robin Weigert; Mike Hogan: Andy Butterfield; Phil Hogan: Raye Birk; James Tyrone, Jr.: Marco Barricelli; T. Stedman Harder: David Arrow; *Directed by*: Laird Williamson; *Set design by*: Rob Morgan; *Costume Design by*: Sandra Woodall; *Lighting Design by*: Don Darnutzer; *Sound Design by*: Garth Hemphill; *Produced by*: the American Conservatory Theater, San Francisco, California; (Carey Perloff, Artistic Director; Heather Kitchen, Executive Director). Regional Theater Revival.

McCarter Theatre Center, Berlind Theatre; Opened: 13 January 2006.
Cast: Josie Hogan: Kathleen McNenny; Mike Hogan: Peter Scanavino; Phil Hogan: Jack Willis; James Tyrone, Jr.: Andrew McCarthy; T. Stedman Harder: Jeremiah Wiggins; *Directed by*: Gary Griffin; *Set Design by*: Eugene Lee; *Costume Design by*: Jess Goldstein; *Lighting Design by*: Jane Cox; *Sound Design by*: Andre Pluess, Ben Sussman; *Fight Direction by*: J. Steven White; *Produced by*: the McCarter Theatre Center, Princeton, New Jersey; (Emily Mann, Artistic Director; Jeffrey Woodward, Managing Director; Mara Isaacs, Producing Director). Regional Theater Revival.

Brooks Atkinson Theatre; Opened: 9 April 2007.
Cast: Josie Hogan: Eve Best; Mike Hogan: Eugene O'Hare; Phil Hogan: Colm Meaney; James Tyrone, Jr.: Kevin Spacey; T. Stedman Harder: Billy Carter; *Directed by*: Howard Davies; *Set Design by*: Bob Crowley; *Costume Design by*: Lynette Mauro; *Lighting Design by*: Mark Henderson; *Sound Design by*: Christopher Shutt; *Original Music by*: Dominic Muldowney; *Produced by*: Elliot Martin, Max Cooper, Ben Sprecher, Nica Burns, Max Weitzenhoffer, The Old Vic Company, Spring Sirkin, Wendy Federman, Louise Forlenza, Ian Osborne, Thomas S. Perakos, and James L. Nederlander. Originally presented by The Old Vic Theatre; Originally produced in London by The Old Vic Company, Elliot Martin, Nica Burns, and Max Weitzenhoffer. Broadway Revival.

Works Cited

Alexander, Doris. *Eugene O'Neill's Last Plays: Separating Art from Autobiography*. Athens & London: University of Georgia Press, 2005.

Annand, Simon. "'Moon for the Misbegotten' feels just a bit off the beam." *USA TODAY*. 10 Apr. 2007. www.usatoday.com.

Atkinson, Brooks. "O'Neill's Last." *New York Times*. 3 May 1957: 21.

_____. "Tennessee Williams' 'Summer and Smoke' Acted by the Loft Players at Their Circle-in-the-Square." *New York Times*. 25 Apr. 1952: 19.

Austin, Jeremy. "Resurrection Blues." *The Stage*. 3 Mar. 2006. www.thestage.co.uk.

Barlow, Judith. *Final Acts: The Creation of Three Late O'Neill Plays*. Athens: University of Georgia Press, 1985.

Barnes, Clive. "Landmark 'Moon for the Misbegotten.'" *New York Times*. 31 Dec. 1973: 22.

_____. "A Less-Than-Heavenly Aida." *New York Post*. 26 Mar. 2000: 33.

_____. "'A Moon for the Misbegotten.'" *New York Times*. 13 June 1968: 55.

Bassett, Kate. "The Old Vic Cometh Back." *The Independent* (London). 1 Oct. 2006. www.independent.uk.com.

Benedict, David. "'A Moon for the Misbegotten.'" *Variety*. 27 Sept. 2006. www.variety.com.

Bennett, Ray. "'A Moon for the Misbegotten.'" *The Hollywood Reporter*. 28 Sept. 2006. www.hollywoodreporter.com.

Bennetts, Leslie. "Jerome Kilty, An O'Neill Fan at Last." *New York Times*. 4 May 1984: C3.

Bentley, Eric. "Trying to Like O'Neill." *O'Neill and his Plays*. Eds. Cargill, Fagin, Fisher. New York: New York University Press, 1961. 331–45.

Bermel, Albert. "'A Moon for the Misbegotten.'" *New Leader*. 4 Feb. 1974: 28.

Billington, Michael. "'A Moon for the Misbegotten.'" *The Guardian* (London). 27 Sept. 2006. www.guardian.uk.com.

_____. "Without the classics, the Old Vic is a farce." *The Guardian* (London). 10 Apr. 2006. www.guardian.uk.com.

Black, Stephen. *Eugene O'Neill: Beyond Mourning and Tragedy*. New Haven: Yale University Press, 1999.

Bolton, Whitney. "'A Moon for the Misbegotten.'" *Morning Telegraph*. 14 June 1968: np.

Boulton, Agnes. *Part of a Long Story*. London: Peter Davies, 1958.

Bovard, Karen. "Complicated Relationships." *Hartford Advocate*. 26 Jan. 2006. www.hartfordadvocate.com.

Brantley, Ben. "A Love Story to Stop the Heart." *New York Times*. 20 Mar. 2000: E1.

_____. "A Moonlit Night on the Farm, Graveyard Ready." *New York Times*. 10 Apr. 2007: E1+.

Brown, Mark. "Lindsay in spotlight for Old Vic's new season." *The Guardian* (London). 10 May 2006. www.guardian.uk.com.

Brustein, Robert. "Plays fat and thin." *The New Republic*. 17–24 Apr. 2000: 64+.

Buckley, Michael. "An Interview with Colleen Dewhurst." *TheaterWeek*. Oct. 1989: 34–35.

Butler, Phyllis. "'A Moon for the Misbegotten.'" *CurtainUp*. May 2005. www.curtainup.com.

Cavendish, Dominic. "An epic journey to the 'Moon.'" *The Daily Telegraph* (London). 13 Sept. 2006. www.telegraph.co.uk.

Cedrone, Lou. "O'Neill Play at Mechanic." *Baltimore Evening Sun*. 29 July 1969: A6.

Chase, Chris. "Colleen Has Broadway 'Moon-Struck.'" *New York Times*. 17 Feb. 1974: sec. 2, 1+.

Chrisafis, Angelique. "Spacey to breath new life into Old Vic." *The Guardian* (London). 6 Feb. 2003. www.guardian.co.uk.

Christiansen, Richard. "'Misbegotten': A Masterful Moonshot in the Making." *Chicago Tribune*. 25 Jan. 2000: D1.

_____. "O'Neill Play Bores Through to Tragedy." *Chicago Daily News*. 17 June 1969: 33.

Clay, Carolyn. "Flip Side of a Masterpiece." *Boston Phoenix*. 23 Jan. 1979: 14+.

_____. "Moonlight Sonata." *Boston Phoenix*. 10 Jan. 1984: sec. 3, 1+.

Clurman, Harold. ""A Moon for the Misbegotten.'" *The Nation*. 19 Jan. 1974: 92.

Coffin, Rachel, ed. *New York Theatre Critics Reviews* 18 (1957): 277–280: Donnelly, Tom. "A Long Night's Moongazing." *New York World Telegram-Sun*. 3 May 1957. Kerr, Walter. "'Moon for Misbegotten.'" *New York Herald Tribune*. 3 May 1957. Watts, Richard, Jr. "Another Moving O'Neill Tragedy." *New York Post*. 3 May 1957.

Coleman, A. D. "'A Moon for the Misbegotten.'" *Village Voice*. 20 June 1968: 62.

Commins, Sax, Collection. Rare Book and Special Collections. Firestone Library. Princeton University.

Cote, David. "'A Moon for the Misbegotten.'" *Time Out New York*. 12 Apr. 2007. www.timeout.com.

Coveney, Michael. "'I know I'm a big target.'" *The Observer* (London). 11 Sept. 2005. www.arts.guardian.co.uk.

Cox, Gordon. "'Moon' gathers solid B'way advance." *Variety.* 30 Mar. 2007. www.variety.com.

Crist, Judith. "'Moon' Is Hopeful, Though Unhappy." *New York Herald Tribune.* 28 Apr. 1957, sec. 4, 1.

Cummings, Scott T. "The Homecoming." *Boston Phoenix.* Mar. 2002. www.bostonphoenix.com.

Dempsey, John. "Haunted O'Neill Actors." *Baltimore Sunday Sun.* 27 July 1969: D27.

"Detroit Closes Eugene O'Neill's Play; Pitt Jumps Over 'Moon' as 'Vulgar.'" *Variety.* 12 Mar. 1947: 7.

Dewhurst, Colleen, and Tom Viola. *Colleen Dewhurst: Her Autobiography.* New York: Scribner, 1997.

Dezell, Maureen. "Jones' Growth and Growing Pains." *Boston Globe.* 2 June 2000: C4.

Diesel, Leota. "'A Moon for the Misbegotten.'" *The Villager.* 20 June 1968: np.

Donnelly, Tom. "The Woman in the 'Moon.'" *New York World-Telegram.* 14 May 1957: 18.

Drake, David. "Cherry Jones." 14 Mar. 2005. www.broadway.com.

Drew, Bernard. "Most Moving Experience Ever at O'Neill Play." *Hartford Times.* 19 June 1968: 4E.

Feinberg, Susan. "A Conversation with Cherry Jones." *Theater Scene.* 18 Jan. 2003. www.theaterscene.net.

Feingold, Michael. "Stepping Lightly." *Village Voice.* 22 Mar. 2000. www.villagevoice.com.

Feldberg, Robert. "Spacey returns to Broadway; magic in short supply." *The Record* (NJ). 10 Apr. 2007. www.northjersey.com.

Finkle, David. "'A Moon for the Misbegotten.'" *TheaterMania.* 10 Apr. 2007. www.theatermania.com.

_____. "'A Moon for the Misbegotten.'" *TheaterMania.* 30 Sept. 2006. www.theatermania.com.

Floyd, Virginia, ed. *Eugene O'Neill at Work.* New York, Ungar: 1981.

Fox, David Anthony. "Half Moon." *City Paper* (Philadelphia). 26 Jan.—1 Feb. 2006. www.citypaper.net.

Freedman, Samuel G. "For Kate Nelligan, Ghosts Haunt the Stage." *New York Times.* 15 Apr. 1984: sec. 2, 1.

_____. "Revisionist 'Moon' by Young Director." *New York Times.* 17 May 1984: C17.

Friedman, Arthur. "A.R.T.'s 'Moon' Shines." *Boston Herald.* 24 Dec. 1983: 28.

Funke, Lewis. "Mann, O'Neill Producer, Gains Fame as Director." *New York Times.* 4 June 1968: 19.

Funke, Phyllis. "Jose Quintero and the Devil of Success." *Wall Street Journal.* 15 May 1974: 20.

Gamerman, Amy. "Of Drunks and Derelicts — O'Neill and Mamet, Two Geniuses of the American Vernacular, Probe the Nation's Dark Side." *Wall Street Journal*. 22 Mar. 2000: A20.

Gardner, Lyn. "But You're Beautiful, Miss Jones." *The Guardian* (Manchester). 19 Jan. 2000: 12.

Garvey, Sheila Hickey. "New Myths for Old: A Production History of the 2000 Broadway Revival of *A Moon for the Misbegotten*." *Eugene O'Neill Review*. 24.1–2(2000) 121–33.

_____. "Not For Profit: A History of the Circle in the Square." Diss. New York University, 1984.

Gates, Anita. "She May Be Slight, but Watch Out." *New York Times*. 22 Jan. 2006: C8.

Gelb, Arthur. "From Opera to O'Neill." *New York Times*. 28 Apr. 1957: X1+.

_____, and Barbara Gelb. *O'Neill: Life with Monte Cristo*. New York: Applause Books, 2000.

Gelb, Barbara. "Jason Jamie Robards Tyrone." *New York Times Magazine*. 20 Jan. 1974: 14+.

_____. "A Mint from the 'Misbegotten.'" *New York Times*. 5 May 1974: D1+.

_____. "A Theatrical History." Foreword. *A Moon for the Misbegotten*. By Eugene O'Neill. New York: Vintage, 1974. iii–vi.

_____. "A Touch of the Tragic." *New York Times Magazine*. 11 Dec. 1977: 43+.

Gent, George. "Flanders, 39, Ages to Cheers in O'Neill Play." *New York Times*. 4 Jan. 1974: 20.

Gerard, Jeremy. "Kevin Spacey Finds Booze, Love, Peace on O'Neill's Moonlit Farm." *Bloomberg News*. 11 Apr. 2007. www.bloomberg.com.

Gibbons, Fiachra. "Movie Star Seeks Old Vic revival." *The Guardian* (London). 27 July 2000. www.guardian.co.uk.

Gibbs, Woolcott. "A Tired Tyrone." *New Yorker*. 11 May 1957: 84+.

Gill, Brendan. "'A Moon for the Misbegotten.'" *New Yorker*. 14 Jan. 1974: 58.

_____. "'A Moon for the Misbegotten.'" *New Yorker*. 14 May 1984: 130.

Goff, John. "'A Moon for the Misbegotten.'" *Hollywood Reporter*. 14 May 1969: 6.

Gottfried, Martin. "'A Moon for the Misbegotten.'" *Women's Wear Daily*. 2 Jan. 1974: 17.

_____. "'A Moon for the Misbegotten.'" *Women's Wear Daily*. 14 June 1968: 37.

Gubernick, Lisa. "The Character Man Up for a Tony." *Wall Street Journal*. 2 June 2000: 13C.

Gussow, Mel. "Jose Quintero's Long Road Back." *New York Times*. 28 Jan. 1974: 34.

_____. "Saving O'Neill and Himself." *New York Times*. 26 Aug. 1998: E1.

Hammerman, Harley J., M.D. The Hammerman Collection. www.eOneill.com.

Hampton, Wilborn. "Theater in Review." *New York Times*. 23 Sept. 1992: C16.

Haun, Harry. "Old Vic/New Spacey." *Playbill*. 2 Apr. 2007. www.playbill.com.

Heilpern, John. "Gabriel Byrne's Great Tyrone Makes this 'Moon' Momentous." *New York Observer*. 10 Apr. 2000: 20.

Henderson, Kathy. "Tony Nominee Eve Best is Over the 'Moon' about Broadway." *Broadway.com*. 20 May 2007. www.broadway.com.

Henning, Joel. "O'Neill in Chicago — Productions, Traditional and Not, Do Homage to America's Poetic, Tortured Playwright." *Wall Street Journal*. 8 Feb. 2000: A24.

Herbert, Ian, ed. *London Theatre Record*. 1983: 485–581. Billington, Michael. "'A Moon for the Misbegotten.'" *The Guardian*. 18 June 1983. Fenton, James. "'A Moon for the Misbegotten.'" *London Times*. 26 June 1983.

Hewes, Henry. "Requiem for a Roué." *Saturday Review*. 18 May 1957: 34.

Hipp, Edward Sothern. "O'Neill Flop Now a Dramatic Hit." *Newark Sunday News*. 10 Nov. 1968: sec. 6, E2.

Huston, John. *An Open Book*. New York: Knopf, 1980.

"Interview with Gary Griffin." McCarter Theatre Company. Jan. 2006. www.mccarter.org.

Isaac, Dan. "A Moon for the Misbegotten." *Village Voice*. 19 July 1973: 53.

_____. "O'Neill's 'Moon.'" *Chelsea Clinton News*. 14 May 1984: 14.

Isherwood, Charles. "Byrne Illuminates Dark Side of O'Neill's 'Moon.'" *Variety*. 27 Mar. 2000: 32+.

Jeffries, Stuart. "It's showtime!" *The Guardian* (London). 27 Sept. 2004. www.guardian.co.uk.

Jones, Chris. "A Moon for the Misbegotten.'" *Daily Variety*. 27 Jan. 2000: 25.

_____. "Two stellar leads make 'Moon' shine." *Chicago Tribune*. 10 Apr. 2007. www.chicagotribune.com.

Kakutani, Michiko. "When Great Actors Put Their Stamp on a Role." *New York Times*. 20 May 1984: sec. 2, 1.

Kalem, T.E. "O'Neill Agonistes." *Time*. 14 Jan. 1974: 42.

Kearse, David. "O'Neill's Intensely Personal Drama, 'Moon for Misbegotten,' Opens." *Baltimore Sun*. 17 June 1969: B4.

Keller, Julia. "O'Neill in '00." *Chicago Tribune*. 23 Jan. 2000: 1.

Kelly, Kevin. "A Misguided 'Moon for the Misbegotten.'" *Boston Globe*. 18 May 1991: D14.

_____. "'A Moon for the Misbegotten' — You'll Hope Dawn Is Early." *Boston Globe*. 3 June 1969: 21.

_____. "O'Neill's 'Moon' at ART." *Boston Globe*. 24 Dec. 1983: D1+.

Kerr, Walter. "It's a Rich Play, Richly Performed." *New York Times*. 13 Jan. 1974: sec. 2, 1.

_____. "Playwrights, Take Heed and Take Heart." *New York Times*. 31 Mar. 1974: sec. 2, 1+.

Kissell, Howard. "A Moon for the Misbegotten.'" *Women's Wear Daily*. 2 May 1984: 23.

Klein, Alvin. "'Moon for Misbegotten' at Yale Rep." *New York Times*. 19 May 1991: C16.

Kroll, Jack. "Bottled in Bondage." *Time*. 14 Jan. 1974: 62.

_____. "Courage of Their Convictions." *Newsweek*. 23 Jan. 1984: 69.

Kuchwara, Michael. "A Marvelous 'Moon' Arrives on Broadway.'" *Associated Press.* 9 Apr. 2007. www.ap.com.

Langner, Lawrence. *The Magic Lantern.* New York: Dutton, 1951.

_____, and Theresa Helburn. "Letter to Investors." The Hammerman Collection. www.eOneill.com.

Lautman, Joan. "Don't Miss 'Misbegotten.'" *Brookline* (MA) *Chronicle Citizen.* 12 Jan. 1984: 1.

Lawson, Mark. "The Ken and Kevin show." *The Guardian* (London). 12 Feb. 2005. www.guardian.co.uk.

Lehman, Jon. "A Brilliant 'Moon for the Misbegotten.'" *Patriot Ledger* (Quincy). 3 Jan. 1984: 33.

Lemon, Brendan. "In vino — or whisky — veritas." *Financial Times* (London). 22 Mar. 2000: 40.

_____. "'Moon for the Misbegotten.'" *Financial Times.* 11 Apr. 2007. www.ft.com.

Leonard, William. "'Misbegotten' Shows O'Neill's Real Power." *Chicago Tribune.* 17 June 1969: np.

LeSourd, Jacques. "Kevin Spacey is luminescent in O'Neill's 'Moon.'" *The Journal News.* 10 Apr. 2007. wwwthejournalnews.com.

Levene, Ellen. "A director hears music in O'Neill's 'Moon.'" *Newsday.* 13 May 1984: sec. 2, 13.

Loveridge, Lizzie. "Resurrection Blues." *Curtain Up.* 8 Mar. 2006. www.curtainup. com.

Manheim, Michael. "O'Neill's Transcendence of Melodrama in *A Touch of the Poet* and *A Moon for the Misbegotten.*" *Critical Approaches to O'Neill.* Ed. John H. Stroupe. New York: AMS, 1988.

Mann, Theodore. "'Moon for Misbegotten' Planned for Year." *Baltimore Sun.* July 1969: np.

_____. "Theodore Mann on O'Neill." Letter. *Village Voice.* 18 July 1968: 6.

Marlowe, Joan and Betty Blake, eds. *New York Theatre Critics' Reviews.* 29 (1984): 290–93. Barnes, Clive. "'Moon' Rises Over B'way, British Style." *New York Post.* 2 May 1984. Watt, Douglas. "O'Neill's 'Moon' still shines brilliantly." *Daily News.* 2 May 1984. Wilson, Edmund. "Misbegotten 'Moon.'" *Wall Street Journal.* 4 May 1984.

McCarthy, Mary. "*A Moon for the Misbegotten.*" *O'Neill and His Plays.* Eds. Cargill, Fagin, Fisher. New York: New York University Press, 1961. 209–11.

McClain, John. "O'Neill Opus Long But Fiercely Great." *New York Journal American.* 3 May 1957: 18.

McDonough, Edwin J. *Quintero Directs O'Neill.* Pennington, NJ: a cappella, 1991.

Meaney, Colm, and Eve Best. Interview. *Onstage.* NY1, New York. 28 May 2007.

Melloan, George. "A Dread Secret Unfolds on a Moonlit Porch." *Wall Street Journal.* 2 Jan. 1974: 16.

Miller, Oscar F. "Letter." *New York Times.* 3 Oct. 1954: np.

Miller, William. *Dorothy Day.* San Francisco: Harper & Row, 1982.

Monterey, Carlotta. Letter to Bennett Cerf. Sheaffer-O'Neill Collection. Connecticut College.

"'A Moon for the Misbegotten.'" *Theatre Arts.* May 1957: 67+.

A Moon for the Misbegotten. Dir. Jose Quintero and Gordon Rigsby. Perf. Colleen Dewhurst, Jason Robards, Ed Flanders. Broadway Theatre Archive (Home Box Office), 1974.

"'Moon' Found Anti-Irish." *Variety.* 12 Mar. 1947: 7.

Morner, Kathleen. "'Moon' a triumph for Salome Jens." *Chicago Sun–Times.* 17 June 1969: np.

Murray, Matthew. "'A Moon for the Misbegotten.'" *Talkin' Broadway.* 9 Apr. 2007. www.talkinbroadway.com.

Nightingale, Benedict. "'A Moon for the Misbegotten.'" *The Times* (London). 27 Sept. 2006. www.timesonline.co.uk.

_____. "O'Neill's 'Moon'—A Flawed Masterpiece." *New York Times.* 6 May 1984: sec. 2, 5+.

Norton, Eliot. "Leading Actors Out of 'Moon'; Sub Falters in O'Neill Play." *Boston Record American.* 3 June 1969: 31.

Novick, Julius. "Moon Over the Morosco." *Village Voice.* 3 Jan. 1974: 67.

O'Casey, Sean. Letter to Brooks Atkinson. 25 May 1957. O'Neill-Sheaffer Collection. Connecticut College.

O'Connor, John J. "Happy Reunion." *Wall Street Journal.* 14 June 1968: C74.

O'Haire, Patricia. "'Moon' Shadow." *Daily News.* 19 Mar. 2000: 11.

O'Neill, Carlotta Monterey Diaries. Beinecke Rare Book and Manuscript Library. Yale University.

O'Neill, Eugene. *A Moon for the Misbegotten.* In *Complete Works.* 1932–1943. New York: Library of America, 1988.

_____. *Selected Letters.* Eds. Travis Bogard and Jackson R. Bryer. New Haven: Yale University Press, 1988.

Oppenheimer, George. "Miss Jens Too Lovely for Earthy O'Neill Role." *Newsday.* 13 June 1968.

Paddock, Terri. "Mendes Builds Bard Bridge from Old Vic to New York." *What's On Stage.* 3 Apr. 2007. www.whatsonstage.com.

Peper, William. "Wendy Hiller in O'Neill Play." *New York Telegram-Sun.* 3 Dec. 1956: np.

Phillips, Michael. "Cherry Jones CROSSROADS." *Los Angeles Times.* 28 Dec. 1999: F1.

_____. "Unspoken Passions Are Vented Under O'Neill's Watchful Moon." *Los Angeles Times.* 20 Mar. 2000: F3.

Pogrebin, Robin. "Byrne Takes Gut-Wrenching Journey to O'Neill's 'Moon.'" *Times-Picayune.* 28 Apr. 2000: L45.

Porter, Darwin, and Danforth Prince. *Frommer's 2000 London.* New York: Macmillan, 2000.

Propst, Andy. "Two Souls, Doomed by Self-Loathing." *American Theater Web.* 10 Apr. 2007. www.americantheaterweb.com.

Quintero, Jose. *If You Don't Dance They Beat You*. New York: St. Martin's, 1988.

_____. Playwrights Theater Forum. Provincetown Playhouse, New York. 9–27 Aug. 1988.

Raidy, William A. "Splendid O'Neill Revival." *Long Island Press*. 13 June 1968: 26.

Rich, Frank. "Kate Nelligan in 'Moon for Misbegotten.'" *New York Times*. 2 May 1984: C21.

Richards, David. "Dewhurst Shines in O'Neill's 'Moon.'" *Washington Star-News*. 6 Dec. 1973: 17.

Riedel, Michael. "Extreme $pacey." *New York Post*. 19 Jan. 2007. www.nypost.com.

_____. "Spacey 'Moon' Landing." *New York Post*. 20 June 2007. www.nypost.com.

Robertson, Campbell. "Irish Lovers, Beneath the Moon." *New York Times*. 13 Mar. 2005: C11.

Rochman, Joanne Greco. "'Misbegotten' Is Memorable Pieta." 6 Jan. 2006. www.eoneill.com.

Rooney, David. "'A Moon for the Misbegotten.'" *Variety*. 9 Apr. 2007. www.variety.com.

Rossi, Carl A. "'A Moon for the Misbegotten.'" *Theater Mirror*. Sept. 2003. www.theatermirror.com.

Saltzman, Simon. "'A Moon for the Misbegotten.'" *Theater Scene*. 21 Jan. 2006. www.theaterscene.net.

Sanders, Kevin. "'A Moon for the Misbegotten.'" WABC-TV. 29 Dec. 1973.

Senior, Jennifer. "Tyrone's Power. *New York*. 14 Mar. 2000: 74.

Shattuck, Kathryn. "Eight to Watch, Onstage and Off." *New York Times*. 25 Feb. 2007: sec. 2, 10.

Shaw, George Bernard. *Pygmalion*. New York: Dover, 1994.

Sheaffer, Louis. "Notes on O'Neill." Sheaffer-O'Neill Collection. Connecticut College.

_____. *O'Neill: Son and Artist*. Boston: Little, Brown, 1973.

_____. *O'Neill: Son and Playwright*. Boston: Little, Brown, 1968.

Sheward, David. "'A Moon for the Misbegotten.'" *Backstage*. 9 Apr. 2007. www.backstage.com.

Siegel, Naomi. "More Dysfunction at O'Neill's Junction." *New York Times*. 29 Jan. 2006: C9.

Simon, John. "A Great Compassion." *New York*. 21 Jan. 1974: 53.

_____. "Three-Quarter *Moon*." *New York*. 2 Apr. 2000: 56.

Solomon, Alisa. "'A Moon for the Misbegotten.'" *Village Voice*. 2 May 1984: 79.

Sommers, Elyse. "'A Moon for the Misbegotten.'" *CurtainUp*. 20 Mar. 2000. www.curtainup.com.

Spacey, Kevin. Interview. *Charlie Rose*. PBS. WNET, New York. 9 May 2007.

Spencer, Charles. "Spacey reaches the moon." *Daily Telegraph* (London). 27 Sept. 2006. www.telegraph.co.uk.

Sullivan, Dan. "'A Moon for the Misbegotten' Opens at Lindy Opera House." *Los Angeles Times*. 14 May 1969: part IV, 10.

"The Sweetest Music the Other Side of Fourteenth Street." *Saturday Review*. 16 May 1953: np.

Taylor, Paul. "Spacey confronts and confounds his Old Vic critics." *The Independent* (London). 27 Sept. 2006. www.independent.co.uk.

"The Theater." *Time*. 3 Mar. 1947. 47–48. [McDermott and *Variety* reviews]

Theatre Guild Collection. Beinecke Rare Book and Manuscript Library. Yale University.

"Theatrical Artist Spotlight: Lighting Designer Jane Cox." McCarter Theatre Company. Jan. 2006. www.mccarter.org.

Tripney, Natasha. "Theatre: 'Cloaca.'" *musicOMH*. 20 Sept. 2004. www.musicOMH.com.

Waldau, Roy S. *Vintage Years of the Theater Guild*. Cleveland and London: Case Western University Press, 1972.

Walker, C.W. "McCarter Presents an intimate 'Moon.'" *Home News Tribune* (East Brunswick, NJ). 26 Jan. 2006. www.thnt.com.

Watt, Douglas. "'A Moon for the Misbegotten' Is Back." *Daily News*. 31 Dec. 1973: 25.

Watts, Richard. "In Memory of a Doomed Brother." *New York Post*. 13 June 1968: 57.

_____. "A Superb Play, Superbly Done." *New York Post*. 31 Dec. 1973: 9.

Welch, Mary. "Softer Tones for Mr. O'Neill's Portrait." *Theatre Arts*. May 1957: 67, 82–83.

Wilson, Samuel T. "'A Moon for the Misbegotten.'" *Columbus Dispatch*. 21 Feb. 1947: 14A.

Windman, Matt. "This 'Moon' Shines." *amNew York*. 9 Apr. 2007. www.amnewyork.com.

Winer, Linda. "'Moon' orbits about Spacey's evolution." *Newsday*. 10 Apr. 2007 www.newsday.com.

Winn, Steven. "Gabriel Byrne Outshines Cherry Jones in O'Neill's Late Classic." *San Francisco Chronicle*. 20 Mar. 2000: E1.

_____. "Nimble pas de deux sparks ACT's just-right reading of O'Neill's 'Moon.'" *San Francisco Chronicle*. 6 May 2005: E1.

Index

Abbey Theatre 39, 44, 84, 111
Academy Theater (Lake Forest, IL) 75, 81, 82
Ah, Wilderness! 30, 52, 110, 111
All God's Chillun Got Wings 110
Altman, Robert 140, 141
American Repertory Theatre 91, 100, 109, 123
"Anna Christie" 27, 37, 101
Antoinette Perry (Tony) Award 60, 91, 93, 106, 109, 110, 125, 155, 156, 158, 170
Atkinson, Brooks 59, 60, 61, 63
Azenberg, Emanuel 100, 106

Bannen, Ian 91, 96, 97, 99, 100, 101, 102, 103, 104, 105, 111
Barlow, Judith 35
Barnes, Clive 67, 83–84, 104–105, 124
Barricelli, Mario 130
Benedict, David 145–146
Bennett, Ray 145
Bentley, Eric 87
Best, Eve 142, 143, 144, 145, 146, 147, 150, 151, 152, 154, 156, 157, 158, 159, 167, 168
Beyond the Horizon 83
Billington, Michael 89, 143–144
Black, Stephen 36
Boulton, Agnes 35, 47, 48
Brando, Marlon 51
Brantley, Ben 117–118, 151–152, 153, 154, 155, 156
Bresnahan, Alyssa 131, 133
Brustein, Robert 91, 96, 122–123
Brydon, W.B. 66, 67, 68, 70

Byrne, Gabriel 111, 113, 114, 115, 116, 117, 118, 119, 120, 121, 122, 123, 124, 125, 126, 127, 131, 147, 161, 166

Camp, Joanne 128
Capalbo, Carmen 53, 54, 56, 58, 59, 61
Cerf, Bennett 55, 89
Chase, Stanley 54
Christiansen, Richard 72, 116–117, 126
Circle in the Square 62, 63, 64, 67, 71, 76, 85
Clay, Carolyn 99, 127
Clurman, Harold 75, 86, 88
Colby, James 133
Coleman, A.D. 69, 129
Commins, Sax 47–49
Connor, William P. 48, 49
Cox, Jane 135
Crowley, Bob 144, 145, 147, 156, 157, 158
Cusack, Cyril 58, 60, 62

Davidson, Jack 71
Davies, Howard 107, 142–143, 144, 145, 151, 155, 156, 161, 168
Day, Dorothy 35–36
Days Without End 30
Dehnert, Amanda 129
de la Tour, Frances 90–91
Dennehy, Brian 110, 113, 114, 126
Desire Under the Elms 38, 64, 75, 76
Dewhurst, Colleen 38, 75, 76, 79, 80–81, 82, 83, 84, 85, 86, 87, 88, 94, 99, 104, 106, 107, 112, 118, 123, 127, 128, 134, 135, 136, 152, 154, 159, 162, 164, 165, 166, 167, 168

Dolan, John "Dirty" 34, 126
Donnelly, Tom 56, 59, 60, 61, 164
Dotrice, Roy 111, 112, 113, 115, 116, 117, 118, 119, 120, 121, 122, 123, 124, 125, 126, 127, 155
Drama Desk Award 88, 106, 125, 158
Drama League 125, 158
Drummer, Mrs. Libby 33, 47
Duclos, Janice 129, 167
Dunn, James 39, 40, 41, 43, 44, 45, 113, 163
Dynamo 30

Edelstein, Gordon 131
Edwards, Ben 82, 114
Ell, Christine 35
Evans, Walker 93, 157

Feingold, Michael 118–119, 121
Feldberg, Robert 154, 155
Finkle, David 147, 154, 155, 156, 168
Fitzgerald, Barry 39
Flanders, Ed 79–80, 84, 85, 86, 87, 88, 107, 155
Friedman, Arthur 97

Garvey, Sheila Hickey 63, 64, 110
Gelb, Arthur and Barbara 33, 51
Gelb, Barbara 27, 78, 89
Gierasch, Stefan 70, 72, 73, 74
Gill, Brendan 85, 103
Gilpin, Charles 38
Goldstein, Jess 135
Goodman Theatre 110, 115
Gottfried, Martin 69, 87
Griffin, Gary 133, 135, 136, 167
Gussow, Mel 63, 79
Gutierrez, Gerald 109, 110

Hammond, Edward Crowninshield 36
Harkness, Edward Stephen 36
Heilpern, John 123–124
The Heiress 56, 109
Helburn, Theresa 28, 42, 44, 50
Hiller, Wendy 51, 54, 56, 58, 59, 60, 62, 84, 109, 118, 122, 164, 168
Howard Johnson's Restaurant 45
Hughie 31, 110
Huston, John 38
Huston, Walter 38

The Iceman Cometh 30, 31, 37, 51, 52, 55, 58, 59, 64, 76, 78, 110, 155, 156
Isaac, Dan 81, 104
Isherwood, Charles 120

Jens, Salome 38, 66, 67, 68, 70, 71, 72, 73, 74, 118, 164, 165
Jones, Cherry 38, 107, 110, 111, 112, 113, 115, 116, 117, 118, 119, 120, 121, 122, 123, 124, 125, 126, 127, 131, 136, 161, 166, 168
Jones, Chris 115, 126, 152, 153–154
Jujamcyn Theatres 109, 110

Kazan, Elia 51, 66
Kelly, Kevin 72, 96–97, 128
Kerr, Walter 59, 60, 61, 84, 85, 88
Kerrigan, James M. (J.M.) 39, 43
Kilty, Jerome 95, 97, 99, 103, 104
Klein, Alvin 127–128
Kroll, Jack 86, 99
Kuchwara, Michael 152, 154, 157, 168

Langner, Armina Marshall 39, 44
Langner, Lawrence 28, 29, 30, 31, 37, 40, 45, 50, 113, 163, 168
Lee, Eugene 114, 118, 119, 121, 124, 135
Lee, Ming Cho 131
Lemmon, Jack 81
Lemon, Brendon 122, 154
Leveaux, David 90, 95–96, 99, 100, 101, 105, 106, 125, 161, 165
Libin, Paul 64, 110
Logan, Josh 39
Long Day's Journey Into Night 31, 32, 49, 55, 56, 58, 59, 64, 107, 155

Mamoulian, Rouben 39
Manheim, Michael, and the transcendence of melodrama 51–52
Mann, Theodore (Ted) 62, 63, 64, 66, 67, 68, 69, 70, 74, 75, 76, 129
Marco Millions 27, 30, 39
Martin, Elliot 81, 88, 107, 109, 110, 143
McCarthy, Andrew 134, 135, 167
McClain, John 59, 60, 61, 164
McDonough, Edwin J. 82, 84
McDormand, Frances 127, 128
McNenny, Kathleen 133, 134, 135, 167
Meaney, Colm 143, 144, 145, 150, 155

Migatz, Marshall 79
Miller, Arthur 66, 109, 140, 141, 161
Miller, Jason 94–95, 96
A Moon for the Misbegotten: appeal of 17, 88–89, 127, 136; as melodrama 18–20, 46; plot 21–25, 32, 46–47, 49; production photograph (1957) 57; production photograph (1968) 65; production photograph (1973) 77; production photograph (1983) 92, 98; production photograph (2000) 109; production photograph (2006) 132
More Stately Mansions 31, 75, 107
Mourning Becomes Electra 30, 75, 110, 142
Murray, Matthew 155, 156, 157

Neeson, Liam 101, 111, 147
Nelligan, Kate 38, 93–94, 97, 99, 100, 101, 102, 102, 103, 104, 105, 106, 118, 123, 131, 164, 165, 166, 168, 169
Nightingale, Benedict 89, 101–102, 103, 144
Nobel Prize (Literature) 31, 44
Nolan, Lloyd 56, 58
Norton, Elliot 42, 71

O'Brien, Paul 128
O'Casey, Sean 59, 67, 90, 103, 123
Old Vic Theatre Company 56, 93, 137, 138, 139, 147, 148, 150, 167
O'Neill, Carlotta Monterey 31, 35, 50, 54, 55, 53, 63, 89
O'Neill, Edmund 32, 33
O'Neill, Ella 32, 33, 49
O'Neill, Eugene Gladstone: cause of death 31; ill health 40, 41, 48, 50; inscription to Carlotta 72; letter to Bennett Cerf 55; letter to son Eugene 36; letter to Theatre Guild 29–30; opening of *The Hairy Ape* 47; reaction to censorship 44, 45; relationship with brother James 17, 33, 34, 47–49; stage directions 161, 169; statement to Barrett Clark 70; *Work Diary* 21, 32, 89
O'Neill, Eugene, Jr. 55
O'Neill, James, Jr. 17, 32, 33, 47, 48, 118
O'Neill, James, Sr. 18, 33, 35, 162
O'Neill, Oona 34, 55, 89
O'Neill, Shane 55, 89
Osterman, Lester 82, 88, 107

Outer Critics Circle Award 88, 125, 158

Page, Geraldine 58, 63
Papp, Joseph 165
Phillips, Michael 121, 126
Propst, Andy 153, 155

Quintero, Jose 55, 58, 62, 63, 64, 66, 75, 76, 78–79, 80, 81, 82, 83, 84, 85, 86, 87, 88, 104, 107, 114, 127, 128, 129

Raymond, Bill 131, 133
Resurrection Blues 140–141
Resurrection Company 75, 88, 112, 165
Rich, Frank 94, 100–101
Richards, Lloyd 127
Riverside Studios 90, 91
Robards, Jason 55, 64, 75, 76, 78, 79, 80, 81, 82, 83, 84, 85, 86, 87, 88, 99, 101, 104, 107, 110, 116, 123, 127, 128, 136, 147, 154, 155, 158
Rooney, David 152, 153, 156
Rossi, Carl A. 128–129
Rubin, Jane 55, 63
Russell, Rosalind 51
Ryan, Mitchell 66, 67, 68, 71

Sandy, Sarah 35
Schmidtke, Ned 80, 81
Scott, George C. 76, 88
Shaw, George Bernard 29, 56
Sheaffer, Louis 34, 40–41, 44–45
Sheward, David 152, 154, 155
Shields, Arthur 39, 40, 44, 45, 70
Shubert Organization 100, 106
Simon, John 88, 118
Snyder, Charles 44
Spacey, Kevin 107, 137, 138, 139–140, 141, 142, 143, 144, 145, 146, 147, 148, 149, 150, 151, 152, 153, 154, 155, 156, 158, 161, 168
Sprecher, Ben 148
Stapleton, Maureen 53, 56
Sterne, Morgan 72, 73, 74
Strange Interlude 27, 30, 45, 58, 64, 76, 89
Strathairn, David 127, 128
Sullivan, Dan (critic) 71
Sullivan, Daniel (director) 110, 111, 114,

115, 116, 118, 119, 120, 121, 123, 124,
125, 161
Sullivan, Fred, Jr. 129

Theatre Guild 27, 28, 29, 30, 31, 37, 38,
40, 41, 42, 44, 45, 49, 50, 51, 61, 87,
168
Theatre World Award 125, 158
Tone, Franchot 58, 60, 61, 62, 84, 122
A Touch of the Poet 31, 107, 125

Vahey, Brien 96, 104

Washington Square Players 28

Watts, Richard 59, 60, 61, 68, 85–86
Weigert, Robin 130
Weiss, Marc B. 103, 104, 106
Welch, Mary 38, 39, 40, 41, 42, 45, 70,
86–87, 163, 164, 166, 168, 169
Williams, Rhys 43
Williams, Tennessee 51, 63, 131
Willis, Jack 133
Winer, Linda 152, 157
Winn, Steven 121–122, 130
Wolheim, Louis 38

Yale University Press 55